The Complete Idiot's Reference Card

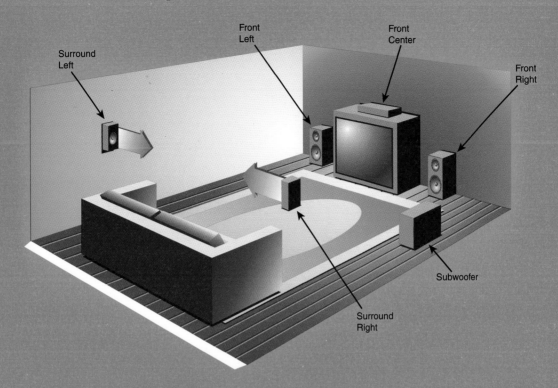

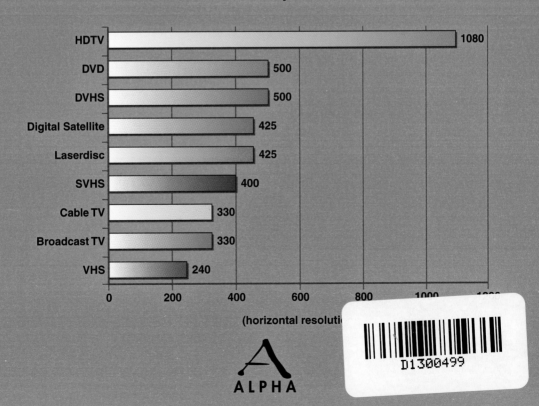

Picture Quality of Video Sources

Source	Horizontal resolution
HDTV	1080
DVD	500
DVHS	500
Digital Satellite	425
Laserdisc	425
SVHS	400
Cable TV	330
Broadcast TV	330
VHS	240

(horizontal resolution)

ALPHA

D1300499

AUDIO/VIDEO CONNECTIONS

CONNECTOR	PLUG	JACK
RF (Antenna)		
Composite Video		
S-Video		
Component Video		Y Pr Pb
Line Audio		R L
Coaxial Digital Audio		
Optical Digital Audio		

THE COMPLETE IDIOT'S GUIDE® TO

Home Theater Systems

by Michael Miller

ALPHA

A member of Penguin Group (USA) Inc.

*To my father, for introducing me to the consumer electronics business—
and for making sure we always had the very latest model television in the
living room during my formative years!*

Copyright © 2000 by Michael Miller

International Standard Book Number: 0-02-863939-1
Library of Congress Catalog Card Number: Available upon request.

04   03   8   7   6   5   4   3

Interpretation of the printing code: The rightmost number of the first series of numbers is the year of the book's printing; the rightmost number of the second series of numbers is the number of the book's printing. For example, a printing code of 00-1 shows that the first printing occurred in 2000.

Printed in the United States of America

Note: This publication contains the opinions and ideas of its author. It is intended to provide helpful and informative material on the subject matter covered. It is sold with the understanding that the author and publisher are not engaged in rendering professional services in the book. If the reader requires personal assistance or advice, a competent professional should be consulted.

The author and publisher specifically disclaim any responsibility for any liability, loss, or risk, personal or otherwise, which is incurred as a consequence, directly or indirectly, of the use and application of any of the contents of this book.

Publisher
Marie Butler-Knight

Product Manager
Phil Kitchel

Managing Editor
Cari Luna

Senior Acquisitions Editor
Renee Wilmeth

Development Editor
Tom Stevens

Production Editor
Billy Fields

Copy Editor
Amy Borrelli

Illustrator
Jody P. Schaeffer

Cover Designers
Mike Freeland
Kevin Spear

Book Designers
Scott Cook and Amy Adams of DesignLab

Indexer
Lisa Wilson

Layout/Proofreading
Svetlana Dominguez
Steve Geiselman

Contents at a Glance

Part 1: Before You Buy: Bone Up on the Basics   **1**

1   It's More Than Just a Big TV: Home Theater Basics   3
When you don't know what you don't know, this is the place to start!

2   What to Buy: Figuring Out What You Have,
What You Need, and What You Want   11
Can you reuse anything from your current system, or do you need to start from scratch!

3   How to Shop: Get the Best Stuff—at the Best Price   19
Is Best Buy the best buy—or should you shop online, or use a custom installer?

Part 2: Picture Perfect: Television Today   **27**

4   Pick a Picture: Choose the Right TV for Your System   29
How big should you get—and do you need a direct view or projection set?

5   The Boob Tube: Direct View Television   41
When price is an issue, go for a set with a big picture tube!

6   Bigger Is Better: Projection Television   47
Hey—these puppies don't look near as bad as they did a few years ago!

7   Thin Is In: Flat-Screen Plasma Television   55
Really neat, really expensive—and really flat!

8   The Next Generation: Digital and High-Definition TV   59
The future of television is digital, and it's here today!

Part 3: Looking Good: Video Sources for Your System   **71**

9   A Picture's Worth a Thousand Words: Choose the
Right Video Sources   73
Which gives you the best picture—videotape, digital satellite, or DVD disc?

10   Digital Pictures on a Disc: DVD Players   85
How can they get that much movie on such a little disc?

11   Tale of the Tape: Video Recorders   103
Everybody has one—so make sure you have the best VCR for your specific system.

12 A Better VCR: Digital Video Recorders 109
Personal TV viewing from a hard disk—it's neater than it sounds.

13 The World on a Dish: Digital Satellite Systems 115
Hundreds of channels with really good picture quality— you might as well cancel your cable subscription right now!

Part 4: Sound Off: Audio Receivers, Players, and Other Components **123**

14 Sound Is All Around: Understanding Surround Sound 125
If you don't know Dolby Digital from Dolby Pro Logic, you're not alone—so read this chapter to learn how to put five (or six!) speakers together for a great-sounding system.

15 More Power, More Inputs: Amplifiers and Receivers 137
The most important component in your system isn't your television—it's your audio/video receiver!

16 Woofers and Tweeters and Horns, Oh My: Speaker Systems 147
You need a lot of speakers for your home theater system— so you better read this chapter to find out which ones to buy!

17 Sound at the Speed of Light: CD Players and Recorders 159
Compact disc players are old hat—especially when you can buy compact disc changers, jukeboxes, and recorders!

18 Make Your Own Kind of Music: Audio Recorders 165
If you want to record your own party mixes, which should you use—an audiocassette recorder, MiniDisc recorder, or CD recorder?

Part 5: Everything But the Popcorn: Building Your Home Theater System **171**

19 Get Ready: Prepare Your Room for Home Theater 173
What can you do to make your room look and sound better for home theater use?

20 Quick and Easy Systems: Home Theater in a Box 179
When you don't want to spend a lot of time or money, buy a prepackaged system!

21 Plug It In: Which Cable Goes Where 183
What's better—composite video, component video, or S-Video? And how do you hook all those components together, anyway?

22   Take Charge: Controlling Your System   197
     Throw away your old remote control—and buy a new one,
     with even more buttons!

23   What to Do When It Doesn't Work: Troubleshooting
     System Problems   209
     Find out how to track down and fix the most common
     home theater-related problems.

24   Home Beautiful: Installing a Custom System   221
     Find out how the pros install those big, expensive sytems—
     and read an interview with an award-winning custom in-
     staller!

25   How Much Can You Afford: Putting Together the Perfect
     System for Your Budget   239
     Six different budgets, six different systems—turn here to
     find the right system for your pocketbook!

Appendixes

A   Glossary   251
     All the buzzwords, explained in plain English.

B   Home Theater Resources   259
     Magazines and Web sites where you can learn more about
     home theater systems.

     Index   263

Contents

Part 1: Before You Buy: Bone Up on the Basics   1

**1 It's More Than Just a Big TV:
Home Theater Basics   3**

What Makes a Home Theater? 4
What Does a Home Theater Cost? 5
How Home Theater Works 6
For Your Eyes Only—Video Displays...........................8
Hear This: Surround-Sound Systems 8
Playing Movies (and Other Programs): Video Sources 9

**2 What to Buy: Figuring Out What You Have,
What You Need, and What You Want   11**

New TV, or Not New TV? That Is the Question. 11
Keep Your VCR, or Throw It Away? 12
New Audio System—or the Same Old Song? 13
Old Speakers for a New System 14
Shiny, Shiny Discs 14
The Other Stuff in Your System 15
Check It Off: Your Home Theater Shopping List 16

**3 How to Shop: Get the Best Stuff—
at the Best Price   19**

Before You Buy: Get Smart! 19
Where to Shop 21
How to Shop 23

Part 2: Picture Perfect: Television Today   27

**4 Pick a Picture: Choose the Right
TV for Your System   29**

Not Your Father's Zenith: New Tech TV 29
The Whole Picture: Wide-Screen Movies and Letterboxing....30

A Better Picture: Digital and High-Definition TV 31
The Future of TV: What's Next?.....................................32
Size Matters: Choosing the Right Size Screen 34
Round, Flat, Front, or Rear: Four Different
Types of TV to Choose From 35
Direct View Televisions 35
Rear Projection Televisions 36
Front Projection Televisions 36
Flat-Screen Plasma Televisions 36
Which Should You Choose? 37
Why Is *That* Set so Expensive? 38

5 The Boob Tube: Direct View Television   41

Direct View Basics 42
The Price Is Right..42
Get Branded 42
Smart Shopping: What to Look For 43

6 Bigger Is Better: Projection Television   47

Affordable Big Screens: Rear Projection Television 47
How Rear Projection Works 48
Should You Buy an RPTV? 49
Really *Big* Big Screens: Front Projection Television...........49
How Front Projection Works 49
Fantastic Four: Different Types of Projectors 50
Should You Buy an FPTV? 52
Front or Rear—Which Should You Buy?........................52
Shop Smart: What to Look For 53

7 Thin Is In: Flat-Screen Plasma Television   55

It's a Gas: How a Plasma Display Works 55
How Good Is the Picture? 57
Why Would You Want a Plasma Display? 57
Smart Shopping: What to Look For 58

8 The Next Generation: Digital and High-Definition TV **59**

Defining Digital 60
Decoding the Different Digital Formats 62
Why Would You Want HDTV? 64
Almost HDTV: Digital-Ready Televisions 64
Coming to Your Town Soon: The HDTV
  Broadcast Rollout 65
Should You Buy ... or Wait? 66
Shop Smart: What to Look For 68

Part 3: Looking Good: Video Sources for Your System **71**

9 A Picture's Worth a Thousand Words: Choose the Right Video Sources **73**

Going Digital: The Latest Video Technology 74
The Picture Makers: Video Sources for Your Home
  Theater System 75
Broadcast Television 76
Cable Television 76
Direct Broadcast Satellite (DBS) 77
DVD 77
Videocassette Recorder (VCR) 78
Personal Digital Video Recorder (DVR) 79
Other Video Sources 80
Video Game System 81
Garbage In, Garbage Out: Searching for
  the Best Picture and Sound 81
Which Should You Choose? 82

10 Digital Pictures on a Disc: DVD Players **85**

Great Picture—and Great Sound 86
What DVD Is—and How It Works 87

Think Different: Different Options Available on DVD......90

Different Aspect Ratios..*90*

Different Audio Formats..*91*

Different Languages *92*

Different Countries..*92*

Different Ratings *93*

Make Your DVD Player Do Double Duty 93

Different Types of DVD Machines 94

DVD Players *94*

DVD Changers *95*

DVD Recorders...*96*

Computer DVD Drives *97*

Audio-Only DVDs *97*

All Those Different Outputs: How Do I Hook
This Up? 98

Smart Shopping: What to Look For 99

11 Tale of the Tape: Video Recorders   103

VHS: Poor Quality, Hard to Use—and
Everybody Has One 104

Better Sound, Same Picture: VHS HiFi...........................104

It's Super, Man: A Better VHS 105

DVHS: Video Recording for the Digital Age 105

Wait! There's More: Camcorders and
Other Formats 105

VHS-C..*105*

8mm *106*

Hi8 ....*106*

Digital 8 ....*106*

Mini DV *107*

Shop Smart: What to Look For 107

12 A Better VCR: Digital Video Recorders   109

A Computer in Your Living Room: How Personal
Digital Video Recorders Work 109

Take Two: Looking at the Different Types of DVRs 110

Fancy Recording, and Then Some: All You
Can Do with a DVR...111

Easy as Pie: Hooking Up a DVR.....................................112

Smart Shopping: What to Look For 113

13 The World on a Dish: Digital Satellite Systems   115

Eye on the Sky: How Digital Satellite
Systems Work..115

DIRECTV and EchoStar: Twin Sons of Different
Mothers 117

The Longest Distance Between Two Points: Getting
Local Stations from the Satellite.................................118

Mounting and Pointing: How to Install a Digital
Satellite System 119

Installing the Dish *119*

Connecting the Receiver *120*

One Dish, Two Rooms: Connecting Multiple Receivers *120*

Today's Best Source for Digital Television: Upgrading
Your Dish for HDTV Broadcasts 121

Shop Smart: What to Look For 121

**Part 4: Sound Off: Audio Receivers, Players,
and Other Components   123**

**14 Sound Is All Around: Understanding
Surround Sound   125**

Surround-Sound Basics: What You Need, and
What Goes Where 126

More Than One Way to Surround: Understanding
the Different Surround-Sound Formats........................127

Lots of Channels, Great Sound: Dolby Digital....................*127*

One More Channel in the Rear: Dolby Digital EX *129*

The Lower-Priced Alternative: Dolby Pro Logic *131*

Not so Popular: DTS *132*

For the Discriminating—and the Rich: THX *133*

Choosing a Surround-Sound Format..............................134

15 More Power, More Inputs: Amplifiers and Receivers   **137**

Making Music: Essential Audio Components 138
   More Inputs: Understanding Preamplifiers.........................138
   More Channels: Understanding Surround-Sound
     Processors...138
   More Power: Understanding Power Amplifiers 138
Everything in One Box: Audio/Video Receivers 139
Specs and Features: Why One Receiver Is Better
   Than Another..140
   Pay for Performance 140
   Dollars for Dolby 141
   Cash for Connections 142
   Coins for Control 144
Shop Smart: What to Look For 145

16 Woofers and Tweeters and Horns, Oh My: Speaker Systems   **147**

Sound in a Box: A Speaker Primer..............................147
   Woofers and Tweeters: Understanding How Speakers
     Work 148
   Bookshelf, Floor, and Wall: Understanding Speaker
     Enclosures 149
   Louder and More Efficient: Understanding Speaker
     Designs 150
What Goes Where: Planning Your Home Theater
   Speaker Layout...151
   Left, Center, and Right: Selecting Front Speakers 153
   To the Rear: Selecting Surround Speakers...........................154
   Let's Get Ready to Rumble: Selecting a Subwoofer 155
Do You Really Need New Speakers for Home Theater? 156
Shop Smart: What to Look For 157

17 Sound at the Speed of Light: CD Players and Recorders   **159**

CD Players 159
CD Changers 160
CD Recorders 161
Playing CDs in DVD Players 162
Better CDs: DVD-Audio and SACD 162
It's Super, Man: Introducing the Super Audio CD *162*
A More Versatile Digital Disc: DVD-Audio *163*
Which Format Wins?...*163*
Shop Smart: What to Look For 164

18 Make Your Own Kind of Music: Audio Recorders   **165**

The Old Standby: Cassette Recorders 165
Sony's Digital Standard: MiniDisc Recorders 167
The Best Way to Record from a CD—
  CD Recorders 167
Record from the Internet: MP3 Recorders 167

Part 5: Everything But the Popcorn: Building Your Home Theater   **171**

19 Get Ready: Prepare Your Room for Home Theater   **173**

Space, the Final Frontier: Creating the Ideal Home
  Theater Room...174
Here, There, and Everywhere: Positioning Your
  System 176
Plugged In and Ready to Go: Assembling All
  the Connections 177

20 Quick and Easy Systems: Home Theater in a Box   **179**

One Box, Lotsa Stuff 179
  What's in the Box? *180*
Smart Shopping: What to Look For 181
Make a Match: Home Theater Speaker Systems 182

21 Plug It In: Which Cable Goes Where   **183**

You Say Component, I Say Composite:
  A Connection Primer...184
  RF (Coax) *184*
  Composite Video *184*
  S-Video *185*
  Component Video...*185*
  RGB Video *187*
  Line Audio..*187*
  5.1 Audio..*187*
  Digital Audio *188*
  Speaker Connections..*189*
  Subwoofer Connections..*190*
  A Selection of Connections: The Best Ways to Hook Up
    Your Home Theater Components *190*
  The Preferred Connection: Feed Your Receiver *191*
  The Number-Two Choice: Let Your TV Do the Switching....*192*
  The Fallback Connection: Everything in a Series *194*

22 Take Charge: Controlling Your System   **197**

Point and Click: Understanding the Different
  Types of Remotes 197
  Gotta Use 'Em All: Standard Remotes *200*
  Rewarding Brand-Loyal Consumers: Multiple-Component,
  Single-Brand Remotes *200*
  Punch In the Codes: Universal Remotes *200*
  Do a Brain Dump: Learning Remotes *201*

Teach a New Dog Old Tricks: Programmable Remotes........202
Total Control: Custom Remote Control Systems 204
Get Control of Your Remotes: Choosing the Right
Remote for Your System 207

23 What to Do When It Doesn't Work: Troubleshooting System Problems 209

He's Dead, Jim: Pondering Power Problems 210
Your Entire System Is Dead................210
A Specific Component Is Dead 211
Your Remote Control Doesn't Work................211
I Can't Hear You: Solving Sound Problems.................212
Your System Has Power, But No Sound 212
One Speaker or Channel Is Dead 212
A Specific Component Has Power, But No Sound 213
You Have a Buzz in Your Audio 213
Your Sound Is Bad (Tinny, No Bass, No Treble, Etc.)..........214
A Specific CD Won't Play in Your DVD Player 214
A Specific CD Skips or Won't Play 215
*An Audiocassette You Recorded Plays Back with
Poor Sound*.................215
There's No Sound Coming from Your Rear Speakers............215
Out of Sight: Verifying Video Problems 216
There's No Picture on Your TV 216
There's No Picture from a Specific Component 216
Your TV's Picture Is Grainy (or Blurry or Fuzzy) 217
*The Picture from Your Satellite Fades or Drops Out
Completely*.................217
A Specific DVD Won't Play in Your DVD Player.................218
A Specific DVD or Laserdisc Skips or Won't Play 218
*A Videocassette Doesn't Play Back Properly in
Your VCR*.................218
*The Picture on Your TV Appears Distorted Horizontally
or Vertically* 219
Calling for Help 219

24 Home Beautiful: Installing a Custom System   221

Flaunt It or Hide It: Where Do You Put Your Stuff? 221
*What You Got Is Good Enough: Using Existing Shelves
and Furniture* *223*
Build It Yourself: Ready-to-Assemble Furniture *223*
All Wood, All the Time: The Fine Furniture Option *224*
Spec It Yourself: Ordering Custom A/V Furniture................*225*
*Interior Design Meets High Tech: Creating a Custom
Installation* *225*
Getting Fancy: More Sophisticated Installations 226
*Audio and Video Everywhere: Installing
a Multiple-Room System*..*226*
*Putting the "Home" in Home Theater: Integrating with
Home Automation Systems*..*228*
When the Job's Just Too Big to Do Yourself:
Thinking About Custom Installers 229
Why Use a Custom Installer?..*229*
Should You Use a Custom Installer? *230*
Find a Firm: How to Choose a Custom Installer 230
How to Evaluate Different Firms *230*
Where to Find a Custom Installer.......................................*231*
Learn from a Pro: An Interview with an
Award-Winning Custom Installer 232

25 How Much Can You Afford: Putting Together the Perfect System for Your Budget   239

Under $1,000: Home Theater on a Shoestring 239
Under $2,500: The Budget System 240
Under $5,000: Improving Performance 242
Under $10,000: Bigger and Better 243
Under $25,000: High Definition 245
Unlimited Budget: Unlimited Performance 248

Appendixes

A Glossary   251

B Home Theater Resources   259

   Index   263

Introduction

When I was about six or seven years old, our family got our first color television. Compared to our old black-and-white sets, this "big screen" (21" diagonal) color set was extremely cool. It was so neat to watch *Batman* and *Get Smart* and all my other favorite shows in "living color," as RCA called it back then. I couldn't imagine anything better.

Of course, things *have* gotten better in the 35 or so years since then. My father owned a television/appliance store, so we were always the first family on the block with all the latest technology. After color TV came solid state TV (much more reliable!), videogames (I played Pong for hours on end), videocassette recorders (the first one in the store sold for $1,400!), stereo television (great for music programs), videodiscs (*much* better picture quality), projection television (lousy picture at first, but really big!) compact discs (I couldn't wait for all the Beatles' albums to be re-released on CD), and on and on and on.

Today, all these technological advances have combined into something we call *home theater*. You take a big-screen TV (probably rear projection, but a big direct view TV will do), connect it to a powerful sound system (complete with surround sound, of course), and feed into it high-quality programming (DVD or digital satellite broadcasts are best). The result is an experience that approaches—and in some cases exceeds—that of watching a film in your local movie house.

I have to admit, re-creating a movie theater experience in a normal living room is something I couldn't have imagined as I watched Batman do the Batutsi in living color back in 1965. Today, however, it's not only easy to imagine but it's also easy to do—and without breaking the bank. You can put together a minimal home theater system for around $1,000, and can build something really impressive for less than $5,000. (Just make sure you have enough money left over to buy all the DVD movies you want to watch!)

What do you get for your money? If you build the right system, you get an entertainment experience second to none. Just pop in the DVD of *Apocalypse Now*, crank up the volume, and hold onto your chair when the helicopters blast by to the thrilling strains of "Ride of the Valkyries." You'll swear you're in the middle of the action as the choppers swoop from front to rear and back again; bombs explode all around you, causing your furniture to shake from the force. Trust me—it's an experience unlike any you've had watching traditional TV.

How do you get started with home theater? First, you have to understand what home theater is, and what equipment you need for a first-class home theater experience. That's where this book comes in. *The Complete Idiot's Guide to Home Theater Systems* will help you understand, choose, purchase, and use the best home theater components for your budget. Whether you have a $1,000 budget or a $100,000 budget, you'll find out what you need to know to build your own personal home theater system.

Of course, to understand home theater, you have to understand the audio and video technologies and equipment that comprise today's state-of-the-art home theaters. As you read this book you'll learn more about all these audio/video components, including …

➤ Direct view and projection television.
➤ Digital TV and HDTV.
➤ DVD players.
➤ Audio/video receivers.
➤ Surround-sound speakers and subwoofers.
➤ Digital satellite systems.
➤ Videocassette recorders.
➤ Personal digital video recorders.
➤ CD players, changers, and recorders.

By the time you reach the final page of this book, you'll have learned which components you need, how to shop for those components, and how to assemble them into a high-performance home theater system. The only thing missing is that blank check you need when it's time to start shopping!

What You'll Find in This Book

The Complete Idiot's Guide to Home Theater Systems is composed of 25 chapters, each of which concentrates on a different home theater-related topic. The chapters are organized into five parts, as follows:

➤ **Part 1, "Before You Buy: Bone Up on the Basics,"** presents a general overview of home theater, and shows you how to shop for the best equipment at the best price.

➤ **Part 2, "Picture Perfect: Television Today,"** discusses the four different types of video displays you can choose for your home theater system—direct view, rear projection, front projection, or plasma—and gets you up to speed on digital television and HDTV.

➤ **Part 3, "Looking Good: Video Sources for Your System,"** introduces you to the many different video components you can include in your home theater system, including DVDs, VCRs, digital satellite systems, and personal digital video recorders.

➤ **Part 4, "Sound Off: Audio Receivers, Players, and Other Components,"** presents the audio components of home theater, including audio/video receivers, surround-sound speakers, CD players and recorders, and audiocassette and MiniDisc recorders.

➤ **Part 5, "Everything But the Popcorn: Building Your Home Theater System,"** brings it all together and shows you how to prepare your room, assemble your components, and hook up your home theater system. You'll also learn all about system remote controls, and whether you should use a custom installer. The final chapter of this section—also the final chapter in the book!—presents sample systems by price range, so you can see what home theater systems you can afford on your budget!

How to Get the Most Out of This Book

To get the most out of this book, you should know how it is designed. I've tried to put things together in such a way as to make reading the book both rewarding and fun.

As you read *The Complete Idiot's Guide to Home Theater Systems,* you are presented with additional tips and advice in little boxes (what we in the publishing business call sidebars). These elements enhance your knowledge, or point out important pitfalls to avoid. Here are the types of boxes you'll see scattered throughout the book:

Product Specs

These boxes contain definitions of terms or technologies you may encounter when building your home theater system.

Overload!

These boxes contain warnings and cautions about things *not* to do when building your home theater system!

Input/Output

These boxes contain additional information about the topic at hand.

Power Up

These boxes contain tips and advice to help you get more enjoyment out of your home theater system—or make a better purchasing decision.

Let Me Know What You Think

I always love to hear from my readers—it's where I get some of the best ideas for my books! If you want to contact me, feel free to e-mail me at books@molehillgroup.com. I can't promise that I'll answer every e-mail, but I will promise that I'll read each one!

If you want to learn more about me and any new books I have cooking, check out my Web site at www.molehillgroup.com. Who knows—you might find some other books there that you'd like to read!

Ready ... Set ... Go!

Still here? It's time to get started, so turn the page and get ready to immerse yourself in the home theater experience!

Acknowledgments

The usual thanks to the usual suspects at Macmillan, including but not limited to Billy Fields, Phil Kitchel, Tom Stevens, Renee Wilmeth, and Marie Butler-Knight. Special thanks to all the industry folks who helped provide background information, equipment, or photographs for this book, including Jim Swearingen of Tom Doherty, Inc.; Michael Shultz and Foy Wilkey of Thomson Consumer Electronics; Mark Pedley and Lori LeRoy of Philips Consumer Electronics; Sam Chesser of Niles Audio Corporation; and Cat Fowler of Escient Convergence Group. Finally, a very special thanks to Harvey and Shirley Jeane for sharing the photograph of their living room—and for sharing their opinions about home theater!

Trademarks

All terms mentioned in this book that are known to be or are suspected of being trademarks or service marks have been appropriately capitalized. Alpha Books and Penguin Group (USA) Inc. cannot attest to the accuracy of this information. Use of a term in this book should not be regarded as affecting the validity of any trademark or service mark.

Part 1

Before You Buy: Bone Up on the Basics

Learn what home theater is (and what it isn't), what it takes to make one, and how to buy one. (Where to get the money to buy one is your business!) If you don't know anything about home theater, make sure you read these chapters first!

Chapter 1

It's More Than Just a Big TV: Home Theater Basics

In This Chapter

➤ What home theater is—and what it isn't

➤ Various display options for your home theater system

➤ How to enhance your picture with surround sound

➤ Using your existing components in a home theater system

➤ What kinds of rooms work best for home theater

If you're sitting in your living room watching sitcoms on a 19" television, you are hopelessly behind the times—and depriving yourself of something truly exciting. This is the era of the home theater system, a complete audio/visual experience that can turn your living room into your own private movie theater.

Imagine your living room filled with dynamic, pulse-pounding sound that travels from front to rear to back again. Explosions shake the furniture with gut-thumping bass, spaceships zoom overhead, and even the quiet moments make you feel like you're in the middle of the scene, not just watching a movie on a super-sharp big-screen TV.

The best home theater systems pull you into the movie, offering both the viewing quality of the best movie theaters and the convenience of your own home. And, best of all, you watch what you want, when you want, and control it all from the comfort of your easy chair.

What does it take to turn your living room into a home theater? That question can't be answered in a single sentence—the answers are in the other 24 chapters of this book! Before we get down to the nitty-gritty details, however, let's look at what home theater really is—and what it isn't.

What Makes a Home Theater?

Home theater means different things to different people. To some, hooking up a hi-fi VCR to a 20" stereo TV creates a home theater. To others, it's a DVD player running through a surround-sound audio system and a projection TV. To still others, it's a dedicated room with theater-style seating, huge front projection screen, and a popcorn machine in the lobby.

The reality is, home theater is whatever you want it to be—as long as it helps achieve one basic goal. That goal is to reproduce, as accurately as possible, the experience of watching a film in a movie theater. How you achieve this goal is at the heart of audio/video system design—and you can spend as much or as little as you want to achieve that goal.

What are the minimum requirements for a home theater system? Rational minds may vary when giving an answer, but in my mind a true home theater system should incorporate the following parts:

➤ Fairly large television or other video display

➤ Multiple-speaker *surround-sound* system

➤ High-quality video and audio sources

Product Specs

Surround sound is a technique that puts the listener in the middle of a three-dimensional sound field, typically through the use of both front and rear speakers. There are several different surround-sound systems available for home theater systems, including Dolby Digital, Dolby Pro Logic, and DTS. See Chapter 14, "Sound Is All Around: Understanding Surround Sound," for more information.

Naturally, there are lots of different choices for each of the basic parts of your home theater system, as well as many other components you can add to your system to increase your viewing and listening enjoyment. For example, how do you define a "fairly large television"? If you're currently watching a 19" TV, a 27" model would seem fairly large to you. Other folks, however, might say that you really need a 35" or larger screen for home theater viewing; still others might spec a 45" rear projection screen as the bare minimum. For all parts of your system, what you end up with depends on your personal tastes, your personal budget, and the type of room you're working with.

As an example, the following picture shows a home theater system put together by Harvey Jeane of Las Vegas, Nevada. This system, which incorporates a rear projection television and surround-sound audio, shows how home theater can peacefully coexist with the trappings of a normal living room. (For more information on how Harvey put together his system, go to his Web site at www.digitaltheater.com/pictures/harv/.)

A typical home theater system with rear projection television and surround-sound speakers (hanging from the ceiling); the piano is optional!

(Courtesy of Harvey and Shirley Jeane)

What Does a Home Theater Cost?

What you choose affects how much your total system will cost, of course. While it's possible to build a bare-bones home theater system for less than $1,000, it's more likely that you'll have to move into the $2,500–$5,000 range to attain acceptable performance—and it's not unheard of for high-end systems to cost $25,000 or more. As with anything else in life, you get what you pay for—and if you want state-of-the-art home theater performance, you'll have to shell out some big bucks.

The following table shows all the equipment you can possibly include in your home theater system, along with typical costs.

Parts of a Home Theater System

Function	Component	Price Range
Video display	27"–36" direct view television or	$350–$2,000
	Rear projection television or	$1,500–$10,000
	Front projection television or	$3,000 and up
	Plasma flat-screen television	$10,000 and up

continues

Parts of a Home Theater System   (continued)

Function	Component	Price Range
Audio system	Audio/video receiver with surround-sound processing	$200–$3,000
	Surround-sound speakers (front left, front center, front right, surround left, surround right)	$500 and up
	Subwoofer (optional)	$150–$1,500
Video source	DVD player or changer	$250–$2,000
	Hi-fi VCR (optional)	$150–600
	Personal digital video recorder (optional)	$500–$1,000
	Digital satellite system (optional)	$200–$400
Audio source	CD player, changer, or recorder (optional)	$100–$1,000
	Audio-cassette recorder (optional)	$100–$500
	MiniDisc recorder (optional)	$250–$400

As you can see, it's possible to assemble the bare-bones components for around $1,000; it's also possible to get into the six figures!

Product Specs

A **receiver** is a system component that combines an amplifier, preamplifier, and control functions in a single unit. An **audio/video receiver** (also called an a/v receiver) also controls the video inputs and outputs in your system. For more information on a/v receivers, see Chapter 15, "More Power, More Inputs: Amplifiers and Receivers."

How Home Theater Works

The basic concept of home theater is pretty simple. As you can see in the following figure, the output signal from your video source (such as a DVD player) is fed into your *audio/video receiver*. The receiver uses its built-in surround-sound decoder to send separate audio signals to all five of your speakers, while at the same time sending the video signal to your television. The result: You view the movie on your TV while listening to the five channels of movie sound from your speakers.

Most home theater systems include multiple video sources. You may have both a DVD player and a hi-fi VCR, for example, or you may have a digital satellite system connected for high-quality television viewing. Most consumers will also feed signals from a television antenna or cable system into the a/v receiver.

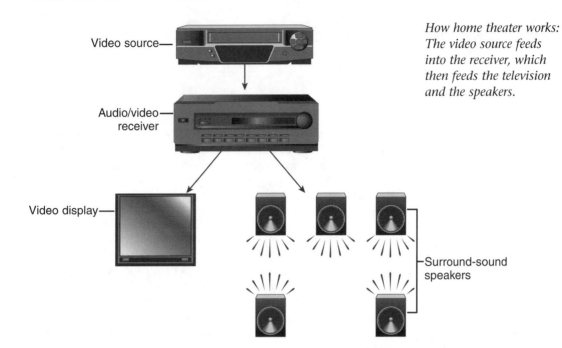

Video source—

Audio/video— receiver

Video display—

Surround-sound speakers

How home theater works: The video source feeds into the receiver, which then feeds the television and the speakers.

Your home theater system is also an audio system, so you'll probably have a few audio sources, such as an AM/FM tuner (probably built into the receiver), CD player, audiocassette recorder, or other audio components. When you select one of these audio-only devices, the sound is fed to your speakers (ideally, only the front-left and front-right speakers) and the television signal is blanked.

While each device in your system (except your speakers!) has its own individual remote control, you'll probably be able to control most of your system functions from the remote control included with your a/v receiver. At the very least, you'll use this multiple-function remote control to switch from one source to another, and to adjust the sound for your entire system.

Input/Output

For advice on the best systems for various price ranges, see Chapter 25, "How Much Can You Afford: Putting Together the Perfect System for Your Budget." This chapter details recommended systems for the following price ranges: under $1,000, under $2,500, under $5,000, under $10,000, under $25,000, and unlimited budgets.

For Your Eyes Only—Video Displays

A home theater system has to have a video display—otherwise known as a television set.

While any larger television can suffice, the best home theaters have video displays with larger screens and sharper pictures—and cost a bit more than a regular TV. At a bare minimum, a home theater system must include at least a 27" diagonal television. Anything smaller just doesn't have a big enough picture area to simulate a true theater experience—and the bigger you get, the better. (This is one area where size *does* matter!)

Input/Output

Another reason to move to a larger screen: Letterbox movies (widescreen movies that use black bars to mask off the unused top and bottom portions of the screen) can get *really* small on a small screen, and can be practically unwatchable on any screen smaller than 25" diagonally.

As for what constitutes "bigger," most mid-priced home theater systems incorporate projection sets with screens in the 45"–60" range—and some ultra-high-end systems can have screens measured in *feet* instead of inches! Home theater video displays can incorporate a variety of display technologies, from standard direct view picture tubes to rear and front projection systems to flat-screen plasma displays.

Which type of display you choose should depend on the size of your room, your personal preference, and the amount of money you want to spend. Typically, you should allocate a quarter or more of your home theater budget for your display. (For more information on video display devices, see Chapter 4, "Pick a Picture: Choose the Right TV for Your System.")

Hear This: Surround-Sound Systems

As to sound, a true home theater surrounds you with sound, just as you are surrounded at a real movie theater. To do this, you must have an audio/video receiver that includes a surround-sound processor, and a minimum of five speakers—front left, front center, front right, surround left, and surround right. More sophisticated systems will also include a sixth speaker, called a subwoofer, for deep bass; the very latest 6.1 surround-sound formats add a third surround speaker between and behind the left and right surrounds.

The audio/video receiver serves as the control center for most home theater systems. All audio and video components—CD players, DVD players, satellite dishes, and so on—are all routed through the receiver. The receiver routes the picture from all these devices to your television or display device, and routes the sound—after decoding the surround-sound information—to your multiple speakers. You use the receiver's remote control to select what you see and hear on your system.

Playing Movies (and Other Programs): Video Sources

Finally, a true home theater system includes a high-quality video source you use to feed your favorite movies to your video display and surround-sound system. This *could* be a hi-fi VCR (although the picture quality on VCRs leaves a lot to be desired), but is more likely to be a DVD player or digital satellite system (DSS).

Today, the sharpest pictures come from devices that store and transmit the picture digitally. Today's digital video sources include DVDs and DSS; older analog sources—such as VCRs and broadcast television—simply can't match the sharpness and clarity of digital pictures.

The best-quality picture, however, is the province of high definition television (HDTV). Unfortunately, televisions capable of HDTV display cost several times more than standard sets, and the amount of HDTV programming (via digital satellite and broadcast) is extremely limited. Still, HDTV is the standard for the future, and I guarantee you that an HDTV system is in your future—*someday*. (For more information on video input devices, see Chapter 9, "A Picture's Worth a Thousand Words: Choose the Right Video Sources.")

Input/Output

For more information on the audio part of your audio/video system, see Part 4 of this book, "Sound Off: Audio Receivers, Players, and Other Components." The five chapters in this part (Chapters 14–18) detail all the different audio components you need in your system, including a/v receivers, speakers, CD players, audio recorders, and more.

The Least You Need to Know

➤ A home theater system attempts to reproduce the experience of watching a movie in a first-class movie theater.

➤ A small-screen television and VCR do not make a true home theater system.

➤ True home theaters include a large video display (television), surround-sound receiver and speakers, and a high-quality video source (such as a DVD player or digital satellite system).

➤ You can spend anywhere from $1,000 to $25,000 or more on a good home theater system—with the best systems incorporating HDTV technology.

Chapter 2

What to Buy: Figuring Out What You Have, What You Need, and What You Want

In This Chapter

➤ Can you use your old TV in your new home theater?

➤ Why you probably need a new receiver—and new speakers

➤ Why it's time to upgrade to DVD

➤ Create your own personal home theater shopping list

If you're reading this book, chances are you're tired of watching movies on that little bitty portable TV with the single tinny speaker, and are ready to replace your current equipment with a full-fledged, high-performance audio/video system. The only things holding you back are the cost and your reluctance to throw away all your current equipment—which is still working just fine, thank you, even if it makes the battle scenes in *Saving Private Ryan* look like the miniature soldiers in *Toy Story*.

Here's some good news for you: You might not have to throw out your old TV—and you may be able to save a few bucks while you're turning your living room into a home theater system. Read on to learn about reusing your old equipment in a new home theater setup.

New TV, or Not New TV? That Is the Question.

Okay, you already have a television set. Everybody does. Do you have to throw it out when you move up to home theater—or can you use your existing TV as the center-piece of your new system?

The answer to this question depends on what kind of set you have. If you have a relatively new and relatively large (27" or more) television, it may be adequate for your home theater needs. However, if you want a sharper or bigger picture, you'll probably have to upgrade.

Newer sets—especially the more expensive newer sets—typically incorporate more sophisticated circuitry and better picture tubes that produce sharper images, more accurate colors, and (in many cases) brighter pictures. In addition, newer sets are likely to contain more advanced features—such as picture-in-picture, built-in program guides, S-Video inputs, and V-Chip parental controls—that can increase your viewing enjoyment.

Of course, if you have a smaller-screen TV and you want a bigger picture for your home theater system, then you need to warm up your checkbook. Fortunately, you'll be pleasantly surprised at the affordable prices on many "very large" screen (32" and larger) televisions these days. Chances are you won't pay much more for one of these sets than you paid for a 25" set just five years ago. So, if you've been wanting a bigger set, now is the time to buy!

Finally, if you want a *really* high-end home theater system—one that's capable of receiving and displaying HDTV programming—then you'll definitely have to buy a new set. No television sold prior to 1999 had HDTV capability, so you'll have to buy a new set to get the new technology.

Input/Output

When you're buying a new TV, you can choose from traditional direct view models, rear projection sets, front projection systems, and the new flat-screen plasma devices. To determine which is the right technology for you, turn to Chapter 4, "Pick a Picture: Choose the Right TV for Your System."

Keep Your VCR, or Throw It Away?

If you have a VHS HiFi VCR (*not* a mono unit!), there's no reason why you can't use it as one of the video sources for your new home theater system. Not as *the* video source, but as *one of* the machines you use to play movies.

The reason you need to supplement your VCR is that the picture quality of VHS recorders is simply not good enough to reproduce the true theater experience in your home. The picture from a DVD player has twice the resolution of a picture from a VCR—and if you're viewing that picture on a 35" or larger television, that's a difference that's *extremely* noticeable!

VHS HiFi VCRs have pretty good sound, however, even though they're limited to the older Dolby Pro Logic surround-sound system. (DVD players incorporate both Dolby Pro Logic and the newer, better-sounding

Dolby Digital—both of which are discussed in Chapter 14, "Sound Is All Around: Understanding Surround Sound.") In any case, you shouldn't be embarrassed playing a VHS HiFi movie through your new home theater system, at least where sound is concerned.

Power Up

The latest video recording technology doesn't use tape—it uses a hard disk, like the one you have in your personal computer! This new technology—called **DVR,** for Digital Video Recorder—uses a large hard disk to record hours and hours of video and audio, digitally. The quality is much better than what you get with a VHS VCR, and you get the convenience of "pausing" your TV viewing with the touch of a button. (The program is stored on the hard disk while the machine is paused.) To learn more about DVRs, see Chapter 12, "A Better VCR: Digital Video Recorders."

If your old VCR *isn't* a VHS HiFi model, then you have lousy sound to accompany the lousy picture and you should spend a few hundred bucks to upgrade to a new VHS HiFi machine. (Unless, of course, you don't plan on doing any recording—or renting any movies on tape.)

Bottom line—you can probably keep your old VCR, but that won't stop you from purchasing a new DVD player, too! (For advice on purchasing a new VCR for your system, turn to Chapter 11, "Tale of the Tape: Video Recorders.")

New Audio System—or the Same Old Song?

If you have an audio system in your home—even if it's a high-end system—chances are it's an audio-only system. This means that it probably doesn't include a surround-sound processor or video inputs.

To control your home theater system—and to decode surround-sound movie soundtracks—you'll need an audio/video receiver that includes surround-sound processing and a four- or five-channel amplifier. In most cases, that means you'll probably have to buy a new receiver.

Even if you already have an audio/video receiver, if it's more than a year or two old you'll probably want to consider investing in a new unit. That's because older a/v receivers incorporated the older Dolby Pro Logic surround-sound system, while newer receivers include both Dolby Pro Logic and the newer, better-sounding Dolby Digital system. Almost all DVDs are coming encoded in Dolby Digital, and once you hear the difference, you'll definitely want to upgrade. (For advice on purchasing audio/video receivers, turn to Chapter 15, "More Power, More Inputs: Amplifiers and Receivers.")

Old Speakers for a New System

If you have an older audio-only system, you most likely also have only two speakers. While you can use those speakers as part of your surround-sound speaker array, you probably don't want to.

The reason is that when you're creating a surround-sound system, it's important that all three front speakers (left, center, and right) be *identical* in their sound properties. It also helps if your surround speakers sound pretty much like those in front—which means that you probably want to use the same type and model speakers for all three fronts, and possibly even for your surrounds.

Overload!

If you decide to use your old speakers in your new home theater system, you should probably use them as your front-left and front-right speakers. Then, when selecting a center speaker model, take care that this new speaker is a close match, sonically, to your existing speakers.

So, unless you can purchase additional quantities of the same speakers you already own, you're probably better off replacing your existing speakers with a completely new—and matched—set of speakers. Besides, you'll probably find that a new set of speakers sounds considerably better than your old set—speakers can get a little mushy sounding over time.

In addition, you should consider adding a subwoofer to your speaker system. A subwoofer reproduces only the very lowest bass frequencies, which are typically used in movie soundtracks for explosions, rumbles, and the low end of the music track. The Dolby Digital system allocates a separate channel for the subwoofer output. (To learn more about purchasing speakers for your home theater system, turn to Chapter 16, "Woofers and Tweeters and Horns, Oh My: Speaker Systems.")

Shiny, Shiny Discs

If your current audio system includes a CD player (and it probably does), good for you—there's no reason to buy a new one for your new system. (Unless, of course, you have a jones for one of those new 400-disc changers!)

If you were an early adopter of DVD technology, you're a step ahead. If you haven't yet taken the plunge into DVD, get ready to leap—you'll definitely want a DVD player as the primary input device for your new system. The picture and sound quality of DVDs outshine anything available previously, including laserdiscs.

If you're a long-time laserdisc fanatic, it's time to give it up. The LD format is sinking fast as everybody and their brother—including high-end aficionados—move to DVD. There's no reason to throw out your extensive collection of discs, however—just realize that most of your new purchases will be on DVD. (To learn more about purchasing a DVD player, see Chapter 10, "Digital Pictures on a Disc: DVD Players." For information about the latest CD players and changers, see Chapter 17, "Sound at the Speed of Light: CD Players and Recorders.")

Power Up

Here's something not everybody knows—every DVD player can also play CDs! That's right—if you have a DVD player, you don't need a separate CD player. Note, however, that most DVD players *can't* play back CD-Rs (those CDs you record yourself from a CD recorder), even though they play back regular CDs just fine.

The Other Stuff in Your System

What else do you have hooked up in your living room? Here's a short list of additional components, and whether you should keep them or go shopping:

➤ **Television antenna.** Over-the-air broadcast signals produce pretty much the worst picture and sound you can imagine—and we won't even go into the limited programming available. While you still might need an antenna to receive your local television stations, you should consider investing in a digital satellite dish for high-quality picture and sound, as well as hundreds of channels of programming. (One notable exception to this rule is if you have an HDTV-capable system; you'll need an over-the-air antenna to receive broadcasts from local stations transmitting in HDTV format.)

➤ **Cable TV.** Some cable systems deliver acceptable picture and sound, some don't. (You know which one *you* have!) In any case, you'll get better picture and sound—and, in some cases, more programming options—from a digital satellite dish.

➤ **Satellite TV.** Lucky you! If you already have a digital broadcast satellite (DBS) dish, you're all set! No need to upgrade to a new unit, unless you want to receive HDTV signals from your digital program provider.

➤ **Audiocassette recorder.** While you *could* upgrade to a CD recorder (or even a MiniDisc recorder—although this is not a widely embraced technology), if you're currently recording your own audio tapes, there's no reason to quit doing so just because you're getting a new home theater system. Use your own best judgment here.

➤ **Turntable.** If you still have a turntable as part of your audio system, you're either (a) hopelessly low-fi and behind the times, or (b) an audiophile from way back who thinks that CDs just don't sound as good as the best vinyl. If you're the former—throw away that monstrosity and get yourself a CD player, for heaven's sake! If you're the latter—there's no need to throw away something you love, although you might want to check out the new DVD-Audio and SA-CD formats for their dramatically improved sound.

➤ **Eight-track player.** Oh, come on—you're kidding me, right?

Check It Off: Your Home Theater Shopping List

Ready to go shopping? Then use the following table as a handy shopping list for those new audio and video components you really need for your home theater system!

Home Theater Shopping List

Function	Why Buy	What to Buy
Video display	Your old TV is too small	27"–35" direct view TV
	Your old TV doesn't have video or S-Video inputs	40" or larger rear or front projection TV Plasma flat-screen display
	Your old TV doesn't have the features you want; you want to upgrade to digital TV or HDTV	HDTV monitor
Audio system	Your old receiver is audio only or isn't Dolby Digital compatible	Audio/video receiver with Dolby Digital surround sound
	You have only two speakers	Five surround-sound speakers
	You want to experience gut-thumping bass	Powered subwoofer
Video source	You only have a VCR or an old laserdisc player	DVD player or changer
	Your old VCR is mono only	VHS HiFi VCR
	You want higher-quality time-shifting	Digital video recorder

Function	Why Buy	What to Buy
	You're tired of watching broadcast TV or your cable stinks	Digital broadcast satellite (DBS)
Audio source	You don't have a CD player or you don't want to use your DVD player for CDs	CD player, changer, or recorder
	You want to record your own music	Audiocassette recorder, CD recorder, or MiniDisc recorder

The Least You Need to Know

➤ If you have a relatively new, relatively big TV, it may work as the centerpiece of your new home theater system; if not, it's time to upgrade.

➤ No matter what kind of audio system you currently have, you probably need to purchase a Dolby Digital-compatible a/v receiver—and buy a whole new set of speakers.

➤ If you want really gut-thumping sound, add a subwoofer to your system.

➤ While there's no reason to throw out your old VCR or laserdisc player, a DVD player is essential to any new home theater system.

Chapter 3

How to Shop: Get the Best Stuff—at the Best Price

In This Chapter

➤ Research before you shop

➤ Where to shop for your home theater system

➤ How to shop for equipment—and the best ways to compare different models

➤ Questions to ask your dealer—*before* you buy!

You've decided to dive headfirst into the wonderful world of home theater. You've determined what equipment you need and checked your bank account, and it's just full enough to pay for what you want. Now it's time to go shopping!

Before You Buy: Get Smart!

Before you hand over your credit card, you need to do some homework. The smarter you are before you buy, the more likely you'll be to purchase the right equipment—at the right price.

The first thing you need to do is determine what types of components you want. Use the checklist in Chapter 2, "What to Buy: Figuring Out What You Have, What You Need, and What You Want" (and the information throughout this book!), to narrow down the equipment you really need.

Once you know what components you want, you need some sort of idea of the price range, brand, and even models that fit your purchasing criteria. This is where the real homework comes in—in the form of additional reading and a little Web surfing.

Appendix B, "Home Theater Resources," lists a ton of magazines and Web sites that you can use to gather background information before you go out shopping. The audio/video magazines are great not only for their articles and equipment reviews, but also because of their advertisements. You can almost use the manufacturer ads as a kind of catalog, showcasing the very latest equipment.

It also helps to check out your local newspapers for ads from your local audio/video retailers. These ads will give you an idea of who carries what brands, and some of the going prices.

Power Up

You need to be careful of the equipment featured in both manufacturer and retailer advertisements. Manufacturer ads (from Sony, RCA, JVC, and the like) will almost always feature equipment from the very top of their lines—in other words, the most expensive models available. Retailer ads (from Best Buy, Circuit City, and so on), however, will almost always feature equipment at the very *bottom* of the manufacturers' lines—in other words, the cheapest (in all senses of that word) available. Don't confuse the two types of advertising and think that the equipment in the manufacturer ads can be had for the prices in the retailer ads; it just isn't so! Besides, you'll probably end up buying equipment that's *middle* of the line—not quite as cutting edge as that in the four-color magazine ads, and a little bit more expensive than that advertised in the newspaper.

You can also find a wealth of information on the Internet. Most manufacturers have a plethora of product information on their Web sites; some manufacturers even include detailed spec sheets and downloadable instruction manuals online.

There are also a number of industry and enthusiast Web sites that include equipment reviews and comparisons. I've listed several of these sites (along with select manufacturers' sites) in Appendix B.

I'd like to draw your attention to two Web sites that I find particularly useful. The first, etown.com (www.etown.com) is a great industry site that features a mixture of informative equipment reviews and product news; etown.com even includes links to purchase most of the equipment featured on its site.

The other site I highly recommend is AudioREVIEW.com (www.audioreview.com). This site, part of the ConsumerREVIEW family, features equipment reviews written by users just like you. I find these reviews—listed by type of equipment and specific model number—extremely honest (painfully so, at times!) and helpful. I can't think of a better site for finding out what other folks think about a particular piece of equipment. You'll discover the real-world pros and cons that a typical salesperson either won't tell you or doesn't know about.

Where to Shop

Now that you have some idea of what you want to buy, where should you buy it? There are many types of dealers available, but I tend to break them down into the following types:

➤ **Internet/catalog merchants.** Just about any model from any manufacturer can be found for sale from an Internet e-tailer or catalog merchant. (Note that many traditional consumer electronics catalogers, such as Crutchfield, also have robust Internet sites.) The advantages of buying online are convenience and price; the disadvantage is a total lack of human interaction and customer service. If you know what you want and just want the best price, shopping online is great; if, on the other hand, you want to compare performance or need some hand-holding and advice, stay offline. Shop here if you know exactly what you want and want the best deal possible.

➤ **Mass merchants.** These retailers—typified by Best Buy and Circuit City—carry a wide selection of low- to midrange equipment, along with a smattering of higher-end models. Their prices are generally quite low, but so is the quality of their sales help, in most cases. Shop here if you know what you want and are looking for a good deal.

➤ **Audio/video specialists.** These stores are usually local or regional, and typically stock midrange and higher-end equipment—but not a lot of low-end gear. You'll find more knowledgeable sales help here and get more hand-holding than you will at a mass merchant. Some a/v specialists even do their own custom installations. Shop here if you want more serious equipment, and don't mind paying a little more for it.

➤ **Custom installers.** Custom installers are the top rung of the retail ladder. These pros fly in some rarified air, and typically handle high-end equipment that you just won't find anyplace else. A custom installer will handle your complete system, from concept through installation—including, in some cases, remodeling your home's interior to best fit your new system. If you're concerned about price, find another place to shop; you'll get superb service here, and you'll pay for it.

Power Up

It's relatively easy to find your local Best Buy or Circuit City, but where do you find a custom installer? The custom-installation business tends to work by word of mouth, but there is a central directory of the very best installers in the country. The Custom Electronic Design and Installation Association (CEDIA) maintains a finder service for custom electronic designers and installers. Just go to the CEDIA Web site (www.cedia.org), click on the Help for Homeowners link, and then click on the Find a Professional link. You can then search for installers by regional area or by company name. While you're on the CEDIA site, check out the articles on "How to Hire a Custom Installer" and "What Can a Custom Designer/Installer Do for You?"

The following table should point you to the right kind of retailer for your particular needs.

Where to Shop for Audio/Video Equipment

What You Want:	Internet/ Cataloger	Mass Merchant	Audio/ Video Specialist	Custom Installer
Rock-bottom prices	Yes	Yes	Sometimes	No
Hassle-free returns	No	Yes	Yes	Yes
Repair service	No	Sometimes	Yes	Yes
Budget equipment	Yes	Yes	No	No
High-end equipment	Yes	No	Yes	Yes
Esoteric equipment	No	No	No	Yes
Side-by-side comparisons	No	Yes	Yes	Yes
Knowledgeable sales help	No	No	Yes	Yes
Delivery and setup	No	No	Yes	Yes
Custom installation	No	No	Sometimes	Yes

How to Shop

Now that you're in the store, how do you choose the right models of equipment for your home theater system? Here are some tips on the best ways to shop for the equipment you need:

➤ **Look—and listen.** Which TV should you buy? That's simple—the one that looks best to you! It's the same thing with speakers or receivers. You should use your time in the store to do plenty of side-by-side comparisons of different products. Don't rely only on product specs—use your eyes and ears to decide which equipment you really like the best!

➤ **Bring your own demo material.** You *could* rely on the soap operas and sitcoms playing on the store's banks of television sets, but it's better if you bring your own comparison material. Pick out a DVD that can put a system through a real workout, and then use that same DVD (and the same scenes on the DVD) when comparing different models. (Movies with lots of action—and big sound—work well, as do quieter films that let you here the nuances in the surround soundtrack.) The same logic applies when comparing audio equipment—pick a CD with broad dynamic range to use as a test disc. (The best CDs to demo are those you're intimately familiar with—you know how they *should* sound—as well as those with plenty of deep bass and high cymbals, played both loud and soft.)

➤ **Adjust it yourself.** Have you ever looked at a wall of TVs in a store and noticed that one or two models really catch your eye? That could be because they're the better sets, or it could be because somebody cranked up their brightness—and your eyes were attracted to the brighter picture. Don't assume that all sets on the floor are adjusted optimally. Pick out the sets you want to compare, and then *adjust them yourself* for their optimal performance. Then—and only then— can you give them a true comparison.

➤ **Remember the room.** When comparing equipment—especially televisions and loudspeakers—try to take into account any peculiarities of your particular space. If your favorite chair is positioned 45 degrees off-angle, make sure you evaluate televisions from that angle, not just head-on. If you have unusual light sources or strange acoustics, take those factors into account when shopping.

➤ **Go ahead—look at the good stuff.** You've been good about setting a budget and narrowing your choices to selected models within your price range. That doesn't mean, however, that you can't at least look at some of the higher-end equipment. If nothing else, you'll gain an appreciation of what spending all that extra money will give you. You might even find that there's something about one of those models that really appeals to you, and reevaluate your purchasing parameters.

➤ **Don't waste the salesperson's time.** I used to sell consumer electronics at retail, and this was a particular pet peeve for me. Don't go to an a/v specialist and pump the salesperson for all sorts of information (and spend beaucoup amounts of time demoing different models) and then head to a mass merchant or Internet e-tailer to save a few bucks on your purchase. If you want sales expertise, be willing to pay for it, and if you're going to buy from a no-frills dealer, don't try to get the frills elsewhere for free!

➤ **Watch out for unbelievable deals.** If you find a price that sounds too good to be true, it probably is. Assuming that you've done your homework, you should know the going prices for the equipment you're looking for. If you find a dealer who is offering that particular model for substantially less than what you find elsewhere, ask why. Maybe the price is for a demo model, or reconditioned unit, or (if you're purchasing online or via direct mail) for a *gray market* model imported from overseas and not intended for sale in the U.S. (and probably not covered under a standard manufacturer's warranty). Believe it or not, most equipment sells for pretty much the same price at all dealers (give or take 10 percent), so any unusual low price should raise your eyebrows.

Product Specs

So-called **gray market** goods are products that are made available outside a manufacturer's normal distribution channels. Most consumer electronics distributors have their own authorized network of distributors and retailers; some retailers, outside the authorized network, obtain merchandise through a variety of means (often from other countries where the manufacturer sells similar merchandise) and sell it at a significant discount. Unfortunately, many manufacturers will not honor the warranties on products obtained outside their dealer network. The best way to avoid gray market goods is to deal only with a manufacturer's authorized dealers; you can typically find lists of authorized dealers on a manufacturer's Web site.

➤ **What if you don't like it—or it breaks?** Before you sign on the dotted line, ask about the dealer's return policy. What if you get the unit home and it doesn't work well with the rest of your system—or your particular room dynamics? How easy is it to return merchandise? Will you be charged a restocking fee? If you're purchasing online or from a cataloger, how do you return the merchandise, and who pays for return shipping? Beyond simple returns, you should also ask about product service—who do you call if your product needs repair? Even though most consumer electronics products are highly reliable, it's good to know who'll take care of you if something does go wrong.

Bottom line: Find a dealer who you're comfortable with, and who'll work with you—whatever your particular needs may be. Don't spend a dime if you're not comfortable or not sure of your decision!

The Least You Need to Know

➤ Before you start shopping, read a few audio/video magazines and check out relevant Web sites to help set your purchase parameters.

➤ If you want advice and service, shop at an audio/video specialist or custom in-staller; if you want sale prices and low-priced equipment, shop online or at a mass merchant.

➤ When shopping, use your own source material to perform side-by-side equip-ment comparisons.

➤ Before you pay for your purchase, find out about the store's return and service policies.

Part 2

Picture Perfect: Television Today

From standard direct view televisions to projection TVs to the newest HDTV sets, you have a bigger variety of video displays to choose from today than at any time in history. Not sure what size screen you need? Confused about rear projection and front projection? Curious about those new flat-screen TVs? Want to know what digital TV is—and whether you need a high-definition system? Then read this part to find out which display is best for you!

Chapter 4

Pick a Picture: Choose the Right TV for Your System

In This Chapter

➤ Is a wide-screen TV better than a square one?

➤ Why the industry is embracing digital and high-definition TV

➤ Selecting what size TV you should have in your home theater system

➤ The four different types of displays—direct view, rear projection, front projection, and flat-screen plasma

➤ What makes one set more expensive than another

The most important part of your home theater system is the video display. The better—and bigger—your video display, the more realistic your home theater experience.

You should allocate at least a quarter of your home theater budget to your video display. This chapter will help you pick the right kind of display for your system. (You can then turn to Chapters 5 through 8 to learn more about specific types of displays—including the latest digital and high-definition TVs.)

Not Your Father's Zenith: New Tech TV

Before we examine the different types of displays you can buy, you need to get up to speed on some of the new technologies available on TVs today. I guarantee you, if you haven't bought a TV set for five years or more, things have changed!

The Whole Picture: Wide-Screen Movies and Letterboxing

When the movie industry felt threatened by the then-new medium of television back in the 1950s, the studios responded by producing films in various wide-screen formats. These formats—Panavision, Cinemascope, and the rest—provided a much wider picture than that presented by television's "little square box."

In reality, television doesn't present a perfectly square picture. The standard television picture has an aspect ratio of 4:3—which means that if a screen is four units of measurement wide, it's also three units tall. Another way to measure this is to say that the standard television screen has a 1.33:1 ratio—the width is 1.33 times the height.

The various wide-screen formats used by Hollywood presented ratios much wider than 1.33:1—1.85:1 was common, but some movies were filmed as wide as 2.35:1. In the widest of these formats, the picture was more than twice as wide as it was tall.

Well, it turns out that television didn't kill movies after all, and both media have learned to coexist. One result is that you now have the opportunity to watch just about any movie ever made on your home TV. But how, you ask, do you display a wide-screen movie on a decidedly unwide television screen?

There are two ways this can work. The most common, until recently, was for a technician to "pan and scan" the narrower television image area over the movie's image—cutting off the edges of the wide-screen picture. This is a somewhat less than satisfactory approach, however, as it often cuts off important parts of the picture, and definitely interferes with the way the director wanted the movie presented.

A more recent approach is to present the movie at its full width—which leaves some unused areas at the top and bottom of your television screen. This approach, called letterboxing, displays the wide-screen movie in a strip across the center of your screen, with long black bars above and below the movie image. Most DVDs present movies in letterboxed versions.

With the move to high-definition television (discussed in Chapter 8, "The Next Generation: Digital and High-Definition TV"), the television industry had the opportunity to resolve this wide-screen problem. The solution was to specify a wider aspect ratio for HDTV broadcasts.

HDTV programming is spec'ed with a 16:9 aspect ratio—or 1.78:1, if you want to measure it that way. With this aspect ratio, wide-screen movies that use the common 1.85:1 ratio can be displayed on screen with little or no letterboxing; even the wider 2.35:1 movies fit better on a screen with a 1.78:1 ratio.

The following figure shows you how the 4:3 and 16:9 TV aspect ratios compare with the more common Hollywood aspect ratios.

Comparing different aspect ratios—HDTV uses the 16:9 ratio.

If you're quick on your feet, you're already wondering how standard television programming—produced in the 4:3 ratio—will be displayed on a 16:9 screen. The answer is simple—vertical letterboxing. That is, the 4:3 picture appears centered on the 16:9 screen, with black bars to the right and left. (Some sets attempt to digitally stretch the 4:3 picture to fill the entire 16:9 screen, but the result is a little odd, to say the least.)

A wide-screen movie letterboxed on a 4:3 ratio screen.

(There's Something About Mary, *courtesy of Twentieth Century Fox Home Entertainment*)

A Better Picture: Digital and High-Definition TV

As you read previously, a wider screen is part of the spec for high-definition television. HDTV is more than just a wider picture, however; it's also a much higher resolution picture—with better sound, to boot. All of this comes courtesy of digital reproduction (as opposed to standard analog broadcasts), and is being phased in over the next decade by the federal government. By 2006, all television broadcasts in the U.S. will be in HDTV—which means that sometime before then, you better buy an HDTV television!

Input/Output

Television screens are always measured diagonally, from one corner to another—even when the screen is a 16:9 aspect ratio. What this means is that if you take two screens with the same diagonal measurement, the 16:9 screen isn't as tall and doesn't have the same viewing area as the 4:3 screen with the same measurement.

Essentially, if you want to keep the same height—and thus preserve the same viewing area for standard 4:3 programming—you want your 16:9 screen to have a diagonal measurement about 23 percent larger than a comparable 4:3 screen. As an example, if you're used to watching a 35" 4:3 screen, when you upgrade to a 16:9 model, you'd want to go with an approximately 43" model. This would give you a set with the same screen height—it would just be a wider screen.

The danger is in purchasing a 16:9 screen with the same diagonal measurement as your old 4:3 set. If you move from a 35" 4:3 set to a 35" 16:9 set, the new screen will be shorter than your old one—which will result in a smaller viewing area when you watch standard 4:3 programming.

In short, when you move up to HDTV—and the resultant 16:9 aspect ratio—you'll have to get a slightly larger screen (as measured diagonally) than what you had before.

However, I wouldn't recommend that everyone rush out and put down 10 grand on a big-screen HDTV set just yet. Today there are few HDTV broadcasts (although television stations serving more than half the U.S. are already HDTV-capable), and the sets are quite expensive. You might want to wait a year or two before you become an HDTV household—or you can buy a lower-priced, high-resolution, digital-ready television today, and add an HDTV tuner at a later date.

HDTV is an important enough development to warrant its own chapter in this book. Turn to Chapter 8 to learn more.

The Future of TV: What's Next?

Writing a book like this, one needs to project out two to three years. What amazing developments in television technology will we see in the first half of this new decade?

To be honest, I'm not that great a prognosticator, so I took the opportunity to talk to Michael Shultz, general manager of TV Product Planning at Thomson Consumer Electronics, the company that produces RCA, Proscan, and GE-branded video and audio products. Shultz pointed out several areas that Thomson thinks will become more important over the next few years, including:

➤ **Digital TV.** This is the obvious one. Customers can easily see the improved picture offered by the various digital formats, even if they're still scared off by the high prices on full-blown HDTV sets. Thomson is seeing strong sales on its RCA and Proscan high-resolution, digital-ready, direct view and rear projection TVs. I checked out RCA's new 35" direct view and 52" rear projection digital-ready models, and can definitely see the appeal.

➤ **Program guides.** Thomson listens to its customers. With millions of digital satellite systems sold each year, Thomson discovered that one of the things users liked best was the system's on-screen program guide. It wasn't too big a leap to conclude that viewers without satellite dishes might also like an on-screen program guide, so Thomson has been steadily adding program-guide technology throughout its various television lines. Expect to see more and more TVs—from Thomson and others—come with automatically updated on-screen program guides.

➤ **Interactivity.** Thomson has announced its intention to enhance the functionality of its television line with various forms of interactivity. Just what is interactive television? It's the capability of pushing a button on your remote while watching a TV show, and having something happen. Television programmers can use interactivity to make you a live participant in a game show, or register your vote in a town hall forum, or let you easily order that videotape advertised at the end of the movie of the week—all with the push of a button. At the top end of the line, that interactivity will probably come from incorporating WebTV technology into the television sets themselves. For a larger number of models, however, Thomson will create "enhanced TV" with simple point-and-click voting, shopping, and e-mail—all accomplished without the need for a phone-based Internet connection. Instead, Thomson will use 900Mhz pager-based technology to connect the television to the appropriate interactive service. I'm looking forward to this one.

Shultz told me that Thomson sees sales of larger and higher-end televisions continuing very strong for the next few years, driven not only by digital TV and HDTV, but also by exploding sales of DVD players and DIRECTV satellite systems. Let's face it—if you add a higher-quality video source to your system, you'll probably want a higher-quality TV to match. That's what Thomson figures, anyway—and I agree!

Size Matters: Choosing the Right Size Screen

The traditional method of "sizing" your TV screen is that you want your viewing distance to be about three times the size of the screen (measured diagonally). As an example, if you sit nine feet away from the TV, divide nine by three to get three feet. Convert that into inches (which is how screen sizes are measured, at least in the U.S.) and you come up with a 36" screen.

However, if you're purchasing a 16:9 set, the traditional diagonal screen measurements go out the window. When reproducing 4:3 ratio programming, a 16:9 screen needs to be about 23 percent times as big (diagonally) to display the same screen area. So if you're buying 16:9, multiply the recommended screen size by 1.23 to get a screen that's as tall as the one you're used to.

The following table provides some more exact guidance in terms of recommended screen sizes.

Recommended Screen Sizes

Viewing Distance	Ideal 4:3 Screen Size	Ideal 16:9 Screen Size
6'	25" diagonal	31" diagonal
7'	27" diagonal	33" diagonal
8'	32" diagonal	39" diagonal
9'	36" diagonal	44" diagonal
10'	40" diagonal	49" diagonal
11'	45" diagonal	55" diagonal
12'	48" diagonal	59" diagonal
13'	52" diagonal	64" diagonal
14'	56" diagonal	69" diagonal
15'	60" diagonal	74" diagonal
16'	64" diagonal	79" diagonal
17'	68" diagonal	84" diagonal
18'	72" diagonal	89" diagonal
19'	76" diagonal	93" diagonal
20'	80" diagonal	98" diagonal

Note that with the higher-resolution pictures of HDTV—and the use of line doublers in some non-HDTV sets—this traditional method of figuring the right screen size isn't quite as reliable. These new technologies pretty much eliminate visible scan lines, which means you can sit a lot closer to an HDTV or line-doubled set than you can to a standard resolution model. It's not uncommon for videophiles to use a 55" or larger 4:3 aspect screen in a room with a viewing distance of 10' or less—with no problems whatsoever.

Product Specs

A standard video signal consists of a series of interlaced lines. One field of 240 *odd* lines (representing half the picture) is flashed on screen, immediately followed by a second field of the remaining 240 *even* lines; the result is one complete 480-line picture.

Interlaced pictures tend to flicker, especially when viewed close up. In fact, get too close to a large TV screen and you can start to see the lines themselves.

The solution to this problem is to "fill in the gaps" between the lines. This can be done with **line multiplier** technology. In its simplest form, a line doubler takes the interlaced video and converts it into a progressively scanned image—effectively displaying the full 480 lines at a time rather than the two 240-line halves. This process increases the apparent (but not the actual) resolution of the picture.

Line doublers—and triplers and quadruplers—are found on most high-end front projection televisions, and are starting to appear in high-resolution, digital-ready, direct view and rear projection televisions.

Round, Flat, Front, or Rear: Four Different Types of TV to Choose From

There are four basic types of display technologies available today: direct view, rear projection, front projection, and flat-screen plasma. Which type you choose depends on your budget, the demands of your room, and your personal preferences.

Direct View Televisions

Direct view television is the traditional type of set you've always had in your living room. A direct view set utilizes a picture tube—also called a cathode ray tube, or CRT—as its video display; you can find direct view sets as small as 5-inch diagonal and as large as 36-inch diagonal.

Direct view sets typically have the brightest picture of any display type, and generally cost less than similar-sized projection or plasma sets. Their main limit is size; if your viewing distance is 10' or more, a direct view set may be inadequate for your needs.

For more information on direct view televisions, see Chapter 5, "The Boob Tube: Direct View Television."

Rear Projection Televisions

Rear projection televisions (RPTVs) are ideal for consumers who have a bigger room and need a bigger screen—but don't want to totally break the bank. You can find smaller RPTVs—in the 45" diagonal range—selling for as little as $1,500.

Input/Output

At one point in time Mitsubishi produced a 40" diagonal direct view set. (I have one in my own home theater system!) It was a monster (in terms of size and weight) and no other manufacturers ever followed suit. When Mitsubishi abandoned the direct view business in the late 1990s (and switched to all projection), the era of the ultra-large tube was over, replaced by more affordable (and lighter) rear projection sets.

An RPTV works by using three CRTs (one each for the colors red, green, and blue) "firing" backwards in the cabinet towards a mirror, which then projects the picture through the front screen. Because of this projection design, RPTVs by nature produce a dimmer image than do direct view sets. In addition, the viewing angle for an RPTV is more restrictive; the more off angle you get, the dimmer the picture becomes.

Still, the picture quality of today's RPTVs is vastly better than that produced by RPTVs just a few years ago—and an RPTV is a good choice for most midrange home theater systems.

For more information on RPTVs, see Chapter 6, "Bigger Is Better: Projection Television."

Front Projection Televisions

Front projection televisions (FPTVs) are used in most larger and professional home theater installations. The advantage of an FPTV is that you can project a *really* large picture—up to 20' diagonal in some super installations.

An FPTV system works similar to an RPTV system, except the three CRTs (or LCDs or other types of projectors) sit in front of the screen, and project the picture across the room directly onto the screen. This type of system is inherently less bright than any other type of display, and also has a somewhat narrow viewing angle. This means that the room has to be dark and narrow for an FPTV system to work—although the room can be very large, of course.

FPTVs typically cost more than RPTVs, as well. You'll find FPTV systems starting at around $3,000, and going as high as you can possibly imagine. (For more information on FPTVs, see Chapter 6.)

Flat-Screen Plasma Televisions

The newest type of display is very thin—and very expensive. Plasma displays sandwich a layer of plasma gas between two thin layers of glass; the glass layers are covered with electrodes. Voltage is applied to the electrodes, causing a single pixel to emit light of a specified color. (This is kind of how neon signs work—electricity causes the gas to light up.)

The result is a display no more than six inches deep, that can be easily mounted on a wall—or on a ceiling! In fact, the main benefit of a plasma display is its versatility in tricky installations with unusual space considerations. (For this reason, plasma displays are more popular in Europe than in the U.S., because European homes are typically much smaller than American homes.)

You'll find that most current plasma displays are HDTV-capable and formatted for the 16:9 aspect ratio. Sizes range from 40" to 60" diagonal, and prices are high—currently $10,000 or more. While you can expect prices to decrease over the next few years, plasma displays will probably remain a niche item for some time. (For more information on plasma displays, see Chapter 7, "Thin Is In: Flat-Screen Plasma Television.")

Which Should You Choose?

When it comes time to select the video display for your system, turn to the following table to help make your decision.

Video Displays—Which Should You Choose?

Consideration	Direct View	RPTV	FPTV	Plasma
Price	$350–$2,000	$1,500–$10,000	$3,000+	$10,000+
Space (depth)	Deep	Deep	Flat	Flat
Picture size	Up to 36"	40"–80"	50"–20'	40"–60"
Picture brightness	Bright	Moderate	Dim	Moderate
Viewing angle	Wide	Moderate	Narrow	Wide
Second unit (projector)	No	No	Yes	No

In short, you should choose the following:

➤ If you have a smaller room, want the brightest possible picture, want a wide viewing angle, or are on a budget, choose a direct view TV.

➤ If you have a larger room but want to make as few compromises as possible in terms of room lighting or viewing angle, choose a rear projection TV.

➤ If you want the largest picture possible, don't mind restricting both viewing angle and room lighting, and price isn't an object, choose a front projection TV.

➤ If you have virtually no space for a television set or projector and price is no object—or if you just want to show off the neat technology—choose a plasma TV.

Why Is *That* Set so Expensive?

Once you choose a specific display type and screen size, you still have to choose from a plethora of different models from different manufacturers. What makes one television better or more expensive than another? There are several factors:

➤ **Screen size.** The bigger the screen, the higher the price—no matter what the display type.

➤ **Picture quality.** However it's achieved—via a better CRT or brighter projector or enhanced electronics or whatever—it generally costs a little more to deliver an enhanced picture.

➤ **Sound system.** The more speakers in the set, the higher the cost.

➤ **Inputs and outputs.** The more jacks in the back, the higher the cost.

Input/Output

If you're hooking up high-quality video sources—such as DVD players and digital satellite systems—to your TV, you'll need more and higher-quality jacks. In particular, look for the following connectors on the back of any set you're considering adding to your home theater system:

➤ RF input (for antenna or cable)

➤ Video and L/R audio inputs (using RCA jacks—most higher-end sets will have at least two separate sets of audio/video inputs)

➤ Video and L/R audio output

➤ S-Video input

➤ Component video inputs with separate Y (luminance), Pr (red), and Pb (blue) inputs

➤ RGB input (used to input computer signals, or in some cases HDTV signals—not always a necessary input)

➤ Speaker outputs

You can learn more about these different types of connections in Chapter 21, "Plug It In: Which Cable Goes Where."

➤ **Remote control.** Virtually all televisions come with some type of remote control; the better sets include remotes that control more functions—and other components.

➤ **Additional features.** The more stuff on your TV, the higher the price. Features such as picture-in-picture, V-Chips, and on-screen program guides add to the set's cost.

In addition, if you're looking for a higher-resolution picture—and a set that's digital-ready for the upcoming HDTV standard—get ready to shell out some big bucks. The circuitry necessary to display HDTV-resolution pictures is mind-boggling, and can add hundreds of dollars to the manufacturing cost of a set. Until digital and high-definition TV become more of a mass market item, expect to pay a premium for the advanced technology necessary in these sets.

The Least You Need to Know

➤ Traditional TV screens have an aspect ratio of 4:3; new digital TVs have a wider 16:9 aspect ratio, which is better for displaying wide-screen movies.

➤ In addition to the wider screen, the new HDTV format delivers a higher-resolution picture and Dolby Digital surround sound.

➤ In general, you should choose a TV with a screen one-third the size as the distance you sit from the screen; if you sit nine feet away from your TV, choose a 36" diagonal screen.

➤ There are four different types of video displays; which you choose depends on the characteristics of your home theater room, your budget, and your own visual preferences.

➤ For smaller rooms (and smaller budgets) a traditional direct view TV is recommended; for larger rooms (and larger budgets), consider moving to a rear projection or front projection TV.

Chapter 5

The Boob Tube: Direct View Television

In This Chapter

➤ How direct view televisions work

➤ Which television brands are the most popular

➤ What you can expect to pay for specific screen sizes

➤ What to look for when you're shopping for a new TV

The most popular video display is the old standby—direct view. Direct view televisions have been around as long as television itself, and are in no danger of being supplanted by any of the other display formats. In fact, the most popular screen size remains the good old 19 incher—which you can now buy for $150 or less.

The almost unbelievable low price for a 19" TV demonstrates one of the most amazing aspects of the consumer electronics industry—continually falling prices and incredible consumer values. It wasn't that long ago that a 19" TV sold for $400; today, that same $400 will get you a full-featured 27" model.

The benefit to you, of course, is obvious. It's now possible to assemble a home theater system—complete with large-screen TV—for a fraction of what it used to cost. Where $1,000 wouldn't have bought much more than a big TV a few years ago, you can now assemble a complete (albeit budget) system for the same price—or spend a few bucks more and get what used to be a high-end system for a midrange price.

Whatever else you might say about the consumer electronics industry, you can't complain about the prices!

Direct View Basics

A direct view display is nothing more than what most folks call a television set. Direct view TVs are ideal for budget and midrange home theater systems; they deliver the brightest picture and the widest viewing angle at the lowest cost of any available display device. The only limitation to direct view television is the screen size; today's direct view sets top off at 36" (measured diagonally, of course), while rear projection sets can go to 60" or more.

Your standard direct view TV includes a picture tube (also called a cathode ray tube, or CRT); a tuner (which is called a terrestrial tuner if it receives broadcast television signals, or a satellite tuner if it receives DSS signals); the various circuitry it takes to convert the television signals into the images displayed on the CRT; a sound system consisting of one or more speakers; and a variety of input and output jacks on the back of the set.

Beyond these basics, you'll find a variety of sets, at a variety of quality levels, at a variety of prices, from a variety of manufacturers. In fact, the choices available can be overwhelming!

The Price Is Right

In terms of prices, here's what you can expect to pay (at minimum) for the most popular large-screen sizes:

> ➤ 27" diagonal: $350 and up
> ➤ 32" diagonal: $600 and up
> ➤ 35" and 36" diagonal: $900 and up

Obviously, the more feature-laden the set, the higher the price; high-end sets from most manufacturers sometimes go for twice as much as the least expensive sets in their lines! Which means, if you do the math, that you can spend up to $2,000 for a full-featured, digital-ready 36" set.

Get Branded

What are some of the best brands of direct view television? You can always find good values in the RCA brand (and in the closely related Proscan and GE brands—all manufactured by Thomson Consumer Electronics), and some of the top-end RCA sets more than hold their own with the best from any manufacturer. Sony is the other major contender, known more for its higher-end models; I particularly like Sony's WEGA series, with its revolutionary perfectly flat picture tubes. At the very high end of direct view offerings is Loewe (pronounced "low-vuh"), a German brand new to the U.S. delivering no-compromise performance.

There are many more brands to choose from, of course. Whichever brand you prefer, make sure to compare similarly priced models from other manufacturers, as well as models from the same manufacturer just above and below the model you're looking at. Make sure all the sets you're comparing are adjusted similarly, then spend as much time as you need evaluating each set—taking care to watch different types of programming, under different viewing conditions. I hate to state the obvious, but the set you buy should be the one you most like to watch—as long as it's within your price range, of course!

Smart Shopping: What to Look For

When it's time to shop for a new TV, what should you look for? Here are some of the technologies and features that should enter into your decision:

➤ **Screen size.** Traditionally, you want your viewing distance to be about three times the size of the screen (measured diagonally). So, if you sit nine feet away from the set, a 36" diagonal set is about the right size. However, if you choose a television with built-in line doubler or with HDTV resolution, then you can use a bigger screen with the same viewing distance. In any case, you're limited to a 36" maximum size with direct view sets—and you may need to think smaller, especially if you're on a budget. Inevitably, you'll be faced with the need to compromise picture quality with picture size; do you go with a high-end 32" model or a midrange 36" set? I can't make this kind of decision for you, but I can advise you to spend some time in a direct comparison of both options; ultimately, you have to choose the combination of size and quality that looks best for you.

➤ **Dark tubes.** The darker the surface of the picture tube, the better the set will reproduce a high-contrast picture. Go for the darkest screen you can find—you'll get both blacker blacks *and* whiter whites!

➤ **Flat tubes.** The flatter the surface of the picture tube, the better the picture in terms of less distortion, less glare, and so on. Late in 1999 Sony became the first television manufacturer to produce a totally flat picture tube, both horizontally and vertically. (It's a stunner!) Expect other manufacturers to follow with their own perfectly flat tubes—but whatever your price range, look for as flat a screen as possible.

➤ **Comb filter.** A comb filter is a piece of circuitry that reduces "dot crawl" along the straight edges of objects in a television picture. The larger the screen size, the more essential it is to have a high-performance comb filter; ragged edges are more prevalent on larger screens. You'll find different manufacturers using different types of comb filters; digital is better than analog, and 3-D filters are better than all the rest.

➤ **Overall picture quality.** You can measure lines of horizontal resolution and check out the various types of comb filters, but when it all comes down to it, picture quality is subjective. Give any set you're looking at a long test drive, and pick the model that looks best to your eyes. Look especially at black areas of the picture (you want true deep black, not dark gray); white areas (bright whites, not dingy whites), and red areas (on lower quality sets, red tends to "bloom"). Also look at the usable picture resolution by watching some movie credits; small white type on a black background is one of the toughest tests to which you can subject a TV.

➤ **Inputs and outputs.** If you're feeding your video sources through an audio/video receiver, all you need is a single set of inputs and outputs—even though these should be the highest possible quality. You should make sure the set has traditional RF antenna jacks, video/audio jacks (using RCA connectors), and at least one S-Video jack. If you're not using an a/v receiver, make sure the TV has enough input jacks to handle all your different video sources (VCR, DVD player, and so on).

➤ **Remote control.** Make sure the remote is easy to learn and easy to use. It doesn't hurt if the unit fits well in your hand, and if the buttons feel logical beneath your fingers. Look particularly for remotes that are preprogrammed with codes for the other components in your system, or for "learning" remotes that you can program yourself to operate your other components.

Input/Output

If you don't like your TV's remote control unit, you can always purchase a third-party universal remote. Many of these add-on remotes can control several of your home theater components, via either preprogrammed codes or learning technology. To learn more about remote controls for your home theater system, see Chapter 22, "Take Charge: Controlling Your System."

➤ **Sound system.** If you're integrating your TV into a home theater system with a/v receiver and separate speakers, don't worry about the TV's built-in sound system—you'll turn off the internal speakers, anyway. If you don't have a separate sound system, however, then you better make sure you listen to—and like—how the TV sounds. Trust me on this one, though—you will *always* get better sound with a separate audio system. Always.

➤ **Physical size.** Just how big is this TV set, anyway? Will it fit in the space you have in your living room? And, if you're picking it up yourself from your local dealer, will it fit in your car? Don't dismiss pure physical size—the last thing you want is to get the darn thing home and find out it won't fit in your a/v cabinet!

➤ **Picture-in-picture.** Picture-in-picture (PIP) technology lets you watch two programs at once—the second in a smaller on-screen window. Higher-end sets will have a second tuner for the PIP window; lower-end sets can only feed signals from a separate device (such as your VCR or DVD) into the PIP window. In either case, it's a good way to monitor TV programming while you're watching a movie on DVD—or, with second-tuner PIP systems, check out that *other* game on a Sunday afternoon!

➤ **Program guides.** Many sets come with built-in guides that display on-screen program listings for your area. All you have to do is push a button on your re-mote, and the set displays current and upcoming television programs, sorted by channel or (in some cases) by type of program. If you've ever used an on-screen program guide, you'll really appreciate this feature; it's a fast and easy way to see what else is on TV at any given time.

➤ **V-Chip parental controls.** If you have kids, look for sets with built-in V-Chips. This technology—when activated by you, the parent—will automatically block out programs rated inappropriate for certain age groups.

➤ **Digital capability.** When you're looking at high-end direct view sets, consider going with a high-resolution, digital-ready model. These sets (discussed in Chapter 8, "The Next Generation: Digital and High-Definition TV") typically in-clude line doublers to improve standard TV pictures and—when wedded with add-on HDTV tuners—are capable of displaying HDTV broadcasts. Some of these sets even have a 16:9 aspect ratio screen, for wide-screen programming. This type of set is a good compromise if you don't want to move all the way to HDTV for a year or more, but still need a large screen, high-quality set in the short term.

The Least You Need to Know

➤ Direct view TVs are the best-performing, lowest-priced display options for your home theater system—as long as you don't need larger than a 36" screen.

➤ Measure the distance from your chair to the TV set, and then choose a screen size that's roughly one-third that distance.

➤ Darker, flatter picture tubes and comb filter circuitry combine to produce sharper, higher-contrast pictures.

➤ You can find a basic 27" direct view set for as little as $350—or you can spend up to $2,000 for a full-featured 36" model.

Chapter 6

Bigger Is Better: Projection Television

In This Chapter

➤ Rear projection versus front projection

➤ How projection TV works—and how much it costs

➤ Four different types of front projectors

➤ Which type of projection—front or rear—is best for your home theater system

➤ What to look for when you're shopping for a projection television

---

When you need a display bigger than 36", you have to move beyond direct view into projection displays. Projection television works by projecting an image from a picture tube or other display onto a screen (or onto a mirror and *through* a screen), thus enabling larger pictures without the expense or impracticality of larger picture tubes.

There are two main types of projection TVs—rear projection (RPTV) and front projection (FPTV). RPTV sets are available in screen sizes ranging from 40" to 80" (diagonal), while FPTV screens can range in size from 50" to 20'. Smaller-screen RPTV sets can be purchased for as little as $1,500; FPTV sets start at $3,000.

Affordable Big Screens: Rear Projection Television

For most home theater enthusiasts, an RPTV is the best choice for their main video display. RPTVs present a good value in terms of price and performance, and come in the right sizes for most living rooms.

How Rear Projection Works

Rear projection sets use three different *cathode ray tubes* (CRTs)—one each for red, blue, and green—shooting backwards in the cabinet to a mirror. The mirror projects the images from these CRTs onto the screen at the front of the unit.

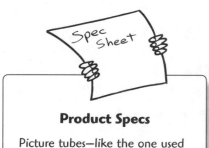

Product Specs

Picture tubes—like the one used in your direct view television set—are also called **cathode ray tubes,** or CRTs.

Today's RPTVs are much better than models sold even a few years ago. If you're used to the fuzzy pictures on a projection TV in your local bar, you're in for a big surprise. The best RPTVs today deliver pictures that rival those from similar-sized direct view TVs.

What affects the quality in a rear projection set? First, look at the set's CRTs; the bigger the tubes, the better the picture. (Most RPTVs use seven-inch CRTs; larger screen sizes incorporate nine-inch CRTs.) In addition, the better the lenses attached to the CRTs, the better the picture. (Glass lenses are much better than plastic ones.) Finally, the screen material can dramatically impact the picture quality; look for darker nonglare screens, when available.

Rear projection TVs use three CRTs projecting off a mirror onto the built-in screen.

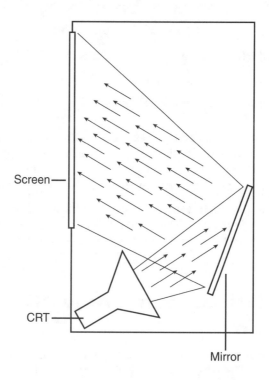

Should You Buy an RPTV?

The main advantages of rear projection are larger picture size (compared to direct view), low cost, and increased room flexibility (when compared to front projection). A rear projection set is also a good choice if you're thinking of upgrading your home theater system to 16:9 HDTV.

The main disadvantage to rear projection is bulk; these units weigh a ton and take up a lot of space. In addition, it helps if you lower the lighting in your room a bit when watching an RPTV; unlike a direct view set, RPTVs can look a little washed out under direct lighting.

If you've decided to go rear projection, the best buys typically are on models in the 45"–55" range. The most popular (and best-performing) brands include Sony, Pioneer, Mitsubishi, and RCA.

Power Up

Even though many HDTV and digital-ready RPTVs use seven-inch tubes, this size tube can't display all available pixels in a 1080i HDTV picture. (See Chapter 8, "The Next Generation: Digital and High-Definition TV," to learn more about 1080i and the other available HDTV formats.) For true HDTV, an RPTV really should use nine-inch projection tubes.

Really *Big* Big Screens: Front Projection Television

If your home theater system dictates a very large screen (80" or larger), you have a single choice: front projection.

How Front Projection Works

FPTVs are two-piece systems, utilizing both a projector and a screen. The projector unit typically contains three CRTs (or other display devices—see the following sections), and is located several feet in front of the large screen fabric screen. Images are projected from the projector unit onto the screen, much the way a movie projector displays images on a movie screen.

The size of the picture in a front projection system depends on the size of the screen, the capabilities of the projector, and the distance between the projector and the screen.

A projector unit can sit on the floor or be mounted on the ceiling; wherever it is, it needs to be carefully installed and calibrated for the best picture. Front projection systems are tricky to set up and typically require professional installation.

Most front projection systems use three CRTs projecting an image that converges on a separate screen.

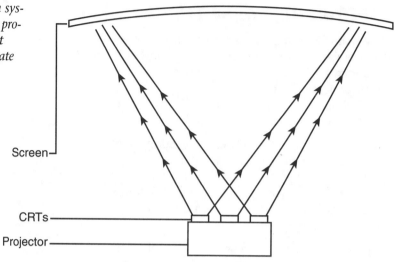

Screen

CRTs

Projector

Input/Output

Most high-end FPTVs utilize **line multiplying** technology to eliminate scan lines, which can be annoyingly visible with very large pictures. As discussed in Chapter 4, "Pick a Picture: Choose the Right TV for Your System," line doublers turn a normal interlaced picture into a progressively scanned picture—essentially doubling the number of scan lines visible at any given instant. Line triplers and quadruplers go a step further by increasing the scanning frequency for each individual picture. The result is a smoother picture, with less flicker and less-visible scan lines.

Fantastic Four: Different Types of Projectors

There are actually four different types of projectors used in FPTV systems. These types include:

➤ **LCD.** An LCD projector uses an internal LCD display to create the picture image, and then projects that image through a lens onto the screen. Since the picture is generated internally, these units don't require any *convergence;* all the adjustments you need can be done with the lens, which also lets you size and zoom the picture. While these units are easy to use, they typically have inferior picture quality, with low contrast and lots of pixellation. (Pixellation is the break up of the picture into chunks of pixels—resulting in a blocky picture, especially during scenes with lots of motion.)

Product Specs

FPTVs and RPTVs that use three CRTs—which includes most projection units—must **converge** the signal from all three light sources. Ideally, light from the red, blue, and green CRTs combine (converge) to create white. The CRTs, however, must be converged across all points of the screen, which can sometimes be a little tricky. To properly converge a projection set, you have to display a set of cross-hatch lines onscreen, and then use the set's service controls to adjust the red/blue/green settings across all the lines. It's possible to have a set converged properly in the center of the screen, yet be off convergence in one or more corners. Properly converging a set is a time-consuming process, sometimes taking several hours. The process is necessary, however, as a misconverged picture will display green or red or blue "fringing" around the edges of objects—definitely not a desirable situation!

➤ **CRT.** This is the traditional front projection unit, using three CRTs (picture tubes) to project the image on the screen. They're difficult to set up (and typically require professional installation and convergence), but deliver a good quality picture.

➤ **Light valve.** Light-valve projectors are relatively new (and relatively expensive), and use three CRTs to create images on three different LCD panels, which are then projected on the screen. Picture quality is sharper and brighter than with a traditional CRT projector.

➤ **DMD and DLP.** DMD (Digital Micromirror Device) and DLP (Digital Light Processing) projectors both work in similar fashion, using thousands of light-reflecting mirrors that are turned on or off to create the picture that is then projected on the screen. These units create a brighter picture than any other front projector, with few if any visible scan lines.

Most home-based FPTVs use CRT projection, although LCD models are starting to catch on (despite their often-inferior picture quality). At this writing, light valve and DMD/DLP projectors are pretty much for business use only.

The following table details the four different types of front projectors.

Types of Front Projectors

Feature	LCD	CRT	Light Valve	DMD/DLP
Price range	$3,000+	$4,000+	$15,000+	$10,000+
Needs convergence	No	Yes	Yes	Yes
Picture quality	Low	Good	Better	Best
Technology	LCDs	CRTs	CRT/LCD combo	Mirrors

Should You Buy an FPTV?

Whichever type of projector you decide on, the main advantage of front projection is size; if you need a super-large picture, this is literally the only way to go. (The million-dollar home theater system discussed in Chapter 24, "Home Beautiful: Installing a Custom System," uses an ultra-high-end front projection system with a 16' by 9' screen—the ultimate 16:9 HDTV system!)

The disadvantages of front projection are numerous—you need a dark room, you must have a narrow viewing angle, you probably should utilize the services of a professional installer, and you'll spend a lot of money. Entry-level FPTVs are more expensive than similarly sized RPTVs; you have to ante up at least $3,000 to get into the game. Prices on higher-end FPTVs can get into six figures.

When you're looking for an FPTV, you move away from the mass market brands into the realm of professional gear.

Front or Rear—Which Should You Buy?

Factoring in cost, size, and ease of use, the right projector for most midrange home theater systems is a rear projector. You'll typically spend between $2,000 and $4,000 for a 45"–60" RPTV model—and get a digital-ready display, to boot.

If you're aiming for a higher-end system—or have a very large room—then front projection is for you. You should pay for professional installation and setup—and make sure your system includes a good line doubler (or tripler or quadrupler)—but then you'll be all set to watch your movies on a *really* big screen!

Shop Smart: What to Look For

Whether you're shopping for a rear projection or front projection TV, here are some things to look for:

➤ **Screen size.** Traditionally, you want your viewing distance to be about three times the size of the screen (measured diagonally). So, if you sit 15' away from the screen, you'll want to go with a 60" model. However, if you choose an RPTV or FPTV with built-in line multiplier or with HDTV resolution, then you can use a bigger screen with the same viewing distance. (Learn more about HDTV and digital TV in Chapter 8.)

➤ **Viewing distance.** If you have your heart set on a super-large screen, you still need to use the old size/distance formula, because it's easy to sit too close to a big-screen TV. How far away do you have to sit before scan lines disappear?

➤ **Viewing angle.** The best picture on a projection TV comes when you're sitting directly in front of the screen (called "on axis"). How far off axis can you get before the picture deteriorates? If your easy chair is off to the side of your room, what will the picture look like from that angle?

➤ **HDTV capability.** Is the model you're looking at capable of receiving HDTV broadcasts—or of being upgraded to full HDTV compatibility? If you choose a digital-ready set, are you satisfied with a 4:3 aspect ratio or do you want to go with a 16:9 screen? If you choose a 4:3 model, will letterboxed movies appear big enough on the screen—or should you go for the next size up?

➤ **Comb filter.** A comb filter is a piece of circuitry that reduces "dot crawl" along the straight edges of objects in a television picture. The larger the screen size, the more essential it is to have a high-performance comb filter; ragged edges are more prevalent on larger screens. You'll find different manufacturers using different types of comb filters; digital is better than analog, and 3-D filters are better than all the rest.

➤ **Line doubler.** The bigger the picture, the greater your need for a line doubler (or tripler or quadrupler) to eliminate visible scan lines. You can add a line doubler to most FPTVs; only higher-end digital-ready RPTVs typically incorporate line-doubling technology.

➤ **Picture quality.** Is the picture bright enough? Sharp enough? Does it have enough contrast? Are the blacks black enough—and does the picture hold the correct geometry from edge to edge? Make sure the picture is adjusted properly before you do a thorough evaluation. Most sets come with color temperature settings; the cool setting will deliver a picture with a reddish tinge, whereas the warm setting delivers a bluer picture. Make sure you select the most appropriate color setting before you put the set through its paces.

➤ **Inputs and outputs.** If you're feeding your video sources through an audio/video receiver, all you need is a single set of inputs and outputs—even though these should be the highest possible quality. You should make sure the set has traditional RF antenna jacks, video/audio jacks (using RCA connectors), at least one S-Video jack, and a set of component video connections.

➤ **Remote control.** Make sure the remote is easy to learn and easy to use. It doesn't hurt if the unit fits well in your hand, and if the buttons feel logical beneath your fingers. Look particularly for remotes that are preprogrammed with codes for the other components in your system, or for "learning" remotes that you can program yourself to operate your other components.

➤ **Sound system.** If you're viewing a 45" or larger picture, you don't want to be limited by the set's built-in speaker system. Use an audio/video receiver and surround-sound speakers and you won't have to worry about the quality of the TV's sound system.

➤ **Physical size.** If you're looking at an RPTV, will the cabinet fit into the designated space in your home theater room? Don't just look at the width, either; these puppies can be quite *deep*, as well!

➤ **Other features.** Don't forget all the features you'd look for on any TV set—program guides, V-Chip parental controls, picture-in-picture, and the like. When you're in this price range, make sure you get your set loaded the way you want!

The Least You Need to Know

➤ Projection TVs project light from CRTs or other sources onto a screen—either from in front of or behind the screen.

➤ Rear projection sets are best for most midrange home theaters, ranging in size from 40" to 80" with prices starting at about $1,500; they're relatively easy to set up and require few compromises in terms of layout.

➤ Front projection systems are better for large and custom-designed systems, ranging in size from 50" to 20' with prices starting at about $3,000; they're difficult to set up (typically requiring professional installation) and require a dark and narrow room.

➤ If you choose a really big screen system, make sure it includes a line doubler, or else you'll be bothered by annoying scan lines.

➤ Higher-end RPTVs are available digital-ready or fully HDTV-compatible with 16:9 screens; most FPTVs can be easily adapted for HDTV reception.

Chapter 7

Thin Is In: Flat-Screen Plasma Television

In This Chapter

➤ The flattest video displays in the industry

➤ How plasma displays work

➤ Why picture quality on a plasma display might not meet your standards

➤ Why you might—or might not—want a plasma display in your home theater system

When you have *no* floor space for a big-screen TV—just bare walls—then it's time to turn to the latest video display technology: plasma flat-screen displays. Plasma displays are thin (six inches deep or less) and can be hung on a wall or even the ceiling. It's like hanging an oil painting, except you're hanging a high-resolution video display!

It's a Gas: How a Plasma Display Works

Plasma displays are so thin because they contain no picture tubes or projection devices. Instead, they contain glass, gas, and electrodes.

A plasma display sandwiches a layer of ionized gas between two thin layers of glass. Each of the glass layers is covered with electrodes that create individual sub-pixels, grouped in threes—for red, blue, and green. When voltage is applied to an electrode, a single sub-pixel is illuminated, emitting light of that specific color. When enough sub-pixels light up in a pattern, a picture is created.

The result is a thin, lightweight (anywhere from 75 to 100 pounds, on average), high-resolution display device, like the one in the following picture, that can display normal television signals, HDTV programming (in full 16:9 format, with many models), and signals from personal computers.

A high-resolution plasma display from Proscan—see how thin it is?

(Courtesy of Thomson Consumer Electronics)

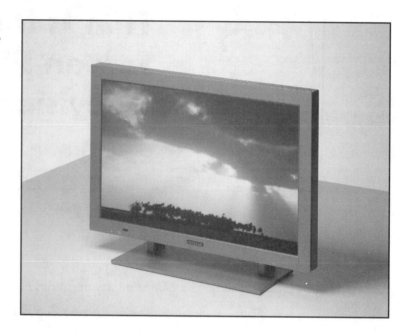

Input/Output

It's tempting to compare a plasma video display to the LCD displays found on notebook PCs (and used in some desktop PC displays, as well). Well, they're not the same. An LCD display isn't near as bright as a plasma display; this extra brightness (and wider viewing angle) comes from the highly charged plasma gas—which also factors into the huge cost difference between LCD and plasma displays. Just remember that LCD flat screens are for computers, and plasma flat screens are for television—it's that simple.

How Good Is the Picture?

Most plasma displays can display the one million or more pixels necessary for an HDTV picture, in 16.7 million colors. However, some of the early plasma units didn't do that good a job of displaying all these pixels.

Early plasma displays had trouble displaying fast action, were prone to color smearing (especially with fine gradations of color), and had difficulty reproducing blacks and details in dark scenes. In short, you paid big bucks, and got a somewhat embarrassing picture.

Newer plasma displays are much improved. Motion artifacts are pretty much gone, although some models are still prone to smearing and other color-related problems. However, it's not unreasonable to expect each new generation of plasma displays to show further improvements in picture quality; decide for yourself whether a specific plasma display meets your personal requirements.

Why Would You Want a Plasma Display?

Given that plasma video displays can cost $10,000 or more—five times as much as comparable RPTVs, why in the world would you want one? I can think of two reasons why you might want to build your home theater system around a plasma display:

➤ You simply don't have the space for a direct view or projection display—so you have to hang your display on the wall. This can be a big deal in homes where space is at a premium—which is why more plasma displays are sold in Europe than in the U.S. In many small European homes, a plasma display is the only way to get a big-screen experience.

➤ You want to impress your friends.

Let's face it—today's plasma displays don't give you much bang for the buck. Not too many home theater enthusiasts want to pay ten grand for an okay but decidedly non-superior picture. However, as prices come down—and picture quality improves—plasma displays might eventually enter the mainstream.

In the meantime, most plasma displays continue to be sold to corporations, for use as fancy wall displays. In addition, since plasma displays can do double duty as computer displays, they're perfect for corporate presentations and trade shows. (And, I suppose, ten grand is pocket change for most large corporations.)

Smart Shopping: What to Look For

If you really want to spend the bucks for a plasma display, here are some things to look for:

➤ **HDTV compatibility.** Most plasma displays can display HDTV signals, although you should check just which HDTV formats are supported; few current plasma displays can support the highest-quality 1080i format, for example. In addition, not all digital plasma displays include HDTV tuners, so you should look for units with built-in tuners—or figure the cost of an add-on tuner to your purchase price.

➤ **Computer compatibility.** If you're going to use your plasma unit as a part-time computer display, make sure the plasma display has the proper RGB input connector.

➤ **Picture quality.** Display quality varies widely from one plasma unit to another—make sure you give your preferred unit an extended in-store test, and that you can live with the picture it produces. In particular, look at how it reproduces fine changes in color; how it reproduces dark scenes; and how it reproduces programming containing fast action, such as sporting events. Also consider the brightness of the display; will you need to adjust the room lighting to facilitate proper viewing?

The Least You Need to Know

➤ Plasma displays use ionized gas sandwiched between two layers of glass to display a high-resolution 16:9 picture.

➤ If you want a TV you can hang on your wall, a six-inch-thick plasma display will do the job.

➤ Picture quality on plasma displays leaves a lot to be desired—as does their $10,000 price tag.

➤ For most home theater enthusiasts, plasma displays don't deliver enougn bang for the buck.

The Next Generation: Digital and High-Definition TV

In This Chapter

➤ The differences between HDTV and regular TV

➤ The many different formats of digital TV

➤ When you'll start receiving HDTV broadcasts

➤ How digital-ready TVs let you add HDTV capability at relatively low cost

➤ If—or when—you should upgrade your home theater system to HDTV

The future has arrived. For decades the consumer electronics industry has been talking about a new broadcasting format that can deliver higher-quality pictures than the antiquated *National Television Standards Committee* (NTSC) format that has been used since the 1940s. Finally, that new format is here.

This new format—called HDTV, for high-definition television—delivers high-definition pictures in digital format. HDTV sets are available today, as is HDTV programming. By government mandate, by 2006 all U.S. television broadcasts will be in HDTV—which means that you *will* own an HDTV set, eventually.

The question is—should you invest in HDTV today?

Defining Digital

First let's clear up something that is a little confusing to most consumers. So-called digital television and HDTV are not necessarily the same thing. All high-definition television is digital, but not all digital broadcasts are high definition. In other words, HDTV is just one form of digital broadcasting. (It's kind of like the "all spaghetti is pasta, but not all pasta is spaghetti" argument.)

We've actually had digital programming available since 1994 or so, via the DIRECTV and EchoStar digital satellite systems (DSS). These systems transmit standard television signals digitally—resulting in a more consistent picture at the high end of the quality range possible in the NTSC system.

DVDs are another form of digital programming. Like DSS, DVDs encode programming in digital format, delivering the best possible NTSC picture.

Input/Output

An analog broadcast transmits programming in a continuous signal that varies in amplitude, depending on the information contained in the picture. This signal can easily deteriorate, which produces a lower-quality picture than the original.

A digital broadcast, in contrast, converts the programming into a stream of digital on/off bits. Each bit represents a small part of the picture; all the bits combine to reproduce a picture identical to the original.

Since it takes more space (called bandwidth) to transmit a digital signal than it does to transmit an analog signal, all digital media compress the signal to fit in a smaller space. HDTV, DSS, and DVDs all use MPEG-2 digital compression, which incorporates computer technology which intelligently senses the changes between frames, thus recording only the important information (and saving valuable bandwidth).

Any compressed signal, if not compressed intelligently, can create problems when decompressed. For example, scenes with lots of motion (think sporting events here) require more bandwidth in their compressed states than do relatively static scenes. If not enough bandwidth is allocated, the playback will appear jerky and pixilated. So even though you're watching in super high-quality HDTV mode (or on a DVD or from a direct broadcast satellite), the possibility exists that the picture will be poor—due to compression issues.

Simply digitizing a picture, however, does not improve upon a mediocre source format. To dramatically improve the picture, the format itself has to be improved. This is what HDTV does—by increasing the picture's resolution, as measured in lines of horizontal resolution.

In addition, the HDTV format changes the aspect ratio of the picture. As explained back in Chapter 4, "Pick a Picture: Choose the Right TV for Your System," the standard television screen has a 4:3 aspect ratio—that is, if the picture is four units wide, it's also three units tall. The HDTV format embraces a wide-screen approach with a 16:9 aspect ratio—for every 16 units of width, you have just nine units of height. The resulting picture is wider than a standard television picture, and more capable of displaying wide-screen movies.

Product Specs

The **National Television Standards Committee** (NTSC) is the industry organization that devised the current television broadcast standards. Because of the historical propensity to deliver crummy pictures with variable color, some wags have dubbed NTSC as "never the same color."

HDTV rear projection television from RCA; note the 16:9 aspect ratio.

(Courtesy of Thomson Consumer Electronics)

Product Specs

A **pixel** (short for "picture element") is a single point on-screen. Video displays are created from thousands (or millions) of pixels, arranged in rows and columns. The pixels are so close together that, from the proper distance, they appear connected—and create a complete picture.

Decoding the Different Digital Formats

Digital television actually comprises 18 different high-resolution formats, each with slightly different specifications. A broadcaster has the option of transmitting digital programming in any one of these formats; all HDTV television sets can receive and decode broadcasts from all formats—although they may not actually display the programming in its native format.

The lowest-resolution digital formats are not technically called high definition; these standard-definition television (SDTV) formats transmit 480 horizontal lines, with each line one *pixel* (a single point on-screen) tall—identical to today's transmission standards, but in digital format (and, in some cases, with a progressively scanned 16:9 aspect ratio). True high-definition television comprises either 720 or 1,080 lines of resolution, with a 16:9 aspect ratio.

The following table details the various digital broadcast formats.

Comparison of Popular Digital Broadcast Formats

Transmission Type	Analog	Digital	Digital	Digital	Digital
Definition	NTSC	SDTV	SDTV	HDTV	HDTV
Name	480i	480i	480p	720p	1080i
Picture Height, in Pixels	480	480	480	720	1,080
Picture Width, in Pixels	640	640	640 or 720	1,280	1,920
Total Number of Pixels	307,200	307,200	307,200 or 345,600	921,600	2,073,600
Scanning	Interlaced	Interlaced	Progressive	Progressive	Interlaced
Aspect Ratio	4:3	4:3	4:3 or 16:9	16:9	16:9
Channel Capacity	1	5–6	5–6	1–2	1
Quality	Standard TV (maximum performance seldom achieved)	Good (DVD or DBS quality)	Better than DVD or DBS	Best possible	Best possible
Adopted by	All current broadcasters	None	Fox	ABC	CBS, NBC, and DIRECTV

In reality, while all HDTV sets receive and decode all 18 formats, many HDTV sets don't display the 720p format, as television manufacturers are assuming that 1080i will become the dominant format for broadcast use. Sets that don't display 720p will typically "upconvert" the signal to display at 1080i—although a few sets "downconvert" the signal to the less-appealing 480i format, so it doesn't hurt to check this out in advance.

Input/Output

Normal television pictures are composed of 480 horizontal lines that scan across the screen in less than the blink of an eye. (While NTSC signals actually transmit 525 lines, some of the lines are used to transmit nonpicture information—resulting in the 480 usable lines.)

One way of putting the lines on-screen is to display two sequential fields of 240 lines each; each odd and even field is scanned in 1/60th of a second, and thus combine for a full picture every 1/30th of a second. This method is called interlaced scanning.

A more visually appealing approach is to scan all 480 lines in a single pass. This method is called progressive scanning, and scans the entire picture in 1/60th of a second—twice as fast as an interlaced picture. The result is improved picture quality; even though the resolution (number of pixels) remains the same, the picture is refreshed twice as fast. This translates into more accurate display when you have fast action on-screen, such as with sporting events.

In HDTV, the 720p format is progressively scanned, while the 1080i format is interlaced. While the 1080i format has higher resolution (and thus a theoretically sharper picture), the 720p format should be better at reproducing fast motion. The reality is both formats look terrific when compared to today's 480i pictures, with the pros and cons of each format pretty much canceling each other out. (The ultimate format, of course would be the highest resolution progressively scanned—otherwise known as 1080p, and on the drawing boards for sometime in the future.)

Why the different digital TV formats? It's simple—the higher the resolution, the more bandwidth necessary to broadcast the program signal. Television stations, cable systems, and DBS broadcasters all have limited bandwidth; the higher resolution the programming they transmit, the *fewer* channels they can transmit. So, some broadcasters (such as the Fox network) are choosing to transmit lower-resolution HDTV signals, and using the leftover bandwidth to either add more channels or to transmit various nontelevision data services. Other broadcasters (including CBS, NBC, and the DIRECTV satellite service) are using the entire bandwidth to deliver the highest-quality programming possible.

Since the government isn't dictating which digital formats broadcasters must use (beyond establishing the four basic formats), if your broadcaster of choice is compromising picture quality for additional programming or services, there isn't much you can do about it. Except to complain, of course!

Why Would You Want HDTV?

There are several reasons why HDTV is appealing to both videophiles and normal consumers. All the reasons tend to boil down to a better viewing experience, and include:

➤ **Sharper picture.** True HDTV (720p or 1080i formats) delivers one million pixels or more of information. Standard TV and DVDs deliver approximately 300,000 pixels. That translates into HDTV delivering a picture more than three times as detailed as what you've been used to watching.

➤ **Less flicker.** The increased number of scan lines per frame (and, in the case of the 720p format, progressive scanning) translates into less-visible scan lines—which means you can sit closer to the screen without seeing flicker in the picture.

➤ **More accurate wide-screen reproduction.** When you display a wide-screen movie on a standard 4:3 TV, the movie is either letterboxed (with black bars at the top and bottom of the screen) or panned and scanned so that only a portion of the movie is displayed on-screen. With HDTV's 16:9 aspect ratio, you can see more of the wide-screen movie with less letter-boxing.

➤ **Better sound.** The HDTV format dictates the Dolby Digital 5.1 surround-sound format, which is much improved over the NTSC stereo standard.

Almost HDTV: Digital-Ready Televisions

Let's be honest—today, HDTV sets are terribly expensive. Do you really want to spend more than twice the price of a regular TV to get a set that can display HDTV broadcasts—when they become more widely available?

Fortunately, there is a middle-ground solution. Several manufacturers are making television sets that are capable of displaying HDTV resolution (up to the full 2 million pixels in some cases), but without the 16:9 aspect ratio—and without a built-in HDTV decoder. These sets are alternately described as high-resolution, digital-ready, or HDTV-ready, and are capable of displaying HDTV broadcasts (either letterboxed or in the 4:3 ratio) when matched with an add-on HDTV tuner.

Today you can purchase a digital-ready television for as little as $1,000, and many of these sets include line doubling technology which converts a normal NTSC transmission into a better-looking 480i display. When you add a $500 (or so) HDTV tuner, you have an almost-HDTV quality system for well under $2,000.

Several manufacturers are making outboard HDTV tuners that can be connected to digital-ready televisions; some models, like the one from RCA, include a terrestrial NTSC tuner (for normal over-the-air broadcasts), a terrestrial HDTV tuner (for over-the-air digital broadcasts), and a DIRECTV satellite HDTV tuner. At prices approaching $500, these units are terrific values—especially combined with a high-resolution digital-ready TV.

Overload!

There is, as yet, no standard for HDTV input and output jacks. As an example, RCA's first HDTV tuner has an RGB HDTV output, while some digital-ready TVs from other manufacturers have component video inputs (with separate red, blue, and green connections), which means one won't work with the other. So, if you want to match an HDTV tuner with a digital-ready TV, make sure the inputs and outputs match. (For more information on the different types of input and output plugs and jacks, see Chapter 21, "Plug It In: Which Cable Goes Where.")

Coming to Your Town Soon: The HDTV Broadcast Rollout

One big question about HDTV is when *you'll* be able to receive HDTV signals. The reality is, more than half of all U.S. households can now receive digital broadcast signals from local stations representing the ABC, CBS, NBC, and Fox television networks. (To be fair, the *quantity* of HDTV broadcasts is still rather slim. Check with your local stations for more details.)

As you can see in the following table, the government has mandated that *all* commercial TV stations begin some form of HDTV broadcasting by May 1, 2002; within 12 months of that date, stations should be broadcasting at least half their programs in HDTV format. In fact, the government wants broadcast stations to completely shift to HDTV format by 2006. At that time, there will be no more analog broadcasts, and the analog broadcast spectrum will be returned to the government for some future use.

Digital Broadcasting Timetable

Year	Goal
1999	Top 4 networks in top 30 markets (53% of all households) HDTV-ready
2002	All commercial stations (100% of all households) HDTV-ready
2003	All PBS stations HDTV-ready
	50% of all content simulcast in HDTV
2004	75% of all content simulcast in HDTV
2005	100% of all content simulcast in HDTV
2006	All stations 100% digital; analog spectrum returned to government for future use

Beyond these transmissions from local broadcast stations, both digital satellite broadcasters are already transmitting programming in HDTV format. In the case of DIRECTV, you need to buy a slightly larger elliptical dish with a second LNB (to pick up the HDTV transmissions from a second satellite) and purchase an HDTV satellite tuner.

Input/Output

Local stations are required to continue broadcasting all content in traditional analog format through 2006. So, even though the number of HDTV broadcasts should steadily increase, anyone with a non-HDTV should be able to continue watching regular programming at least through 2006.

Once you have the right equipment set up, you'll be able to receive special HDTV transmissions from HBO and other satellite networks.

Unfortunately, HDTV programming from your cable system has been slower in coming. The cable industry has only recently agreed on a standard interface for digital cable boxes, so until the cable industry and television manufacturers ramp up to the new standard, you have to use an antenna or a dish to receive HDTV broadcasts. (This new digital cable interface standard, which utilizes so-called "FireWire" connections, isn't fully compatible with the first generation of HDTV televisions.)

Note, however, that—at least for now—HDTV is purely a *broadcast* format. DVDs do *not* display HDTV-quality signals. However, HDTV-compatible DVDs are technically possible, and expect a second high-resolution DVD format to emerge within the next several years.

Should You Buy ... or Wait?

HDTV sets are available now; if you want one, you can buy one. However, at this very moment, HDTV sets are very expensive in relation to comparable non-HDTV sets, and HDTV programming is somewhat limited. Still, any HDTV set you buy today should be a viable video display for many years.

That doesn't mean you should put down this book and rush right out and buy a super-expensive HDTV right this minute. The reality is, HDTV sets *will* come down in price, and *will* improve in performance. The HDTV set you buy a year from now will likely cost 25–50 percent less than the HDTV sets on the market today. The longer you wait, the less you'll pay.

Of course, the longer you wait, the longer you'll be missing out on that wonderful HDTV experience, too. So it's a compromise—when do you bite the bullet and spend the money, knowing that you would have spent less if you waited another year?

If you want HDTV performance without today's stratospheric HDTV price tags, think about buying a high-resolution digital-ready TV. As described previously, many of these sets deliver enhanced performance and—when supplemented by add-on HDTV tuners—can faithfully display HDTV programming, all at a much lower price than you'd pay for a full-blown HDTV unit. The main drawback is the standard 4:3 ratio screen of digital-ready sets (as opposed to the 16:9 screens on HDTV sets), the inconvenience of having a two-piece system (television plus separate tuner), and, in some cases, a lower-resolution HDTV picture. Still, it's a more affordable compromise, at least for the short run.

Overload!

As this book is being written, the cable industry has just established a standard interface for digital cable boxes. This interface will incorporate an IE1394 FireWire connection, which has not been standard on first-generation HDTV televisions. If you want to watch HDTV via cable, you'll want to make sure your HDTV television incorporates an IE1394 FireWire connection.

Power Up

While you can't turn an older TV into an HDTV receiver, there is a way to receive HDTV broadcasts on your old TV—although at normal non-HDTV resolution. Most add-on HDTV tuners, such as the RCA model, include standard-resolution output jacks that you can hook up to any existing television. When you hook up one of these tuners to your current TV, you'll be able to receive all HDTV broadcasts on your regular TV, downconverted to standard non-HDTV resolution. While an HDTV broadcast sent to a non-HDTV will look better than standard broadcast television (the picture will be equivalent to that of a DVD or DBS), it won't be HDTV quality—only because your old TV isn't HDTV quality.

All that said, here are my bottom-line recommendations:

➤ If you currently have a relatively new, relatively large (35" or larger, direct view or projection) television set that's in good working condition, hold off buying an HDTV set for a year or so, until all the standards have been set and the price comes down a little.

➤ If you currently have a smaller TV, a poor-performing set, or an older TV that you simply feel you *must* upgrade, buy a 35" or larger high-resolution digital-ready TV (in either direct view or rear projection formats); you'll get a superior picture in the short term, and when the time is right you can add an outboard HDTV tuner and have a near-HDTV system—at a fraction of the cost of today's full-blown HDTV sets.

➤ If you absolutely, positively, always have to have the latest and greatest equipment in your system, then by all means buy one of today's HDTV sets; be prepared for some incompatibility with future HDTV transmissions from your cable system, however.

Shop Smart: What to Look For

If you do want to buy an HDTV set today, here are the features to look for:

➤ Capable of displaying 1080i format; some manufacturers will call this 2 million pixel resolution

➤ Capable of displaying 720p format or upconverting it to 1080i; avoid units that *downconvert* 720p to 480i

➤ Full 16:9 aspect ratio

➤ Line doubling of normal NTSC signals

➤ IE1394 FireWire connection for digital cable boxes

If you want to buy a digital-ready HDTV set today, look for the highest resolution possible (which will be less than 2 million pixels if the aspect ratio is 4:3 instead of 16:9), built-in line doubling of normal NTSC signals, and (most important) input/output compatibility with whichever HDTV tuner you may purchase.

Power Up

The current generation of VHS videocassette recorders is not capable of recording high-definition programming. However, the new Digital VHS (DVHS) format is perfect for HDTV recording—when used in conjunction with an add-on HDTV tuner. See Chapter 11, "Tale of the Tape: Video Recorders," for more information on the DVHS format.

The Least You Need to Know

➤ HDTV—with 18 different specified formats—is a form of digital television, delivering higher resolution picture, Dolby Digital sound, and a 16:9 aspect ratio.

➤ Half of all U.S. television stations are offering some HDTV broadcasts today, and all broadcasts will migrate to HDTV format by 2006.

➤ Since HDTV sets currently cost twice as much (or more!) than standard non-HDTV televisions and all aspects of the HDTV standard have yet to be established, it may be wise to hold off for a year or two before you purchase a full-blown HDTV television.

➤ An affordable way to make your home theater system HDTV-capable today utilizes a high-resolution digital-ready television and an add-on HDTV tuner/converter.

Part 3

Looking Good: Video Sources for Your System

VCR. DVD. PVR. DSS. Read this part to learn more about these TLAs (three-letter acronyms), with special attention given to the latest digital delivery systems. Have you splurged for a DVD player yet? Ever want to can the cable and install a satellite dish? Fed up with poor VCR picture quality? Get answers to these and other questions—and find out which video sources deliver the best picture and sound quality to your HTS (home theater system).

Chapter 9

A Picture's Worth a Thousand Words: Choose the Right Video Sources

---

In This Chapter

➤ Why digital pictures are better than analog

➤ The various video sources available today—including broadcast television, cable television, digital satellite, DVDs, VCRs, and digital video recorders

➤ Which video sources have the best picture and sound

➤ How to choose the right video sources for your system

A big-screen television is for big pictures—movies and concerts, especially. After all, you're not paying all that money just to watch old reruns of *Gilligan's Island* on your high-resolution, surround-sound home theater system, are you?

The picture you feed into your home theater's video display can come from a number of sources—from regular TV broadcasts to high-resolution DVDs. You should allocate at least 10 percent of your initial home theater budget to purchase video source equipment—and at least $100 a month to feed a constant stream of programming into your system.

Read on to compare all the different video sources you can use in your home theater!

Going Digital: The Latest Video Technology

Before we look at individual video source devices, let's look at an underlying technology that's changing the face of the home video industry. That technology—used in everything from DVDs to satellites to the new HDTV systems—is digital video.

Digital video takes a picture and describes it in terms of bits of information. Each bit is a 1 or a 0, representing either "on" or "off" states. When enough of these 1s and 0s are put together, an exact copy of the original picture is displayed.

Input/Output

The highest-resolution digital picture available today comes from the new high-definition television (HDTV) system. HDTV incorporates digital broadcast signals and is capable of displaying more than three times the resolution of DVD or DBS, today's other digital formats. To learn more about high-definition digital television, see Chapter 8, "The Next Generation: Digital and High-Definition TV."

Digital video by itself doesn't necessarily translate into a better picture—it translates into *more accurate reproduction*. That's because a 1 or a 0 transmitted from point A to point B remains a 1 or a 0; bits don't fade.

Older analog transmissions—such as those you receive from over-the-air broadcasts—are prone to signal degradation, most often seen in the form of fuzzy or noisy pictures. Digital pictures don't get fuzzy or noisy—unless the original picture was fuzzy or noisy to begin with.

If we divide available video sources into digital and analog camps, we get the following:

Digital and Analog Video Sources

Video Source	Digital	Analog
HDTV broadcasts	X	
DVD	X	
Digital broadcast satellite	X	

Video Source	Digital	Analog
Laserdisc		X
Broadcast television		X
Cable television		X
VHS		X

As you'll see later in this chapter (see the section "Garbage In, Garbage Out: Searching for the Best Picture and Sound"), today's digital sources also happen to have the highest resolution pictures. The bottom line is that if you want the highest-quality, most-accurate pictures for your home theater system, go with a digital source!

Input/Output

Some cable operators are advertising new "digital cable" systems. To receive this so-called digital cable, you need a new digital set-top box; once this box is installed, you're capable of receiving over 100 different channels of programming.

The problem with today's digital cable is that it's all about quantity, not quality. Television signals are indeed fed through the cable in digital format, but in a way that enables the cable system to squeeze more channels into your box. The picture quality of the cable programming is essentially unchanged from what you had before; you just have access to more channels.

Don't confuse today's digital cable with tomorrow's true digital cable boxes. These new boxes will be necessary to receive true digital TV and HDTV cablecasts, and will connect to your digital-ready or HDTV sets via an IE1394 FireWire connection.

The Picture Makers: Video Sources for Your Home Theater System

Everything you watch on your TV comes from a specific video source. All the different sources you can hook up to your home theater system have their pros and cons; some have a better picture, some have better sound, some are higher priced, and some are more affordable. In addition, the programming available for each source differs—you may choose or dismiss a source solely on the availability of specific programming (or lack thereof).

Let's take a closer look at some of the more popular video sources you can incorporate in your home theater system.

Broadcast Television

Good old broadcast television is the most watched video source in the world. Received via a set-top or outside antenna, local television broadcasts bring both network and local programming into your living room.

The chief advantages of broadcast television include

➤ Convenient access; practically everyone can receive some over-the-air broadcasts.

➤ Cost—it's free!

The chief disadvantages of broadcast television include

➤ Low-resolution picture.

➤ Poor reception, accompanied by ghosting, snow, and picture noise.

➤ Non-digital sound.

➤ Lack of first-run programming.

Cable Television

Cable television is, for want of a better description, broadcast television piped through a cable and augmented by specialty programming. Cable picture quality is no better than the best over-the-air broadcasts—although without the ghosting and snow caused by poor reception.

The chief advantages of cable television include

➤ Elimination of reception problems.

➤ Wide variety of programming.

➤ First-run programming.

The chief disadvantages of cable television include

➤ Low-resolution picture.

➤ Nondigital sound.

➤ Monthly fees.

➤ Dealing with the cable company (not a joke!).

Direct Broadcast Satellite (DBS)

Think of DBS as cable television without the cable—and with much better picture and sound. DBS programming is beamed off a satellite to a small round or oval dish that is then connected to your television and home theater system. The picture quality on DBS broadcasts are of near-DVD quality, and there is zero snow or noise or other picture degradation. While most DBS programming utilizes the older Dolby Pro Logic sound system, some pay movies are being broadcast in the newer Dolby Digital format.

About that programming—with DBS you get hundreds of channels, including dozens of pay-per-view movies and events. Currently, DBS is available in two different-but-similar flavors, DIRECTV and EchoStar (also known as the DISH Network). Both use 18" dishes and carry similar programming packages.

Going forward, both DIRECTV and EchoStar will be offering HDTV broadcasts through a separate satellite. To receive these broadcasts—along with the standard broadcasts—you'll need a slightly larger oval dish and an HDTV-compatible receiver.

The chief advantages of DBS include

➤ High-quality digital picture.

➤ Dolby Digital sound (with some programming).

➤ Wide variety of programming.

➤ First-run programming.

➤ HDTV-capable.

The chief disadvantages of DBS include

➤ Complicated installation.

➤ Monthly fees.

(For more information about DBS, see Chapter 13, "The World on a Dish: Digital Satellite Systems.")

DVD

DVD is the latest format for prerecorded video, and offers the best picture and sound of any non-HDTV source. A DVD disc looks just like a compact disc (CD), except it holds up to six times the amount of data. Picture and sound are encoded digitally on the disc, and then read back via laser. The picture quality bumps up against NTSC's theoretical 500-line limit, and most sound is in the Dolby Digital 5.1 format (although some older movies are encoded with Dolby Pro Logic).

As to programming—the sky's the limit! Your local video or consumer electronics store carries thousands of DVD titles, with dozens of new (and old) titles being released weekly. Most DVDs sell for $25 or so, and can be rented for about the same price as videotapes.

The simple fact is that every home theater system should include a DVD player as its primary video source for movies and other prerecorded programming.

The chief advantages of DVD include

> ➤ High-quality digital picture.

> ➤ Dolby Digital sound.

> ➤ Wide variety of low-cost programming.

> ➤ First-run programming.

> ➤ Availability of discs for both sale and rental.

> ➤ Ease of use.

The chief disadvantages of DVD include

> ➤ Not HDTV-capable (in the current format).

> ➤ Can't record on a disc (yet ...).

(For more information about DVD, see Chapter 10, "Digital Pictures on a Disc: DVD Players.")

Videocassette Recorder (VCR)

Most households have a VCR connected to their main TV. While VCRs were designed to record television programming, most VCRs are used solely to play back prerecorded movies. The entire video rental industry was created in response to this demand for affordable prerecorded videotape rentals.

Input/Output

Note that there is a new videocassette format on the horizon that delivers HDTV–quality picture and sound. Digital VHS (also known as DVHS) machines, when connected to an HDTV tuner, will be able to both record and play back HDTV programming in full 1080i resolution and 16:9 aspect ratio.

Don't confuse DVHS with the totally new category of personal digital video recorder (DVR) from Philips and others. DVRs use a hard disk drive to time-shift television programming; they're not for watching prerecorded programming.

Today's crop of VHS-format VCRs is, in the grand scheme of things, ancient technology. Signals are recorded on tape in analog fashion, and at extremely low resolution. To be blunt, the worst quality picture and sound you feed into your video system will come from your VCR.

Still, prerecorded rental tapes are in plentiful supply, and the home VCR is the best way to play back the tapes you record with a camcorder. So, it's unlikely that VCRs will disappear any time soon—even with consumers embracing DVD players in ever-increasing numbers.

The chief advantages of VHS VCRs include

➤ Wide availability of programming.

➤ First-run programming.

➤ Availability of tapes for both sale and rental.

➤ Ease of use.

➤ Low-cost hardware.

The chief disadvantages of VHS VCRs include

➤ Low-resolution picture.

➤ Nondigital sound.

➤ Not HDTV-capable (in the current VHS format).

(For more information about VCRs—including the new DVHS format—see Chapter 11, "Tale of the Tape: Video Recorders.")

Personal Digital Video Recorder (DVR)

The newest recording device for your system doesn't use tapes or removable discs—it records television programs on a big hard disk, like the kind you find inside your personal computer. These so-called personal digital video recorders (also called "personal TV receivers," for some unknown reason) can record up to 30 hours of television programming with near DVD-quality picture and sound. You can use a DVR to "pause" live TV programming, or to record selected programming, automatically.

The chief advantages of DVR include

➤ Records high-quality digital picture and sound.

➤ Can "pause" live programming.

➤ Can be easily programmed to automatically record selected programming.

The chief disadvantages of DVR include

➤ Can't play back prerecorded programming.

➤ High cost when compared to VCRs.

➤ Monthly subscription required.

(For more information about DVR, see Chapter 12, "A Better VCR: Digital Video Recorders.")

Other Video Sources

In addition to all these devices, there are a number of other sources you can connect to your home theater system, including

➤ **Laserdisc**. Laserdisc was the predecessor to DVD, presenting high-quality movies on a shiny disc. The movies were analog rather than digital, however, and the discs were 12" in diameter—just like an old vinyl LP. (Also like old LPs, laserdiscs had to be flipped mid-movie, as material was recorded on both sides of the disc.) Pre-DVD, laserdiscs presented the best picture and sound available for your home theater system; this format peaked in 1994, however, and in today's DVD-driven world, laserdiscs are fast becoming obsolete.

➤ **WebTV**. WebTV puts the Internet on your TV. WebTV Classic units enable you to surf the Web and send e-mail from the comfort of your easy chair, while WebTV Plus units include a television tuner for enhanced interactivity with selected programs. (For example, you can use your WebTV Plus unit to play along with Wheel of Fortune over the Internet!) In addition, newer WebTV Plus units now include hard disk recorders, so you can gain all the benefits of digital video recorders with the convenience of Web-based program guides and interactivity. While one can't really consider a WebTV unit an *essential* component for your home theater system, it's something to consider—especially if you want to make safe Internet surfing a true family activity. (To learn more about WebTV, check out my recent book on the subject, *The Complete Idiot's Guide to Surfing the Internet with WebTV*, available wherever books are sold!)

Power Up

If you plan on hooking your camcorder up to your home theater system, look for a television or a/v receiver that has front-panel input jacks. It's much easier to temporarily plug your camcorder into the front of your system than it is to fumble with all the messy rear-panel connections.

This same advice applies if you want to hook up a digital still camera or video game system to your home theater—anything that isn't a permanent component is more easily connected to front-panel jacks.

➤ **Camcorder.** If you own a camcorder, it's possible to hook your unit directly to your home theater system. While you probably won't use your camcorder as a permanent video source, you should make sure your TV or receiver has a free connection available.

Video Game System

Finally, if you're a big video game player—or your kids are—you should consider your video game unit an integral part of your home theater system. Most video game systems output high-quality stereo sound, so it makes sense to devote a set of inputs on your TV or a/v receiver for your game-playing pleasure.

Garbage In, Garbage Out: Searching for the Best Picture and Sound

The best television in the world will display a cruddy picture if the video source you're feeding to it is subpar. If you want the best possible picture for your home theater system, you have to use a high-quality video source.

Short of HDTV broadcasts, the best picture and sound quality today is available from the DVD format. This high-quality source delivers 500 lines of video information, accompanied by Dolby Digital 5.1 surround sound.

Cable and regular TV broadcasts deliver much lower resolution (in the 330-line range) and are plagued by typical analog signal degradation and reception difficulties (in the case of broadcast signals). Suffice to say, I probably don't need to convince you that broadcast and cable quality often leaves something to be desired.

That said, the absolute worst signal you can feed into your home theater comes from that old standby, the VHS VCR. (The 8mm format used by some camcorders is no better, by the way.) Standard VHS can only pump out 240 lines of information (which fades to 220 lines in EP mode), which translates into less than half the resolution you get from DVD programming. Trust me—once you've seen the picture quality of DVD, it will be difficult to go back to VHS-quality viewing.

The following table compares the picture resolution and sound quality of several popular video formats:

Picture and Sound Quality for Various Formats

Video Source	Maximum Video Resolution	Best Possible Sound
HDTV broadcasts	720 or 1,080 lines	Dolby Digital
DVD	500 lines	Dolby Digital

continues

Picture and Sound Quality for Various Formats   (continued)

Video Source	Maximum Video Resolution	Best Possible Sound
DVHS	500 lines	Dolby Digital
Digital 8	500 lines	Dolby Pro Logic
Digital broadcast satellite	425 lines	Dolby Digital
Laserdisc	425 lines	Dolby Digital
SVHS	400 lines	Dolby Pro Logic
Hi8	400 lines	Dolby Pro Logic
Cable television	330 lines	Dolby Pro Logic
Broadcast television	330 lines	Dolby Pro Logic
VHS	240 lines	Dolby Pro Logic
8mm	240 lines	Dolby Pro Logic

The best way to see the differences between these video sources is to compare them your-self. When you head out to your local consumer-electronics retailer, pick a television set similar to the one you'll have in your home theater system, and then ask to have each of these video sources hooked up to that set. Pick similar programming for each source, and then start switching from one to another. You'll soon see why you want your main feeds into your home theater to be the higher-quality DVD and DBS programming—and why you'll probably be decreasing the numbers of videotapes you rent in the future.

Power Up

Remember, you're not limited to just one video source in your home theater system. Most better-quality televisions have multiple inputs, and most audio/video re-ceivers can accommodate four or five different video sources. So, it's okay if you hook up a cable box or broadcast antenna, a digital satellite feed, a DVD player, and a VCR—the more, the merrier!

Which Should You Choose?

Which video sources should you include in your home theater system? Here are some things to keep in mind as you make your choice:

➤ In order to receive local television broadcasts, you'll need to have a broadcast antenna or cable box connected to your system, no matter what.

➤ For the simple reason of compatibility with all those old tapes sitting in your closet—not to mention the movies your kids want to rent at Blockbuster this weekend—you'll need some sort of VCR in your system. To make the best of a bad situation, I recommended upgrading to a VHS HiFi model, especially if your old VCR is more than a few years old.

➤ If you're fed up with poor-quality cable signals, make the leap to DBS. The initial cost of the 18" satellite dish is low, and you'll receive a much better-quality picture—and a wider selection of programming, to boot.

➤ For the best home theater experience, add a DVD player to your system. DVD players can be had for as little as $200, and the discs are cheap to either buy or rent. I'll go as far as to say that no home theater system today should be without a DVD source.

➤ As to the other available sources, include them in your system as necessary. If you already have a laserdisc player, for example, there's no reason to throw it away just because you bought a new DVD player—especially if you also have a substantial collection of laserdiscs. Every home theater system is unique, so the video sources you include can—and should—be unique to your personal needs and situation.

The Least You Need to Know

➤ You can connect multiple video sources to your home theater system.

➤ Digital video sources (such as DVD and DBS) tend to have better picture and sound quality than analog sources (such as broadcast TV and cable).

➤ VHS VCRs have the lowest resolution picture, but are cheap and have a wide variety of available programming.

➤ If you want the best quality picture and sound for your home theater system, you should use a DVD player or a direct broadcast satellite (or both!) as your main video source.

Chapter 10

Digital Pictures on a Disc: DVD Players

In This Chapter

➤ How DVD players work—and how a movie is encoded on a five-inch disc

➤ Options and extras available on DVD discs

➤ How you can play your CDs on a DVD player

➤ Different types of DVD machines

➤ How to hook up a DVD player to your home theater system

Almost 20 years ago, digital technology entered the living rooms of the world. This technology—using computer-like bits and bytes to carry programming information—came on a silvery five-inch disc, and was read by a low-powered laser beam.

Chances are, you probably have one of these digital devices, and several of the silvery discs. You call them compact discs, or CDs, and you use them to listen to digitally recorded music.

It's hard to think of compact discs as "old technology," but that they are. Today a newer technology—looking outwardly identical to a CD—is offering the next generation of digital entertainment. This new technology, unlike the CD, offers both sound and picture, both with high-quality digital reproduction.

What's the name of this hot new technology? It's called *DVD*—and it's taking the world by storm.

Product Specs

You're probably curious as to what the initials **DVD** stand for. The answer isn't that straightforward. You see, early on the format was called "digital video disc," thus the abbreviation. However, after the format was broadened to include computer-data storage and future audio-only discs, digital *video* disc seemed too restrictive, and some companies started calling it the digital *versatile* disc. However, that name didn't really stick, so today DVD simply stands for ... DVD. In other words, the initials don't stand for anything. (I told you it wasn't that straightforward!)

Great Picture—and Great Sound

You don't need to understand all the technical details behind the DVD format to appreciate what it brings to your home theater system. Put simply, a DVD player is an essential video source for your home theater—and should be your primary source for watching movies and other prerecorded entertainment.

The picture quality of a DVD is the best you can feed into your home theater system, short of moving to HDTV. DVDs are capable of 500 lines of resolution, which is much better than VHS (240 lines), broadcast or cable television (330 lines), or even laserdiscs (425 lines). If you're used to watching movies on a VCR, the picture quality of a DVD is more than twice as sharp; if you're used to watching movies on HBO or Showtime, DVD's picture is 50 percent better than what comes over cable, and 25 percent better than what you get off of satellite.

The sound quality of DVDs is also spectacular, with movies typically presented in full 5.1 Dolby Digital sound. This surround-sound format (discussed in Chapter 14, "Sound Is All Around: Understanding Surround Sound") presents five discrete channels of sound (front left, front center, front right, surround left, and surround right) plus a separate bass channel just for subwoofers. The sound is delivered digitally, and is of CD quality.

Input/Output

Today's generation of DVDs adhere to the NTSC standard, and not to any of the new HDTV or digital TV standards. It is possble—and likely—that future generations of DVDs will encode programming in the higher-resolution HDTV format, but as of this writing no standards for HDTV DVDs have been established. (It wouldn't be unreasonable to look for HDTV DVDs by mid-decade, however.)

If your home theater system doesn't include a Dolby Digital recorder, you can still enjoy high-quality sound from your DVDs. All DVD players can take a 5.1- or 6.1-channel Dolby Digital soundtrack and "downmix" it to two channels—which can then be sent to a two-channel stereo receiver or to an a/v receiver equipped with Dolby Pro Logic sound.

Input/Output

Some DVD players come with built-in Dolby Digital decoders and 5.1-channel analog (not digital!) outputs. If you have one of these players, you don't need a receiver with built-in Dolby Digital decoding to enjoy full 5.1 surround sound. Assuming you have an a/v receiver or television that is 5.1-ready, you can connect the 5.1 outputs on your DVD player to the 5.1 inputs on your TV or receiver and enjoy full Dolby Digital surround sound. (If your a/v receiver has its own built-in Dolby Digital decoder, you simply bypass the decoder in the DVD player.)

In addition to the great picture and sound quality, the huge storage capacity available on DVD enables many discs to come with lots of extras. These can include having both 4:3 and letterbox versions of the movie on the same disc, commentaries on a second (or third!) audio track, foreign-language versions of the film, deleted scenes, production notes, and "making of" documentaries.

What DVD Is—and How It Works

DVD was developed by some of the same companies that developed the original compact disc technology. It works similar to the way a CD works, storing information in rows of miniscule pits on a five-inch disc; these pits are "read" by a laser beam, and the information contained within the pits decoded to produce audio and video signals.

Overload!

Not all DVD movies are presented in the Dolby Digital format. Some older movies may be presented in the older Dolby Pro Logic format, or in two-channel stereo, or even in mono. Make sure you carefully read the DVD packaging to determine the format used on that disc.

While DVD discs look like compact discs, DVDs can store more than 12 times the amount of digital data found on a CD. This extra capacity is what enables a complete movie to be stored on a disc—in high-quality digital resolution.

DVDs are capable of storing all this information on a five-inch disc because the microscopic pits on the disc are much smaller and more closely spaced than those of a CD, as shown in the following figure. To accurately read these densely packed pits, DVD players use a red laser with a tighter beam. In addition, the information contained in the pits is compressed (so that more information can be stored in a smaller space) using *MPEG2* video compression.

DVDs store more information than CDs because they have more (and smaller) pits.

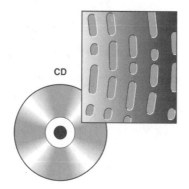

CD

DVD

Product Specs

MPEG2 is the digital video-signal compression standard used for both DVD and digital satellite broadcasts. MPEG2 uses a variable bit-rate process to allocate more storage for complex scenes involving a lot of motion, while minimizing the storage necessary for static scenes. Some DVD players can display an on-screen "bit rate meter," which shows the disc's current data flow in the form of a bar graph.

Even more capacity comes from dual-sided and dual-layer DVD discs. Dual-sided discs incorporate a "sandwich" design to store data on both sides of a disc; typically, disc manufacturers put different versions of a movie on either side of a dual-sided disc, such as a letterbox version on one side and a 4:3 aspect version on the other.

In addition, each side of a disc can contain either a single layer or a dual layer of information. Dual-layer discs can store more information, thus enabling the presentation of longer movies or programs with lots of extras and options.

When you combine two sides with two layers, you get a disc that can contain up to 15.9 gigabytes of information! The following table describes the different combination of sides and layers you'll find on various DVD discs.

DVD Side and Layer Combinations

Side/Layer Combination	Need to Flip?	Capacity	Typical Uses
Single-sided, single-layer	No	4.7Gb	Normal movies up to 133 minutes long
Double-sided, single-layer	Yes	8.75Gb	One side holds 4:3 aspect version, one side holds letterbox version
Single-sided, dual-layer	No	8.0Gb	Longer movies, or movies with more extras and options
Double-sided, dual-layer	Yes	15.9Gb	Longer movies with two different versions

DVDs, in addition to their higher-quality picture and sound, offer almost-instantaneous access to any point on the disc. That means you can jump to any "chapter" in a movie with a push of a button, or even program some players to play specific sections of a disc in a specific order.

DVDs also offer crystal-clear special effects. Whether you're using pause, slow-motion, or forward or reverse scan, the picture you see during the operation is perfect—with none of the lines or choppiness typical with VCR-based special effects.

Input/Output

Almost simultaneous with the launch of the DVD format, electronics superstore Circuit City attempted to launch a "compatible-but-not" variation called DIVX. In essence, a DIVX was a low-cost DVD-like disc that would play just once in a DIVX player, unless you paid extra money to "unlock" the program. This format was viewed as an alternative to traditional video rentals; you'd essentially buy the rental (for a minimal price) up front, but then have to pay the program manufacturer every time you watched the disc. As you can imagine, this scheme wasn't well received by the public, nor was it endorsed by any of Circuit City's retail competitors, and it died a fast and painless death.

Input/Output

Unlike laserdiscs, which require you to flip discs to watch all of a movie, DVDs almost always store an entire movie on one side of a disc. When you encounter a double-sided DVD, the second side is generally used to store a different *version* of the movie—typically with the letterboxed version on one side, and the 4:3 pan-and-scan version on the other. The result is that you don't have to get up to flip a movie in mid-viewing!

Input/Output

Some—although not many—DVDs also offer the option of multiple camera angles for certain scenes. If a program has been produced utilizing this feature, you can press the Angle button on your remote to switch to another view of the current scene. (This seems to be a popular feature with adult films on DVD disc, but is relatively little used in other types of programming.)

Think Different: Different Options Available on DVD

I mentioned earlier that the huge storage capacity of DVDs enables manufacturers to package lots of extras and alternate versions with a DVD movie. When you insert a DVD into your player, you're first presented with an on-screen menu of all the disc's extra features. Most players also let you access this disc menu with a button on the remote control. You use this menu to select which of the disc's special features you want to use or watch.

All the extras on a disc are typically listed on the back of the DVD packaging. While not all discs include all (or any) of these extras, most discs include *some* added-value features, even if it's just the film's theatrical trailer and a menu of scenes. (If a disc includes a scene menu, you can jump directly to a particular scene by selecting it from the menu.)

Specific types of extras are explained in the following sections.

Different Aspect Ratios

Most DVDs present movies in their original wide-screen aspect ratio, using letter-boxing. Some dual-sided DVDs present the letterboxed version on one side, and the pan-and-scan version (in 4:3 aspect ratio) on the other; if you find yourself watching the wrong version, just flip the disc over in your machine. (Learn more about the various aspect ratios available on DVD in Chapter 9, "A Picture's Worth a Thousand Words: Choose the Right Video Sources.")

If you have a television with 16:9 aspect ratio screen, look for discs that present movies in anarmorphic wide-screen format. This is a type of wide-screen display that provides more picture detail when played on 16:9 TVs.

It works like this: A normal letterboxed movie only fills up part of the screen, with black bars displayed on the top and bottom. Those black bars, however, are part of the picture, and take up valuable pixels. When a normal letterbox movie is displayed on a 16:9 screen, the main part of the picture is enlarged—and the black bars cut off or reduced. Since the black bars were part of the picture, however, the total number of pixels available is actually on *reduced* 16:9 TV.

A typical DVD menu—you can play the movie, go directly to your favorite scenes, and access all sorts of special features.

(Monty Python's Life of Brian, courtesy of The Criterion Collection)

The anamorphic mode works by essentially eliminating the black bars from the original picture storage, thus reallocating their pixels to the main part of the picture. This makes for a higher-resolution picture when displayed on a 16:9 set.

When you play an *anamorphic* disc on a regular 4:3 TV, you have the choice of using normal letterbox or anamorphic modes. You should choose the normal letterbox mode, since the anamorphic picture will appear horizontally squeezed on a 4:3 display.

Product Specs

Anamorphic discs may be identified as such on the DVD packaging, or simply labeled "optimized for 16:9 viewing."

Different Audio Formats

While the DVD format is capable of producing full Dolby Digital 5.1 or 6.1 surround sound, a single DVD disc may provide the option of different audio formats. It isn't unusual to have the option—from the disc's main menu—to select one or more of the following types of audio:

➤ Dolby Digital 6.1

➤ Dolby Digital 5.1

➤ Dolby Pro Logic

➤ DTS 6.1

➤ DTS 5.1

➤ Stereo

➤ Mono

If given the option, you should select the format that best fits your home theater system.

Different Languages

Just as you can often choose from different audio formats, some DVD discs let you choose from multiple languages. When you select a different language from the disc's main menu, you'll hear the movie dubbed into the selected language.

Each language is assigned its own separate audio track. The DVD format allows for up to eight separate audio tracks. In addition to using the extra audio tracks for foreign-language versions, some DVDs include audio commentary about the movie on a separate audio track. As an example, the DVD of *Monty Python's Life of Brian* includes a running commentary from John Cleese and Michael Palin on one audio track, and a separate commentary from Terry Jones, Terry Gilliam, and Eric Idle on a second audio track. You can select which audio track you want to listen to from the disc's main menu, or you can use the Audio button on your DVD player's remote control to switch between audio tracks during the movie.

In addition to different languages, many DVD discs contain one or more tracks of subtitles. Although I've never seen anywhere near this many used on a single disc, the DVD format allows for a disc to contain up to 32 different subtitle tracks!

Power Up

Enabling on-screen display of subtitles is quite useful if you're listening to an audio commentary on a subsidiary audio track. You can listen to the commentary while "reading" the film's dialog—so you know what's going on while the experts are talking over the movie!

Different Countries

This one really isn't a feature. The DVD standard allows for what are called region codes. These codes—insisted upon by the motion picture industry—determine in which regions of the world any given disc may be played.

You see, the theatrical and home video releases of movies don't always occur simultaneously worldwide. For example, a film might open in theaters in the U.S. in June, yet not open in Europe until November. If the U.S. home video release is in October, then it would be possible for Europeans to import the U.S. video and see the film before it appears in theaters there.

By giving each disc a region code—and then forcing DVD player manufacturers to sell players in a region that only play discs coded for that region—the movie moguls effectively halt the cross-country "pirating" of their movies. When you buy a DVD player intended for sale in the U.S., you're only able to play discs coded for U.S. playback. If you try to play a disc with another region code—a disc intended for the Japanese market, for example—it won't play on your machine.

The following table lists all available DVD region codes.

DVD Region Codes

Region	Code
USA & Canada	1
Western Europe and Japan	2
Southeast Asia	3
South America and Australia	4
Eastern Europe, Russia, and Africa	5
China	6

Different Ratings

Some DVD discs literally contain more than one version of a movie. If a movie has been edited to a version that receives a different rating—if it's available in both an R and a PG-13 version, for example, or a rated and a nonrated version—then the capabilities of the DVD format enable a manufacturer to code both versions onto a single disc, if so desired. When you choose a particular version, the DVD player will skip over certain scenes or play an alternate audio soundtrack, thus creating the differently rated version of the movie.

For discs that include this feature—which are few, due to the cost of the programming required for the second version—parents can select their own personal identification number to keep their children from accessing the racier version of the film.

Power Up

DVD players enabled for a particular region code are supposed to be sold only within that region. If you want to play discs intended for another region, look for a "code-free" DVD player. These players—typically from smaller suppliers, not the major manufacturers—are capable of playing DVD discs encoded with any region code.

Make Your DVD Player Do Double Duty

If you have a DVD player, you can throw away your old CD player—because all DVD players are "backward compatible" with audio compact discs! There's no need cluttering

Overload!

While DVD players can read normal prerecorded music CDs, any CDs you record yourself with a CD recorder (discussed in Chapter 17, "Sound at the Speed of Light: CD Players and Recorders") *cannot* be read by most DVD players. Unless your DVD player has a second laser just for CD-Rs, any discs you record on a CD recorder are unrecognizable by your DVD player. The reasons are quite technical and have to do with the depth of the encoded information on the disc, but the end result is that you can't play home-grown CDs (including MP3 discs) in your DVD player.

Power Up

While DVDs don't play in normal laserdisc players, Pioneer (the leading proponent of the laserdisc format) does make one combination player that plays all three formats—laserdisc, DVD, and CD. It's an expensive unit, since it uses separate lasers for each function, but it will do double duty for you.

up your system with two different but similar players when a single player—your DVD player—can play both types of discs.

All you have to do is load a CD into your DVD player, and press the Play button. You don't even need to turn on your TV—just switch to audio-only mode and listen to your favorite music on the same machine you use to watch your favorite movies.

While you can play CDs in a DVD player, it doesn't work the other way; you can't play DVDs in a CD player. (Nor can you play them in a laserdisc player, in case you were curious.) You can only play DVDs in DVD players (and in computer DVD-ROM drives).

Different Types of DVD Machines

There is more than one type of machine that can play DVDs. You can choose from DVD players, DVD changers, DVD recorders (not yet available, but coming soon!), and DVD-ROM drives for computers. Let's look a bit at each type of machine.

DVD Players

DVD players do just what you think they do—they play DVD discs. One at a time.

When you go shopping for a DVD player, you'll find prices that range from $200 to $1,200. What makes the thousand-dollar model so much better than the cheaper one?

In most cases it's a matter of features rather than performance. More sophisticated DVD players include on-screen menus that contain more options, remote controls that give you more control over disc playback, and front-panel and on-screen readouts that provide more information about what's being played.

In other cases it's a matter of performance. While all DVD players will deliver a 500-line picture that blows away anything you're used to watching, there are some subtle differences in picture quality between the lower-priced and the higher-priced models. In addition, higher-priced models are more likely to be mechanically sturdier, more reliable, and better at playing scratched or damaged discs.

At the very high end are *progressive-scan* DVD players. While a normal DVD player plays back discs with 500-line resolution using *interlaced* scanning, a progressive-scan player plays back discs with 500-line resolution using *progressive scanning*, which puts those 500 lines on your screen twice as fast. The result—when hooked up to a TV with progressive-scan inputs—makes the typically sharp DVD picture appear to look even sharper, without a trace of flicker or visible scan lines.

Input/Output

As explained back in Chapter 8, "The Next Generation: Digital and High-Definition TV," a normal television picture is displayed in two halves—the "odd" scan lines are displayed first, followed by the "even" scan lines. This happens so fast that the two halves blend together to form a single picture. In the case of a normal DVD picture, you actually see two 250-line halves **interlaced** together to create the 500-line DVD picture.

With progressive scanning, all lines are displayed at the same time, with no interlacing. This puts the whole picture on screen in half the time—which reduces picture flicker and reduces visible scan lines. Progressive scanning produces a noticeably better picture if you have a very large screen display, if you're sitting very close to your television screen, or if you're viewing scenes with lots of motion.

Still, while some videophiles may be able to discern these subtle differences between players, the average consumer will be more than happy with even the most basic DVD player.

DVD Changers

Just as you can buy CD changers that let you queue up multiple compact discs, you can now buy DVD changers that let you insert anywhere from 5 to 300 DVDs into either a carousel or jukebox-type device. With a DVD changer you can watch one movie at a time (of course!), or program the changer to jump from scene to scene on different discs, either randomly or in a preprogrammed order.

Why, you ask, would anyone need to load up a half-dozen or more movies into a single player? Granted, this sounds excessive, but there are some instances where a DVD changer makes a lot of sense:

➤ You have kids, and they watch a lot of Disney movies. Just load up the machine and keep the rug rats happy all day long!

➤ You use your DVD player to play CDs. As you learned earlier in this chapter, your DVD player can also play audio-only CDs. Loading up a changer with multiple CDs not only gives you continuous music for several hours, but—when you use the "shuffle" or random-playback feature—can play a variety of songs from different CDs, in a nonlinear fashion.

➤ You have a lot of DVDs. If you have a hundred or more DVDs, you can load them all into a DVD jukebox and let the jukebox be your storage bin for all your discs. You don't need to walk over to a storage cabinet, pick a disc, and then load it into your machine; with a DVD jukebox, just use your remote to browse through *all* your discs, and then play the one you want with the press of a button.

The only problem with a DVD jukebox is figuring out just *where* that one movie is among the hundreds stored in the changer. That problem can be solved by a high-end DVD disc-control system, such as Escient's PowerPlay. This system reads each disc in your changer, accesses an Internet-based database of titles, and downloads disc and movie information into a base unit. This unit displays DVD covers, titles, and other information on your TV screen, enabling you to easily choose which movie you want to watch. PowerPlay isn't cheap—pricing starts at $5,000—but it is a great way to manage extra-large DVD collections! (Escient also manufactures TuneBase, a similar system for managing large CD collections and multiple CD jukeboxes. For more information on TuneBase, see Chapter 17 or go directly to Escient's Web site at www.escient.com.)

DVD Recorders

As I write these words, the DVD medium is strictly for playback only. That's about to change, however, as several manufacturers are readying to launch their first DVD recorders.

Just as CD recorders use a higher-powered laser to record pits on blank compact discs, DVD recorders will be able to record programming on blank DVD discs. While the motion picture industry will no doubt insist on some sort of copy protection scheme (to at least prohibit direct digital recording of digital material), you should be able to use DVD recorders to time-shift television programming and record your own home movies.

While the initial DVD recorders will no doubt have high price tags, expect prices to come down rapidly as the technology improves and consumer demand increases.

Input/Output

You don't need a DVD recorder to copy DVD movies—you can use your VCR for that task. Or you'd think you could, anyway.

There are two major stumbling blocks to recording from DVD to VHS. The first is that picture quality dramatically suffers in the process; your 500-line DVD picture is cut in half to the 240-line resolution of VHS tape. Why would you want to do that?

The second stumbling block is pretty much out of your control. All DVD players include an anti-copy circuit which will distort the picture if your VCR includes the corresponding circuit—which most do. That means that copying from DVD to videotape is practically impossible. (This copy protection circuit may actually prevent you from connecting your DVD in between your VCR and your TV—even if you're not recording!)

Computer DVD Drives

If you have a personal computer (and you probably do), you're familiar with the CD-ROM drive that plays back special CDs encoded with computer data. In many newer computers, CD-ROM drives are being replaced by DVD-ROM drives, which play back DVDs designed for computer use. Just as normal DVDs contain much more data than do CDs, DVD-ROMs contain much more computer data than do CD-ROMs—enabling computer software manufacturers to replace multiple CD-ROMs with a single DVD-ROM disc.

As an added bonus, most DVD-ROM drives can also play back regular DVD movies. This doesn't go the other way, however; DVD players and changers cannot play back computer DVD-ROM discs.

Audio-Only DVDs

The DVD format was envisioned as a high-quality audio/video format. But why can't this new format be adapted to audio-only discs, utilizing the extra storage capacity to provide ultra-high quality music reproduction?

The answer to that question, of course, is that it can, and it has. The new DVD-Audio format uses DVDs to store and reproduce music with a sonic realism and detail that must be heard to be believed. The DVD-Audio format has a higher signal-to-noise ratio, wider frequency response, and wider dynamic range than traditional CDs, and is capable of reproducing up to six channels of surround-sound audio.

While DVD-Audio is extremely new technology, many industry experts believe that it will eventually replace the compact disc as the music medium of choice.

Input/Output

The DVD-Audio format is competing with another "super audio" format on five-inch disc. Sony's Super Audio CDs (SA-CD) offer similar high-fidelity performance, and the promise (not delivered in first-generation units) of surround sound. To learn more about DVD-Audio and SA-CD, see Chapter 17.

All Those Different Outputs: How Do I Hook This Up?

Once you get your new DVD player home, it's time to hook it up. However, there are a huge number of different connectors on the back of a typical DVD player, and choosing which sets of connectors to use for the best possible hookup can be a tad challenging.

Which particular set of outputs you use depends on the available inputs you have on your television or a/v receiver. Here are the options typically present for connecting your DVD player's video:

➤ **Component video.** This is a three-jack connection (for brightness, red, and blue—typically labeled Y, Pr, and Pb) that provides the ultimate in color accuracy. Only high-end TVs have component-video inputs—but if your TV *does* have a component-video input, this type of connection provides the best quality picture.

➤ **S-Video.** If you can't use the component-video output, use the S-Video output. S-Video provides superb picture quality—almost, but not quite, as good as component video, and superior to traditional composite video.

➤ **Composite video.** If your TV or a/v receiver doesn't have an S-Video connection, it's sure to have a composite-video connection. Composite video—often labeled just "video" and using an RCA jack connector—isn't nearly as sharp as S-Video, but it's better than connecting via an RF connection.

➤ **RF (coax).** If your TV only has a single connection on the back—labeled "Antenna"—then you're forced to use the RF connector on the back of your DVD player. Since this connection combines audio and video signals and feeds them through your television's tuner, the resulting picture is substantially inferior to what the DVD format is capable of reproducing. Still, it's better than broadcast TV or VHS!

There are fewer options for connecting your DVD player's audio. You'll typically find two or possibly three different types of audio connections:

➤ **Digital audio.** Most DVD players include at least one digital audio output for sending the Dolby Digital bitstream directly to a Dolby Digital decoder. This connection provides the best quality audio output, and should be used if you're connecting your DVD player to an a/v receiver that includes Dolby Digital surround sound.

➤ **Traditional audio.** These are the traditional right and left audio outputs, using RCA jacks. You connect these output jacks to the right and left input jacks on an audio or a/v receiver. You use these jacks if you're connecting your DVD to an a/v receiver or TV that *doesn't* include Dolby Digital sound; the output from these jacks will pass through both stereo and Dolby Pro Logic signals.

➤ **5.1 audio.** If your DVD player has a built-in Dolby Digital surround-sound decoder—and your a/v receiver *doesn't*—you can connect these outputs to a separate receiver or preamplifier to play back the decoded surround sound.

Smart Shopping: What to Look For

Now that you're ready to purchase your first DVD player, what features should you look for? Here are some buying tips:

➤ **Easy operation.** Some DVD players have clean front players and simple remotes; some have enough buttons and knobs and joysticks to confuse professional jet pilots. Look for a model with a clean front panel, a remote control that doesn't require a 200-page instruction manual, and easy-to-follow on-screen menus.

➤ **Single-play or changer.** If all you want to do is watch movies, choose a single-play DVD player. If, on the other hand, you want your DVD machine to do double duty as a CD player, think about a multiple-disc DVD changer.

➤ **Do you need a decoder?** Many DVD players come with built-in Dolby Digital recorders. If you have a Dolby Digital a/v receiver, however, you'll never use this built-in decoder—so there's no need to consider it an essential feature.

➤ **Check your connections.** If you have a real high-end system—and a TV with component video inputs—choose a model with component video outputs. Otherwise, you're probably safe with models that max out with S-Video.

➤ **For the true videophile.** If you have an *ultra* high-end system, check out one of the rarified-air models that features progressive scanning. If your video display can handle progressively scanned DVDs—and since not all can, it helps to ask— the picture from a progressive scan player is noticeably cleaner than from a normal player.

Unless you're talking about progressive-scan DVD players, all other DVD players share very similar specs for both picture and sound. While it doesn't hurt to evaluate player performance before you buy, the differences you find will be slight.

Input/Output

Originally I was going to include a section in this chapter about where to find DVD discs. I decided against that once I realized that you can find DVD discs *everywhere*. You can find discs for purchase at any major consumer electronics store (such as Best Buy or Circuit City), most of the major music chains, many video specialty stores, and at a number of Web sites—including CDNow (www.cdnow.com), Amazon.com (www.amazon.com), and my personal favorite, DVD Express (www.dvd.com). You can also find DVD discs for rent at just about any video store, including Blockbuster Entertainment and online at NetFlix (www.netflix. com).

The Least You Need to Know

➤ DVDs deliver the best NTSC-compatible picture and sound to your home theater system—500 lines of resolution (compared to 425 lines for laserdisc or digital satellite, or 240 lines for VHS) and Dolby Digital 5.1 surround sound.

➤ An entire movie can fit on one side of a DVD disc—along with such extras as dual 4:3 and letterbox versions, alternate audio tracks, subtitles, documentaries, production credits, and more.

➤ Picture and sound quality are similar for all DVD players—the difference in price typically comes from additional features.

➤ All DVD players can also play CDs, so you can use a single DVD player for both DVD and CD playback.

➤ When you're connecting a DVD player to your home theater system, use the component video output if your TV has a component video input; otherwise, use the S-Video connection.

➤ If you have a Dolby digital surround-sound system, use your DVD player's digital audio outputs; otherwise, use the normal left and right audio outputs.

Chapter 11

Tale of the Tape:
Video Recorders

In This Chapter

➤ Why the picture and sound quality on VHS recorders might not be good enough for your system

➤ VHS HiFi and Super VHS—better-quality VCRs for your home theater system

➤ VHS-C, 8mm, Hi-8, Digital 8, and Mini DV—the alphabet soup of camcorder formats

➤ DVHS—a new format for recording HDTV broadcasts

Videocassette recorders (VCRs) are a staple in just about every American household. They're relatively inexpensive (some sell for less than $100) and somewhat easy to use (except for setting that darned timer!), and there is plentiful prerecorded programming available for them (there's a video rental store on just about every corner these days).

The only problem is, the ¹/₂-inch VHS-format VCR is very old technology—more than 20 years old, to be precise. The format doesn't offer digital sound or picture, the picture resolution is below even broadcast television, and it doesn't offer much in the way of added features or high-tech bells and whistles.

Still, everybody has one, and millions of new ones are sold every year. So, it's likely that you'll include a VCR as part of your home theater system—but not as your sole video source, hopefully!

VHS: Poor Quality, Hard to Use—and Everybody Has One

The VHS format uses ¹/₂-inch tape in convenient videocassettes to record and play back standard NTSC programs. A VCR can play back prerecorded programming, or you can use it to record programming off the air or from a video camera.

The main problem with VHS VCRs is the picture and sound quality. On tapes recorded at the fastest speed (SP, which delivers the best possible quality), horizontal resolution is only 240 lines. Compare this to the 330-line resolution of normal broadcast or cable television, or the 500-line resolution of DVD, and you can see why a VCR's picture looks dull and noisy next to that from other video sources.

In addition, standard mono VHS sound is … well, it just sucks. I can't put it any other way; sorry. It has abominably high levels of *wow* and *flutter,* an extremely low *signal-to-noise ratio,* and a *frequency response* similar to that of AM radio.

Still, you pretty much have to have a VHS VCR hooked up to your TV—if nothing else, to play back all those tapes you've accumulated over the years. Just be prepared to be really disappointed when you play a videotaped movie back through a high-end, high-resolution, big-screen TV!

Product Specs

Wondering what **wow** and **flutter** are? Fuzzy about **frequency response?** Speculating about **signal-to-noise ratio?** Then turn to Appendix A, "Glossary," for some definitions.

Better Sound, Same Picture: VHS HiFi

If you must include a VCR in your home theater setup, at least upgrade to a VHS HiFi model. VHS HiFi delivers the standard-quality VHS picture, but upgrades the sound to near-digital quality. VHS HiFi features a wider frequency response (a full 20–20,000 Hz), higher signal-to-noise ratio, less wow and flutter, and full stereo sound. VHS HiFi can also reproduce Dolby Pro Logic surround sound—although it *can't* reproduce the newer Dolby Digital soundtracks.

Input/Output

Owning an SVHS VCR won't improve the picture quality on the prerecorded movies you play, because they're all recorded in standard VHS. Sorry.

You won't pay that much more for a VHS HiFi VCR than you will for a standard VHS mono model. You should be able to find some very good VHS HiFi models in the $150–$200 price range.

It's Super, Man: A Better VHS

If you want to record a better picture, you can step up to the Super VHS (SVHS) format. This variation of VHS—which uses the same size videocassettes, but requires a higher-priced tape formulation—can record up to a 400-line resolution, which is much better than standard VHS 240-line resolution. If you want to record programming from a digital satellite system or DVD, this is the format to go with.

SVHS VCRs—which can also play back standard VHS tapes—cost a bit more than standard VHS decks, with prices starting around $300. You also won't find a lot of selection—most manufacturers only include one or two Super VHS models in their line.

DVHS: Video Recording for the Digital Age

What if you want to record one of the new HDTV broadcasts? Well, if you have a standard VHS or Super VHS deck, you're out of luck—they're totally incapable of recording any of these new digital television broadcasts.

Rest assured, there is a solution. A new VHS format—dubbed Digital VHS, or DVHS—is capable of recording digital and high-definition television, in their native 16:9 aspect ratios. DVHS is capable of 500-line resolution, so it won't be quite as sharp as the original digital material, but it's still pretty good.

Right now DVHS decks are few and high priced, but expect that to change as more manufacturers enter this area and HDTV becomes more mainstream.

Wait! There's More: Camcorders and Other Formats

While the home VCR is pretty much a one-format (VHS—with the aforementioned variations) game, when you get into camcorders, the number of formats multiplies. A camcorder, of course, is that unique blend of camera and video recorder that lets you make home movies on videocassettes. Read on to learn a little about the recording/playback formats you'll run into when shopping for a new camcorder.

VHS-C

Early camcorders were big, heavy hogs that used full-size VHS videocassettes. Manufacturers quickly learned that consumers wanted smaller, lighter-weight units, and the VHS-C (compact VHS) format was born.

The VHS-C format uses standard VHS videotape, but in a smaller cassette. Thus, anything recorded on VHS-C is fully compatible with your home VHS deck. All you have to do is place the smaller VHS-C cassette into a special adapter for playback on your home deck.

Power Up

You may think you have to stick with a VHS-C camcorder to maintain compatibility with your home VCR. You'd be wrong. While other format cassettes won't fit in your home deck, of course, you can easily "dub" movies from one format to another. Just connect a cable between the audio and video output jacks on your camcorder and the audio and video input jacks on your home deck, press Play on the camcorder and Record on the home VCR, and you're dubbing. Of course, you can also plug your camcorder directly into your television or audio/video receiver via standard composite video and audio jacks, or (in some cases) an S-Video connection.

As you might expect, VHS-C delivers the same abysmal picture and sound quality as regular VHS—but with only 30 minutes of recording time (90 minutes at the even lower-quality EP speed).

8mm

The most popular camcorder format today is 8mm videotape. This format offers slightly better picture and sound quality, much longer recording time, and a smaller cassette than VHS-C. 8mm camcorders can record up to 2.5 hours in standard mode, or 5 hours in LP mode.

In addition, 8mm camcorders typically use less power than do VHS-C models—which results in less battery changing. Some new 8mm models can record up to 15 hours on a single battery!

Hi8

If you want significantly better picture quality, go with the Hi8 format, which offers a 50 percent sharper picture (400 lines vs. 240 lines). In fact, you can think of Hi8 as the "Super VHS" equivalent of the 8mm format. Hi8 uses the same size cassettes as does 8mm, but with a higher-priced tape formulation.

Digital 8

For even better picture quality, move up to the new Digital 8 format. This format delivers up to 500 lines of resolution, along with digital stereo sound. Digital 8, since it records digitally, also produces high-quality copies, which is important when you're editing and dubbing your home movies. While these units come in at the high-end of the camcorder price ranger (typically $1,000 or more), you get a lot of bang for your buck, especially if you do a lot of semi-pro recording.

The only drawback to Digital 8 is its recording time. Since it records on standard 8mm or Hi8 cassettes—but stores twice as much information on the tape—the storage capacity of each tape is effectively cut in half.

Mini DV

The very best camcorders today incorporate the Mini DV format, which uses an ultra-compact video-cassette to record picture and sound digitally. Mini DV provides the highest resolution, accuracy, and color richness of any consumer camcorder format—on *really* small cassettes. Most Mini DV camcorders include a lot of computerized editing features—and can be easily connected to a personal computer for further editing and enhancement.

Shop Smart: What to Look For

If you want to upgrade the VCR in your home theater system, here are some features to consider:

➤ **VHS HiFi.** If you're serious about home theater, you can't seriously consider a regular mono VCR. Spend two bills and upgrade to a VHS HiFi model.

➤ **Super VHS.** If all you do is watch prerecorded cassettes, you can ignore the Super VHS format. If, on the other hand, you do a lot of recording—and if a lot of that recording is from higher-quality sources, such as a digital satellite system—then consider spending an extra hundred bucks for the 400-line resolution of a Super VHS deck.

Power Up

When you want to connect your camcorder to your home theater system, the last thing you want to do is fumble through the jumble of back-panel connections. It's much easier to connect a camcorder to front-panel connections, on either your audio/video receiver or television set. Normal composite video and audio connections are fine for VHS-C and 8mm camcorders, but you probably should use an S-Video connection to realize the full potential of the Hi8, Digital 8, or Mini DV formats.

Power Up

If you plan to work with video on your PC, look for a camcorder with either a serial PC connector (which is fairly slow) or the much faster IEEE 1394 FireWire connection—referred to as an i.LINK jack by some camcorder manufacturers.

➤ **Automatic clock set.** If you still haven't figured out how to set the clock on your VCR, look for a model that uses EDS (Extended Data Service) data embedded in the video signal of your local PBS station to automatically set the correct time.

➤ **VCR Plus+.** If you have trouble figuring out how to set your VCR's timer for unattended recording, consider getting a deck with the VCR Plus+ feature. VCR Plus+ lets you easily record programs using a series of preassigned codes; just punch in the code to record a specific program.

➤ **Editing features.** If you shoot a lot of movies with your camcorder, consider a VCR that can help you edit your raw footage down to a more watchable version. Look for features like flying erase heads, insert editing, and front-panel audio/video inputs.

➤ **Control of other devices.** If you have a digital satellite system or a cable box, look for a VCR that includes a separate infrared controller (also called an "infrared blaster" or "cable mouse"). This device hangs over the front of your satellite receiver or cable box and sends channel-changing signals from your VCR directly into the remote control receiver of your other device.

➤ **Four heads.** This will probably be a standard feature—especially if you're looking at a VHS HiFi deck—but check to be sure. You need four heads for the best possible picture quality and special playback effects.

The Least You Need to Know

➤ VHS VCRs offer the lowest quality picture and sound quality of any video source—but you probably have to have one in your home theater system, anyway.

➤ VHS HiFi offers better sound and Super VHS offers better picture, both while maintaining compatibility with all prerecorded VHS videocassettes available today.

➤ Standard VHS can't record 16:9 HDTV broadcasts; for that, you need the new DVHS format.

➤ If you have a camcorder (any format), look for an a/v receiver or television that has front-panel connections for easier temporary hookups.

Chapter 12

A Better VCR: Digital Video Recorders

In This Chapter

➤ How a hard disk records TV programs—digitally

➤ Create your own custom TV channels—and pause "live" broadcasts

➤ Compare DVR hardware and services from TiVo and ReplayTV

If you've had it up to here with substandard VHS picture quality, yet you still want to time-shift broadcast and cable programs, there's a new type of home theater component you need to take a look at. This new breed of recorder uses a hard disk—like the kind in your personal computer—to record television programs digitally. And these digital video recorders (DVRs) do more than just record a program for later viewing; you can use a DVR to pause "live" programs, and to create your own custom programming "channels."

Digital video recording—sometimes called personal video recording—looks to be the next big thing in the consumer electronics industry. Forrester Research (a leading market analysis firm) predicts that 14 million people will be using these devices by 2004, which could change the way a lot of people watch TV!

A Computer in Your Living Room: How Personal Digital Video Recorders Work

Digital video recording technology was developed pretty much simultaneously by two different companies, TiVo and ReplayTV. Not surprisingly, both the TiVo and ReplayTV units work in similar fashion.

No matter what kind of DVR you have, television programming (from an antenna, cable box, or satellite receiver) is fed into the unit, which then stores that programming on its hard disk. The programming is stored digitally, using MPEG2 compression.

To view something you've recorded, you just play it back from the hard disk through your TV and home theater system. After you've viewed a stored program, you can continue to store it on the disk, or you can delete it—freeing up space to record other programs.

Input/Output

There appears to be no industry-wide consensus as to what to call these hard-disk-based recorders. TiVo calls its unit a personal television receiver (PTR), while ReplayTV calls its a personal video recorder (PVR). I call them all digital video recorders (DVRs), but you can call them whatever you want.

Overload!

Note that these digital video recorders are great for time-shifting programs, but they can't play back any prerecorded material—the hard disk is totally self-contained.

When you record something on the hard disk, you get to choose the quality level of the stored material. (Well, you choose the quality of the picture, not necessarily of the program itself!) If you choose a lower-quality picture (similar to VHS quality) the program takes less storage space, and you can store more programming on the hard disk. If you choose a higher-quality picture (near-DVD quality) the program takes more storage space, reducing the amount of programming you can put on the hard disk.

Depending on the manufacturer (and the size of the unit's hard disk), a DVR can record from 14 to 30 hours of digital video in its lowest-quality mode. Low-quality recording takes about a third the disk space as the high-quality mode; that 30-hour capacity turns into 10-hour capacity if you're finicky about picture quality.

Take Two: Looking at the Different Types of DVRs

There are two flavors of digital video recorders—TiVo and ReplayTV. Both use very similar technology and offer very similar programming services.

TiVo's DVR units are sold by Philips in most major consumer electronics stores. The ReplayTV unit is available only from ReplayTV or from online retailers such as Amazon.com (www.amazon.com) and ROXY.com (www.roxy.com).

DVRs from either TiVo or ReplayTV currently sell in the $400–$700 range. ReplayTV's monthly programming service is free; TiVo's service runs $9.95 a month.

Input/Output

To learn more about the TiVo and ReplayTV recorders, go to their respective Web sites at www.tivo.com and www.replaytv.com. There's also a great comparison of the two units at the E! Online Web site (www.eonline.com/Features/Features/Tivo/)—they like TiVo best!

A look at TiVo's selection screen—pick a program and click your remote to record.

(Courtesy of Philips Consumer Electronics Company)

Fancy Recording, and Then Some: All You Can Do with a DVR

Something most users don't realize is that when you watch "live" broadcasts through your DVR, it actually records everything you watch, before it passes on the signal to your TV. So, when you watch programming through your DVR, you're actually watching what the DVR has recorded—*not* the live signal. Because you're watching a recording—on a one- or two-second delay—you can utilize all sorts of neat playback features in near-real time.

For example, you can pause a "live" recording as you're watching through your DVR deck. The recording of the actual program continues while the playback is paused; when you release the pause, you continue watching from where you stopped.

A similar capability gives you crystal-clear slow motion, in near-real time. And, if you start watching a program on your DVR several minutes after the start of the program, you can fast-forward through the slow bits of the program—like, say, the commercials.

Speaking of commercials, some DVR units feature a smart scan that lets you automatically skip any commercials you've recorded. Some units even feature an instant replay button to automatically review what you've just watched.

If all you wanted to do was pause the program you're watching, we could stop here. DVRs are capable of much more than TV pause, however, when used with their accompanying programming services. These services let you create your own "customized channels" filled with your favorite shows. All you have to do is choose the shows you want to watch from the on-screen program guide, and the service will automatically program the DVR to record those shows, for your viewing at a later time. (This is different from recording from a VCR, where you tell it what *time* you want to start recording; DVR recording is programmed by actual program, not by time.)

Input/Output

TiVo and ReplayTV technology is also being incorporated in other audio/video devices. For example, EchoStar is selling a special DISHplayer satellite receiver that includes both hard disk recording and WebTV capability. In addition, Philips and other WebTV manufacturers have new WebTV units that merge Internet access with hard drive TV recording.

With some units, choosing what to record is even easier than that. Let's say you like *Frasier*. It's easy enough to tell your DVR to record *Frasier* off network TV this coming Thursday, but you can also tell it to record the program *every* Thursday. You can also have it record both the network and the syndicated showings of *Frasier*—without you having to look up specific channels and times. Beyond that, you can also tell the service to record other programs that feature specific actors and actresses from *Frasier;* you could have it record every show starring David Hyde-Pierce, for example. When you're done with all this, you'd have your own custom *Frasier* channel—all *Frasier*, all the time!

In addition, the DVR service will automatically suggest other shows you might want to record, using a smart search feature based on your personal preferences. The TiVo remote control even has a "thumbs up/thumbs down" button so you can vote on specific programs; the service uses your voting results to suggest new programming.

Easy as Pie: Hooking Up a DVR

Hooking up a TiVo or ReplayTV is as simple as inserting it between your video source (antenna, cable box, or satellite receiver) and your TV (and a/v receiver). For the best possible picture quality, you should utilize the unit's S-Video connectors; alternately, you can use component video or RF connections.

Since the DVR has to access either the TiVo or ReplayTV service, the unit also has to be connected to your phone line. Once you get everything hooked up, you'll be walked through the automatic setup process—which can take anywhere from 30 minutes to an hour.

Smart Shopping: What to Look For

If you want to add a personal hard disk recorder to your home theater system, here are some items to consider:

➤ **Hard disk size.** The bigger the hard disk, the more programming you can store. And since live programming is constantly being recorded—in high-quality mode, to boot—don't be surprised to see your hard disk fill up quicker than you might have thought.

➤ **On-screen displays.** Finding your way around the system is done differently between TiVo and ReplayTV. The remotes also work a bit differently. Check out all the displays and operations to make sure they're comfortable and understandable for you.

➤ **Programming service.** TiVo's service costs $9.95 a month. ReplayTV's is free. You do the math.

One last thing. This book was written in the spring of 2000, and it's probable that pricing on both the TiVo and ReplayTV units will get more affordable over time. It's also probable that newer units will include even larger hard disks and more features—so keep your eyes peeled for the latest developments in this exciting new area!

Overload!

Here's one thing you can't do with your brand-new TiVo or ReplayTV recorder—record one program while you watch another. Since the DVR doesn't have its own tuner—it accepts input from other video sources in your system—it can only record what it's sent. Until DVRs start incorporating their own tuners, this will be one advantage an old-fashioned VCR has over this newfangled technology.

The Least You Need to Know

➤ A digital video recorder—also called a personal recorder—records television programs on a hard disk, using MPEG2 video compression.

➤ The two major DVR systems are TiVo and ReplayTV; hard disk sizes range from 14Gb to 30Gb, and prices range from $400 to $700.

➤ Since a DVR "buffers" live programming on its hard disk, you can watch programming with crystal-clear special effects—including pause, slow motion, fast forward, and instant replay.

➤ The TiVo and ReplayTV programming services enable you to easily select programs to record—and create your own "custom channels" of preselected programming.

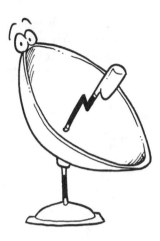

Chapter 13

The World on a Dish: Digital Satellite Systems

In This Chapter

➤ How digital satellite broadcasting works

➤ Which is better—DIRECTV or the DISH Network?

➤ Installing your own satellite dish

➤ Receiving local programming and HDTV broadcasts via satellite

---

If you've added a bigger or higher-resolution television to your home theater system, you want to watch the best-quality picture available. If you're like me, however, you find that the picture quality from broadcast and cable leaves something to be desired. There has to be a *better* way to watch your favorite programs—isn't there?

Well, there is. All you need is a small round dish, a set-top receiver, and a subscription to a satellite broadcasting service—and then you can watch network and cable programming with 25 percent greater resolution!

Eye on the Sky: How Digital Satellite Systems Work

Today there are more than 10 million users of digital satellite systems—with millions more added each year. These digital systems use relatively small (18" or so in diameter) round dishes to receive high-quality digital programming via satellite. Unlike the older C-band satellite dishes—which used 10' or larger dishes—these digital satellite dishes are easy to install and even easier to use.

As you can see in the following picture, a complete digital satellite system consists of a small dish and a set-top satellite receiver. The dish mounts outside your house (pointed toward the proper satellite) and the receiver connects inside your house to your television and home theater system.

The components of a digital satellite system: Mount the dish outside, and connect the receiver to your TV and home theater system.

(Courtesy of Thomson Consumer Electronics)

Product Specs

An **LNB** is a Low Noise Blocker, a type of amplifier that blocks low-end frequencies and receives the high-end frequencies used in digital satellite transmissions. The LNB is located at the end of the arm projecting from the satellite dish; if your dish receives signals from multiple satellites—or if you want to feed signals to more than one receiver—you may have more than one LNB attached to the arm.

The entire system starts with programming signals transmitted from a central broadcasting complex to a series of high-powered geosynchronous satellites in orbit 22,000 miles above Earth. The satellites beam the signals back earthward, where they're collected by your small satellite dish and focused on an *LNB* mounted on a small arm attached to your dish. The LNB then sends the collected signals via a coax cable to the satellite receiver box. This box separates the satellite signal into normal audio and video signals, and feeds them to your TV and a/v receiver. You use a handheld remote control to change channels and perform other operations with the receiver.

Since your satellite system receives only a subset of available programming—assuming you don't subscribe to *everything* that's available!—your receiver has to be instructed as to what signals to block. These instructions are sent via phone lines to your receiver box, which is identified via a unique access card that is plugged into a slot in the front or side of your unit. Your receiver also uses your phone line to contact the programming service when you want to watch a pay-per-view movie; when you push the "I want to watch this movie" button, that information is transmitted via phone to your program provider, which then charges your credit card and sends an unlock signal for that channel back to your satellite receiver.

The picture and sound available via satellite are superb—just short of what you expect from DVD. Both video and audio are transmitted digitally, and picture quality can approach 425 lines of resolution. Audio can be broadcast in Dolby Digital 5.1 (if you have a higher-end satellite receiver with 5.1 outputs), although most programs are transmitted with Dolby Pro Logic surround.

DIRECTV and EchoStar: Twin Sons of Different Mothers

There are two different flavors of digital satellite systems—DIRECTV and the DISH Network (from EchoStar). Both use 18" diagonal dishes to receive digital audio and video programming, both carry similar pricing, and both offer more than 200 different ent programs, including the various cable channels, pay-movie channels, pay-sports channels, music-only channels, and a variety of pay-per-view broadcasts. Programming from both services is sold in packages which start as low as $19.99/month.

Given the similarities, which system should you choose? For what it's worth, DIRECTV appears to be the system of choice for most home theater enthusiasts, but that may be a factor of ease-of-purchase. DIRECTV systems are manufactured and sold by RCA, Sony, Hughes, and others—and several television manufacturers are producing sets with built-in DIRECTV tuners. EchoStar systems, in contrast, are available direct from EchoStar only.

While the dishes used are pretty much the same from manufacturer to manufacturer, there are plenty of differences between their satellite receivers—and between different receivers from the same manufacturer. Higher-end receivers tend to include fancier on-screen guides, more complex remote controls, an infrared controller for programmed VCR recording, and Dolby Digital sound. (All receivers can receive Dolby Pro Logic, but only some receivers have the decoder and outputs for the 5.1 surround-sound system.) EchoStar even makes a receiver that includes built-in TiVo hard disk drive recording (discussed in Chapter 12, "A Better VCR: Digital Video Recorders") and a WebTV Internet terminal.

Input/Output

These small-dish satellite systems are sometimes called digital satellite systems (DSS) or direct broadcast satellite (DBS) systems. Use whichever three-letter acronym (TLA) you prefer.

Overload!

If your satellite receiver isn't connected to your phone line, you won't be able to order pay-per-view programs.

In any case, compare the features of the receivers carefully, because this is where the real differences between hardware lies.

The Longest Distance Between Two Points: Getting Local Stations from the Satellite

Up until recently, satellites were great for nationwide programming, but lousy for local programming. That was because the "birds" beamed down the same programming on everybody—and what would be the point of sending local North Carolina programming to viewers in Oregon?

Overload!

DIRECTV and DISH Network services are not currently available in Hawaii, Puerto Rico, or Canada. You can subscribe to DIRECTV in Alaska, but you need a 10' dish to receive the signals!

Input/Output

Originally, there was a third service—PrimeStar—competing with DIRECTV and EchoStar. DIRECTV acquired PrimeStar, just as it acquired former programming partner USSB. (USSB and DIRECTV each used to offer different programming over the same satellite; now, all the programming comes from DIRECTV.) So now it's just DIRECTV and EchoStar.

That didn't stop users from asking for the big television networks via satellite, and DIRECTV and the DISH Network responded by rebroadcasting signals from a handful of local network affiliates to their subscribers across the nation. This, however, ticked off all the other local affiliates—and the networks themselves—who felt they were losing local viewers when satellite subscribers could get the same programming from another affiliate over satellite. These affiliates successfully forced DIRECTV and the DISH Network to drop these rebroadcasts from their programming plans.

Viewers, however, still hated having to connect an antenna or cable box just to get a handful of network stations, and made a lot of noise about it. The result was the Satellite Home Viewer Improvement Act of 1999, signed into law on November 29, 1999. This law gives satellite TV providers the right to offer local stations, at their discretion.

Now DIRECTV and DISH Network are in the process of rolling out local network channels to their subscribers. The way it works is that the local channels are beamed off the satellite along with the rest of their programming, but are blocked out of all regions except their own local broadcast area. So if you're in Chicago, you can only receive the Chicago stations—not the New York or San Francisco stations.

The problem is, there is only enough bandwidth available on the systems' satellites to include a handful of local stations. Both DIRECTV and EchoStar can only fit stations for the top 20 or so largest cities onto their main satellites. For smaller TV markets, the services are using additional satellites to transmit those local channels. Which, if you're a user in a smaller market, means you need to buy a larger dish—DIRECTV Plus or DISH 500—to receive signals from both the main satellite and the auxiliary satellite used for your local channels.

Once you get properly hooked up and subscribed, however, you can throw away your antenna and disconnect your cable box, because you'll get your local channels along with your satellite channels, all from the same receiver.

Mounting and Pointing: How to Install a Digital Satellite System

When you buy a digital satellite system, you have to deal with two different facets of installation—installing the dish and connecting the receiver. We'll look (briefly) at both issues.

Installing the Dish

Unlike the old 10' (or larger!) satellite dishes, today's pizza-box-sized dish can be installed by anyone with a few useful tools and a free afternoon. (Or, if you're a total klutz—like me!—you can spend a few bucks and have a professional installer do the job for you.)

Input/Output

You can compare the features of the DIRECTV and DISH Network systems at their respective Web sites, www.directv.com and www.dishnetwork.com.

DIRECTV also markets the DIRECTPC system, which uses a slightly larger elliptical dish that adds high-speed Internet access to your standard DIRECTV programming. Just connect the DIRECTPC dish to a special card in your personal computer (and your computer to a phone line, for uploading files and sending e-mail) and you'll be downloading files and surfing the Web—*fast!*—in no time.

Here are the general steps you take to install your digital satellite dish:

1. Mount your dish—typically on the side of your house, with a clear view of the southern sky (meaning no signal-blocking trees, buildings, hillsides, and so on).

2. Assemble the LNB and mounting arm onto the dish.

3. Run a length of coaxial cable from the LNB to your satellite receiver, and then connect your receiver to your TV. (See instructions in the next section.)

4. Point your dish roughly towards the satellite, following the instructions that came with the dish.

5. Using the menu options on your satellite receiver, adjust the dish's direction and elevation until you maximize the signal strength from the satellite.

Some satellite dishes, including models from Sony, include a "signal seeker" LED on the LNB, which blinks more rapidly the closer you aim at the satellite. This makes for an easier installation than having someone inside the house yelling out the window as you get closer to—or farther away from—the satellite.

Overload!

Since you need a clear line of sight between your dish and the satellite, anything big in between can cause a deteriorated or dropped signal. While you typically think of trees and buildings as potential signal blockers, liquid can also block signals. So, if there's a heavy rainstorm or snowstorm between you and the satellite, you could experience "rain fade," where the satellite signal starts to pixelate, freeze, or ultimately cut off altogether. If this happens to you, just wait for the precipitation to let up and your satellite signal will return—right as rain!

Connecting the Receiver

The simplest way to connect your satellite receiver to your TV is to use the RF coax connector, just as you'd connect your cable TV box. However, this method also provides for the lowest-quality picture and sound—with a lower-resolution picture than the satellite system is capable of.

A better connection is via the composite video and R/L audio connections. Better yet is to use the receiver's S-Video connection, along with R/L audio connections. (If your receiver is Dolby Digital-ready, use the digital audio output to feed into your a/v receiver.)

Once your system is completely installed, you then have to officially activate it. You do this by calling the 24-hour toll-free number for either DIRECTV or the DISH Network; your programming service will be activated immediately.

One Dish, Two Rooms: Connecting Multiple Receivers

What do you do if you want to watch the signal from your satellite in more than one room?

The cheap and easy solution—and the only solution if your dish has a single LNB—is to run the receiver's composite video and audio outputs to one TV and the RF output to the second set. The only problem with this setup is that you have to watch the same program on both TVs—which isn't a problem if one set is in your home theater system and the other you only watch at night in your bedroom.

If you want to watch different satellite programs on two different sets, you need to buy a dish with dual LNBs. You can feed the signal from one LNB to one TV, and the signal from the second LNB to a second set. Both sets need their own receiver boxes, and you'll have to pay a little extra each month to view your programming through both receivers. Still, this is the best solution for multi-room satellite viewing.

If you want to watch satellite programming on three TVs, you just upped the complexity quotient—but not by much. ChannelMaster, RCA, and other manufacturers sell add-on components called multiplexers that, when connected to a dual-LNB dish, enable you to easily hook up three, four, or more satellite receivers. (Using a $150 multiplexer is much preferable to the older, clumsier, and more costly method of installing a second dish to use a third receiver!) You can hook up any receiver to any of the multiplexer's outputs—so you can have a top-of-the-line model in your home theater system, and a lower-priced receiver in your guest room.

Today's Best Source for Digital Television: Upgrading Your Dish for HDTV Broadcasts

Both DIRECTV and the DISH Network are starting to include HDTV programming as part of their services. (Actually, it's an extra-charge addition to their normal services, but you know what I mean.) In both cases the HDTV broadcasts come from a second satellite, and require the use of the larger DIRECTV Plus or DISH 500 multiple-LNB dishes and new HDTV-ready satellite receivers.

The initial HDTV programming is coming from the pay cable networks HBO and Showtime. Both are broadcasting HDTV channels with high-resolution 16:9 pictures, but are skimping on the audio by using Dolby Pro Logic instead of the more appropriate Dolby Digital. Expect this to change as viewers demand the best of both worlds—and expect the variety of HDTV programming to increase, as well.

Shop Smart: What to Look For

If you want to add a digital satellite system to your home theater system, here are some things to look for—whether you're looking at DIRECTV or EchoStar:

➤ **On-screen menus and program guides.** All digital satellite receivers feature a variety of easy-to-use menus and program guides. These on-screen guides differ in how they look and how they work, however, so look at each before you buy and pick the one that you like best.

➤ **Installation.** If you're like me, you'll look for someone else to install your system for you. If you're more ambitious, consider buying one of the many DSS installation kits available from the DSS manufacturers and third parties; these kits

include all the materials you need for installation, as well as step-by-step instructions.

➤ **Dolby Digital.** Lower-end satellite receivers lack the digital audio or 5.1 outputs necessary for Dolby Digital broadcasts. If you want Dolby Digital sound, go for a more expensive system with the proper decoding and outputs.

➤ **Local channels—and HDTV.** If you live outside one of the top dozen or so major metropolitan areas, you'll need a slightly larger dish—such as the DIRECTV Plus or DISH 500 units—to receive channels from the second satellite used to beam down the signals for your local television channels. In addition, HDTV signals come from a *third* satellite, again requiring the slightly larger dish (and an additional LNB). If you want both local signals and HDTV broadcasts, your system will need to be configured with the bigger dish and *three* LNBs!

➤ **Second receiver.** If you want to watch satellite programming in two different rooms, you'll want to purchase a dish with a dual LNB and then add a second receiver—which means you'll have to pay a little more for the service each month.

The Least You Need to Know

➤ Digital satellite systems use 18" diagonal dishes to receive high-quality digital audio and video signals broadcast via satellite.

➤ The two major digital satellite systems are DIRECTV and EchoStar (a.k.a. the DISH Network).

➤ Local network stations are now available via satellite, but unless you live in one of the top dozen or so TV markets, you'll need a slightly larger (and slightly more expensive) dish to receive the signals.

➤ Both DIRECTV and the DISH Network are using a second satellite to broadcast HDTV signals; you'll need that larger dish and a special HDTV satellite receiver to receive and decode the HDTV broadcasts.

Part 4

Sound Off: Audio Receivers, Players, and Other Components

A home theater system is more than just a big picture; you need good sound and lots of speakers to get a real theater-like experience. Thinking about buying a fancy audio/video receiver? Confused about all those different Dolby surround-sound systems? Not sure what kinds of speakers you need—or even how many? Then read these chapters to learn more about the audio part of your audio/video system.

Sound Is All Around: Understanding Surround Sound

In This Chapter

➤ How surround sound can enhance your home theater system

➤ All the different surround-sound formats, including Dolby Digital, Dolby Pro Logic, DTS, and THX

➤ How to choose the right surround-sound format for your home theater

A great picture is only half of the home theater experience. The other half is sound—gut-thumping, room-filling sound.

Ideally, your home theater should expand beyond the two-dimensional plane of stereo into the three-dimensional world of surround sound. To truly re-create the movie theater experience, you need to surround yourself with the sounds of the movie—the swelling music, the booming explosions, the roaring engines and the subtle background noises that put you in the middle of the scene.

True surround sound requires a surround-sound decoder, a multiple-channel amplifier, and a battery of speakers on all sides of the room. Read on to learn how to add surround sound to your home theater system—and start experiencing *real* home theater!

Surround-Sound Basics: What You Need, and What Goes Where

Surround sound, put simply, is any combination of electronics and speakers that surround your listening position with sound. Obviously, simple two-channel stereo—with its front-left and front-right speakers—can't surround you with sound. For true surround sound, you need a combination of front and rear speakers.

At its most basic, a surround-sound system includes two front speakers (positioned to the front left and front right of the listener) and two surround speakers (positioned to the rear left and rear right)—just like the now-obsolete quadraphonic audio systems of years past. With this simple four-channel setup you can create an accurate stereo soundstage both in front of and behind you; the rear speakers are used to reproduce sounds occurring away from the main screen, behind the audience.

Input/Output

Any receiver or preamplifier equipped with any surround-sound decoder will also play normal mono and stereo recordings in their original one- or two-channel glory. Some decoders include digital signal processing (DSP) chips that can take non-surround sources and simulate different surround-sound environments and sound fields; while audiophile purists decry these artificial "enhancements," many users like the increased presence added by these DSP chips.

All of today's surround-sound technologies expand on this simple four-speaker setup in a number of ways. The most common addition is that of a center speaker, located adjacent to your video display in between the two existing front speakers. This center channel is used to anchor dialogue and other key sounds to the actors on-screen; the front-left and front-right speakers can then be used to expand the soundstage to either side of the screen with special effects and music. (Learn more about center speakers, subwoofers, and other speakers for surround-sound systems in Chapter 16, "Woofers and Tweeters and Horns, Oh My: Speaker Systems.")

Another common addition is that of a subwoofer, used to reproduce the extreme low bass frequencies common in today's movie soundtracks. Without a subwoofer, a home theater system might sound empty or ungrounded; a subwoofer adds the punch that makes your system boom and rumble.

All surround-sound technologies encode the audio information on the movie's normal soundtrack. Older technologies (such as Dolby Pro Logic) "hid" the rear-channel information within the front-channel information, using matrixing algorithms to mix the different channels together for storage or transmission, and then separating the information on playback. Newer technologies (such as Dolby Digital) dedicate discrete data tracks for each channel of information, thus providing more precise positioning and eliminating channel leakage. (Although, just to be confusing, the newest formats—Dolby Digital EX and DTS ES—add a sixth "surround rear" channel that is matrixed within the discrete surround left and surround right channel information.)

Input/Output

Just because you have a surround-sound system—and are playing a movie with a surround-sound soundtrack—doesn't mean you'll always hear sound from your rear speakers. When sound is mixed for a movie, the sound designer uses the surround channels to create an environment. Some environments require the use of the surround channels, others don't—so don't panic if any particular part of a movie appears to be front-channel focused!

More Than One Way to Surround: Understanding the Different Surround-Sound Formats

Over the past decade there have been several different technologies used to provide surround sound for movies and other prerecorded material in the home environment. Let's take a look at some of the most popular surround-sound technologies—and then determine which is best for your home theater system.

Lots of Channels, Great Sound: Dolby Digital

Dolby Digital—also called Dolby Digital 5.1—is the surround-sound technology incorporated on most of today's DVDs. It is also used on some digital satellite broadcasts, and is the sound standard for all future HDTV broadcasts. Unlike the older Dolby Pro Logic system, Dolby Digital offers six discrete audio channels, as follows:

➤ Front left

➤ Front center

➤ Front right

➤ Surround left

➤ Surround right

➤ Low frequency effects (subwoofer)

Input/Output

In any 5.1 system, the speakers commonly referred to as rear speakers are more accurately called surround speakers. While the Dolby Pro Logic system recommends positioning the rear speakers behind the listener (for better dispersion of the mono surround effects), the Dolby Digital and DTS systems recommend positioning the surround speakers to the *sides* of the listener, to help the listener better position individual sounds on the soundtrack.

The "5.1" designation comes from the five "normal" channels plus the one effects channel. Each of the five front and rear channels is full bandwidth, reproducing a 3–20,000 Hz frequency range. The low frequency effects channel sends a 3–120 Hz frequency range to your subwoofer.

The following figure details a typical Dolby Digital installation.

Dolby Digital sends separate signals to all five speakers, plus the subwoofer.

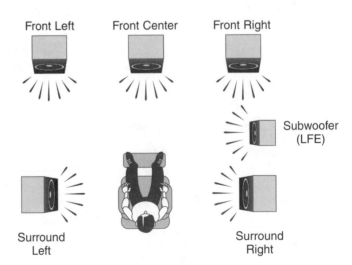

One of the noticeable differences between Dolby Digital and Dolby Pro Logic is that Dolby Digital has two discrete surround channels, whereas Dolby Pro Logic only has a single surround channel—even though it's typically sent to multiple rear speakers. Although you might have a rear-left and rear-right speaker in a Dolby Pro Logic system, both speakers reproduce the exact same material; in a Dolby Digital system, the surround left and surround right speakers reproduce separate and distinct information. This enables movies encoded in Dolby Digital to more precisely position sounds to the sides and rear of the listener.

To play back movies encoded in Dolby Digital, you need a component that includes a Dolby Digital decoder. That component is probably an audio/video receiver, but some televisions and DVD players include built-in Dolby Digital decoders.

Input/Output

The single low-frequency effects channel can actually be sent to more than one subwoofer. Since the sound from a subwoofer is nondirectional, you can add any number of subwoofers to increase the low-end punch, and position them anywhere in your room.

Input/Output

If you've ever listened to a movie on a good Dolby Pro Logic system, you'll swear that you heard sounds move back and forth between the two rear speakers—even though both speakers were receiving the exact same signal. This is a bit of audio slight-of-hand caused by sounds from the front speakers *perceptively* positioning corresponding sounds from the rear speakers. As an example, a sound moving from the front-left speaker to the single rear channel will appear to move to the rear-right speaker (not the left), since that's the direction from which the sound initially appeared. In spite of this perceptive positioning, you need to move to Dolby Digital in order to experience true positioning on a left and right-rear soundstage.

One More Channel in the Rear: Dolby Digital EX

The latest, greatest surround-sound system takes the 5.1-channel Dolby Digital and adds a sixth main speaker for 6.1-channel sound. This extra speaker—dubbed "surround rear"—is positioned between and behind the surround left and surround right speakers, or directly behind the listener. This fills in the gap of the normal Dolby Digital 5.1 system, and surrounds the listener in a full 360-degree listening envelope.

The extra surround channel in Dobly Digital EX isn't a discrete channel like the other 5.1 channels; it uses matrixing technology to extract a signal from the surround left and surround right channels. By using a matrixed channel, the a/v industry doesn't need to retrofit all those 5.1-channel jack panels; all you need is a new receiver with Dolby Digital EX decoding and an extra speaker, and you're in business!

Of course, not all movies utilize that extra rear speaker. When you're listening to a 5.1-channel movie on your 6.1-channel system, you'll hear a blend of the left and right surround channels through the rear surround speaker. (Don't expect to find DVDs labeled as Dolby Digital EX, either; the few EX-encoded DVDs released to-date have been unlabeled!)

The following figure details a typical Dolby Digital EX installation.

Power Up

If you have a receiver with a Dolby Digital decoder, you can also enjoy movies recorded in Dolby Pro Logic, since every Dolby Digital decoder chip also includes Dolby Pro Logic decoding.

Note the additional speaker positioned behind the listener in this typical Dolby Digital EX installation.

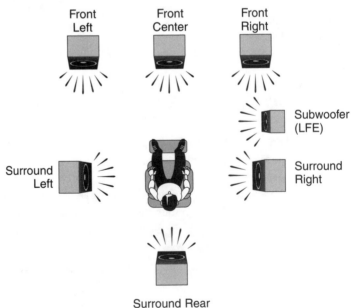

The Lower-Priced Alternative: Dolby Pro Logic

Where Dolby Digital reproduces six discrete channels (plus one matrixed channel, in the case of EX), the older Dolby Pro Logic system offers just four channels—with those four channels matrixed together for storage on two left and right channels. Dolby Pro Logic is used to reproduce surround sound on standard television and cable broadcasts, most digital satellite programming, some older DVDs and laserdiscs, and VHS HiFi videotapes.

Let's look first at the four channels of audio information available with Dolby Pro Logic. Unlike the Dolby Digital system, there is only a single surround channel (even though it's commonly fed to two speakers) and no low frequency effects or subwoofer channel. The four channels of Dolby Pro Logic are as follows:

➤ Front left

➤ Front center

➤ Front right

➤ Surround (mono)

Input/Output

Technically, the *process* of encoding four channels of information into two tracks is called Dolby Surround, and the *technology* used to decode this material is called Dolby Pro Logic. To reduce confusion, I'm calling both the encoding and decoding processes Dolby Pro Logic; to those sticklers in the audience, I apologize for my very slight technical inaccuracy for the sake of clarity.

The following figure details a typical Dolby Pro Logic setup.

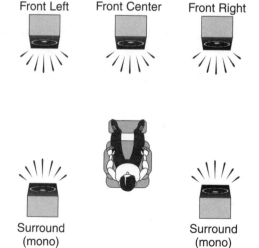

Front Left   Front Center   Front Right

Surround
(mono)   Surround
(mono)

Dolby Pro Logic includes three front channels and a single rear channel, which is typically split between two speakers.

Even though the Dolby Pro Logic system only includes four channels, it was designed to utilize five speakers; the single surround channel is typically sent to two different rear speakers. This mono channel generally includes ambience and special effects, and is nondirectional from a left-and-right perspective. (Interestingly, my initial Dolby Pro Logic home theater actually included three rear speakers, for a better dispersion of the mono surround effects.)

Dolby Pro Logic is a popular system because it encodes these four channels of information onto the standard two channels present in most stereo programming. By mixing four channels into two, Dolby Pro Logic signals can be easily carried along with any videotape, satellite, or television broadcast. Then, during playback in your home theater, your receiver's Dolby Pro Logic decoder converts the encoded signal back to its original four channels, and applies adaptive matrix steering logic. This process increases channel separation by boosting the level of the dominant channel at each instant, so the sounds go where they're supposed to.

To play back Dolby Pro Logic programming, you need a component equipped with either a Dolby Pro Logic or Dolby Digital decoder. If you play back Dolby Pro Logic programming through a two-channel receiver or television, you'll only hear the front-left and front-right channels.

Input/Output

Just because Dolby Pro Logic doesn't include a separate channel for a subwoofer doesn't mean that you can't use a subwoofer in a Dolby Pro Logic system. You can still connect a subwoofer to your receiver's subwoofer output—even though there's no separate channel to feed it, the subwoofer will receive all low-frequency bass from all sources connected to your receiver.

Not so Popular: DTS

DTS—which stands for Digital Theater Sound—is a 5.1-channel surround-sound alternative to Dolby Digital. While the professional DTS system is in wide use in movie theaters, the home version has seen less success. Put simply, there is little DTS-encoded programming available today, and few components that include a DTS decoder.

DTS works just like Dolby Digital, reproducing six discrete audio channels:

➤ Front left

➤ Front center

➤ Front right

➤ Surround left

➤ Surround right

➤ Low frequency effects (subwoofer)

DTS differs from Dolby Digital in that it uses less compression to store its signals—a 3:1 compression scheme as opposed to Dolby Digital's 12:1 compression. This should result in better sound, although there are few complaints about the more highly compressed Dolby Digital format.

To play back DTS programming, you need a component that includes a DTS decoder. Few a/v receivers today include DTS circuitry, and those that do are primarily higher-end models. It is unlikely that DTS will overtake Dolby Digital as the preferred 5.1-channel system for home theaters.

For the Discriminating—and the Rich: THX

Technically, THX is not a surround format. Instead, THX is a set of minimum standards and methods that ensure accurate home reproduction of a theatrical release's soundtrack. Since all soundtracks today incorporate surround sound, THX is typically discussed along with Dolby Digital and other surround-sound formats.

Developed by the discerning folks at Lucasfilm, the home THX standards have a firm foundation in the production processes associated with all feature film material. You may be aware that some movie theaters also carry the THX designation; these theaters incorporate the minimum equipment and design necessary to meet Lucasfilm's professional THX standards.

When examining home reproduction of movie soundtracks, Lucasfilm identified two major areas it felt needed improvement:

Input/Output

Just as Dolby Digital 5.1 has a 6.1-channel counterpart in Dolby Digital EX, DTS has a 6.1-channel version called DTS ES. It works pretty much the same as Dolby Digital EX, with the extra rear surround channel using information matrixed from the surround left and surround right channels. This extra channel is positioned directly behind the listener.

➤ A need to correct the audible tonal and spatial errors caused when soundtracks designed for playback in large auditoriums are played in smaller home listening environments

➤ A need to more accurately reproduce the complex sound fields present in multi-channel soundtracks

To address these needs, Lucasfilm created a series of specifications for speakers, amplifiers, and surround-sound decoders; equipment meeting its specs is officially THX-certified.

There are actually two different home THX standards, THX Select and the higher-end THX Ultra. THX Select is more appropriate to the home theater environment, as it uses a 2,000-cubic-foot room as its target environment. The THX Ultra specification is for larger rooms (3,000+ cubic feet) and more professional installations.

Both THX Select and THX Ultra provide minimum-performance specifications for a number of different types of equipment, including

➤ Speakers.

➤ Acoustically transparent video screens.

➤ Equalizers.

➤ Interconnect cables.

➤ Laserdisc players.

➤ DVD players.

➤ Receivers.

➤ Amplifiers.

➤ Preamplifiers.

Input/Output

Some laserdiscs were produced under the THX Laserdisc Program. This process ensured the highest-quality reproduction of the disc's soundtrack. THX laserdiscs can be played on any system—including both THX and non-THX systems—just as THX systems will play back any prerecorded material, including but not limited to those THX-certified laserdiscs.

Receivers and preamplifiers are sometimes referred to as Home THX Controllers, as they include the surround-sound circuitry (and are associated THX-specified electronic enhancements, such as Reequalization, Timbre Matching, and Decorrelation) to successfully reproduce a multichannel film soundtrack.

Why should you invest in THX-certified equipment, which happens to be on the high end of the home theater price range? For one, THX systems tend to reproduce a more "natural" sound, without the unnatural brightness sometimes associated with home theater systems. In addition, THX systems reproduce more intelligible dialogue, and don't overwhelm the listener with artificially prominent rear-channel effects. THX tends to improve sound localization and create a more uniform sound envelope.

In short, the price you pay for THX components gives you a slightly better-sounding system.

Choosing a Surround-Sound Format

Of the available surround-sound technologies—Dolby Digital, Dolby Digital EX, Dolby Pro Logic, DTS, DTS EX, and THX—which should you choose for your home theater system?

Here's some advice:

➤ If you're on a strict budget, go with Dolby Pro Logic. The surround effects are satisfactory, and the cost of an a/v receiver with a Dolby Pro Logic decoder won't bust the bank.

➤ For most systems, go with Dolby Digital. Dolby Digital is the de facto standard for home surround sound, most DVDs are coming with Dolby Digital encoding, and all future HDTV broadcasts will be in Dolby Digital—what more convincing do you need? How about the fact that Dolby Digital has demonstrably better rear-channel positioning, and just plain sounds more dynamic than Dolby Pro Logic? A/v receivers with Dolby Digital decoders can be had for as little as $300 if you look hard, which puts the better technology in a quite affordable price range.

➤ If you're already on the high end and have a few more bucks, look for a receiver with Dolby Digital EX and invest in an additional surround rear speaker. While there aren't a lot of movies (yet) that utilize that extra channel, if you want the ultimate home theater experience, you'll want to include all the channels you can!

➤ If you're building an ultra-high end system— and money is no object—go with THX-certified components. They're expensive, sure, but you're virtually guaranteed the best possible home theater experience.

One last piece of advice: Don't worry about DTS or DTS ES. There just isn't that much DTS-encoded programming, and what does exist is typically dual-encoded with both DTS and Dolby Digital soundtracks. Besides, if you purchase a higher-end a/v receiver, it should come with both Dolby Digital and DTS decoders, just in case.

Input/Output

Some lower-end a/v receivers are billed as "5.1-ready." These receivers don't include a Dolby Digital decoder, but do include a set of 5.1 inputs on the back panel. You can connect these inputs to the 5.1 outputs from a separate Dolby Digital decoder (such as those found in many mid-range DVD players) and run the surround sound through the receiver.

The Least You Need to Know

➤ Surround-sound systems put you in the middle of the movie experience by adding a center speaker and two rear speakers to the traditional left and right stereo speakers.

➤ All surround-sound systems encode surround-sound information on the film's soundtrack; you have to use a surround-sound decoder (found in most a/v receivers) to decode these channels.

➤ The most popular surround-sound format today is Dolby Digital, which features 5.1 discrete audio channels.

➤ A newer version of Dolby Digital—dubbed Dolby Digital EX—adds a surround rear channel for 6.1-channel sound.

➤ If you can't afford Dolby Digital, the older Dolby Pro Logic system delivers acceptable sound, using a single surround channel.

Chapter 15

More Power, More Inputs: Amplifiers and Receivers

In This Chapter

➤ Which components you need to process and amplify signals from your audio and video sources

➤ Why most home theater owners choose audio/video receivers over separate components

➤ Key specs and features for a/v receivers

➤ How much power you'll really need

➤ Shopping for the best a/v receiver

When you press the Play button on your video source (DVD player, VCR, or whatever) several things have to happen before the picture appears on your video display and the sound emanates from your surround-sound speakers.

First, the audio/video signals from your input device have to be routed to your output devices. Next, the soundtrack has to run through a digital signal processor (DSP) to decode all the surround-sound information. Finally, the audio signals need to be amplified.

Sounds like a lot of work, doesn't it?

To perform all these tasks you can employ a number of separate audio components, or you can use a single component that integrates all these functions, and then some. That single component is called an audio/video receiver, and it is both the control center and power center of your home theater system.

Making Music: Essential Audio Components

The necessary audio/video control and power functions can be performed by a single component, or by separate components. We'll look at the separate components first, since an a/v receiver is really a combination of these separate component functions.

More Inputs: Understanding Preamplifiers

A preamplifier is that component (or component part of your receiver) that controls the inputs of your home theater system. When you select a specific component as your current video or audio source, it's the preamplifier that's doing the switching.

In addition, a preamplifier brings the low-level output signals from your video and audio sources up to the line level your amplifier needs to operate. Preamplifiers do not amplify signals high enough to send directly to speakers, of course; that's what an amplifier does.

More Channels: Understanding Surround-Sound Processors

Some preamplifiers also include a surround-sound decoder, although the decoder (also known as a digital signal processor) is technically a separate component. This processor decodes the surround-sound signals sent from your source component and separates them into different channels, which are then sent to separate amplifiers (one amplifier per channel).

Surround-sound processors come in several different flavors. Lower-end units are compatible with the Dolby Pro Logic system, while higher-end units can decode both Dolby Pro Logic and the newer Dolby Digital 5.1 system. Some units can also decode the less-popular DTS system. (To learn more about the different surround-sound formats, see Chapter 14, "Sound Is All Around: Understanding Surround Sound.")

Some digital signal processors also create simulated surround-sound effects from normal two-channel stereo material. These computer-generated sound fields are used to reproduce the sound of music in various concert halls and theaters.

More Power: Understanding Power Amplifiers

Once the low-voltage audio signal from your source component has been selected, processed, and preamplified, it needs to be amplified to a level that can be sent to your system's speakers. That job is done by a power amplifier.

An amplifier is the brute force component in your system. The more power an amplifier generates, the louder the potential sound your speakers can reproduce.

You need a separate amplifier for each output channel in your system. If you have a simple stereo system, you can use a two-channel amplifier. If you have a 5.1

surround-sound system, you need a five-channel amplifier; if you have a Dolby Digital EX 6.1 system, you'll need a six-channel amplifier. (Your subwoofer contains its own amplifier—all it needs is a line-level output signal, without any additional amplification.)

Amplifier power requirements are highly dependent on room size and speaker sensitivity. A smaller room requires less power than it takes to fill a larger room; smaller speakers are generally more efficient than larger speakers, and require less power to reach their peak output.

Know that small increases in power don't correlate to noticeable differences in loudness. To double the volume level in your system (measured in terms of sound pressure levels) requires *10 times* the power—so the difference between an 80-watt amplifier and a 100-watt amplifier is negligible.

As you shop for receivers, keep in mind that even if you don't listen loud, you may still want a more powerful amplifier. In fact, the biggest benefit of higher power isn't volume, it's increased dynamics and improved sound quality—more powerful amplifiers generally deliver cleaner sound at lower volume levels.

Everything in One Box: Audio/Video Receivers

While you could purchase a separate preamplifier, digital signal processor, and amplifier (and throw an AM/FM tuner in for good measure), most home theater owners prefer to go with a single component that combines all these functions. This component is called a receiver—and if the receiver also switches video sources, it's called an audio/video receiver (or a/v receiver, for short).

Most users prefer an a/v receiver to separate components for many reasons—the relative ease of connecting one component, the lower cost of a single component, and the integrated control of all functions via a single front panel or remote control. While it's true that separate components can deliver superior performance (at least at the very high end), most of today's quality receivers perform at more-than-acceptable levels.

Here's what you'll find in a typical audio/video receiver:

➤ Inputs for multiple video sources

➤ Inputs for multiple audio sources

➤ Preamplifier functions

➤ Surround-sound processor with some simulated concert hall effects

➤ Multiple-channel amplifier

➤ AM/FM tuner

➤ Outputs for multiple speakers, a subwoofer, and headphones

➤ Outputs for one or more video displays

➤ Remote control

Specs and Features: Why One Receiver Is Better Than Another

Audio/video receivers range in price from less than $200 to more than $3,000. As you might expect, performance and functionality can differ wildly from one receiver to another. Here are the factors that make one receiver better (or higher priced) than another.

Product Specs

Some manufacturers make **integrated amplifiers,** which are essentially receivers without an AM/FM tuner. An integrated amplifier typically includes preamplifier, digital signal processor, and amplifier functions, and should be evaluated similarly to a/v receivers.

Power Up

In general, the louder you like to listen, the larger your room is, and the less efficient your speakers are, the more power you need. For home theater in an average-sized room, 60–80 watts is probably enough. However, if you really like to pump up the volume, go for 100 or more watts per channel.

Pay for Performance

First off, you want to evaluate how an a/v receiver actually performs. While the best judge of performance is the set of listening devices attached on either side of your cranium (your ears!), there are some measurable specifications you can evaluate when comparing one or more a/v receivers.

Here are some of the specs to look for:

➤ **Power.** Output power for a receiver is measured for each channel, in watts. A typical spec might read "100 watts per channel × 5," indicating that this unit delivers five channels of 100 watts each. Make sure that you're looking at *continuous*, or RMS, power. (Don't bother with so-called "peak power" ratings—you listen to music continuously, not in short peaks!) Stereo receivers will measure power for two channels; Dolby Pro Logic receivers will typically display separate power ratings for front and rear channels, with the rear channel amps delivering less power than the front (this is normal—Dolby Pro Logic doesn't require a lot of oomph for the surround channel), and Dolby Digital receivers should list equal power ratings for five channels (the 5.1 system requires similar performance for all five channels). As you might expect, more power is better.

➤ **Bandwidth.** This measures the range of frequencies a component can reproduce. Most receivers reproduce a full 20–20,000 Hz range, which is generally considered to be the entire frequency range of human hearing; be wary of any units that start higher than 20 Hz or top off lower than 20,000 Hz.

➤ **Total harmonic distortion (THD).** This measures an amplifier's accuracy, and refers to the amount of internally generated noise. The lower the THD, the better.

➤ **FM sensitivity.** If you're concerned about receiving FM broadcasts through the receiver's AM/FM tuner, look at this rating, which measures the ability to pick up FM signals—a lower number is better.

Behind the specs is a wealth of technology. In fact, when you get into the high end of a manufacturer's models, you'll see a wide variety of proprietary and cool-sounding technology. Some of these fancy technologies are just so much marketing hype, but others actually do help to create "cleaner" sound—which is difficult to measure, but relatively easy to hear. Just make sure you give whatever receivers you're looking at a thorough listening test!

Dollars for Dolby

An audio/video receiver can offer some combination of three different surround formats (plus plain old stereo). The surround decoder operates via a digital signal processing chip, and different chips have different levels of performance—and often offer other sound enhancements, in the form of simulated listening environments. (In fact, more expensive receivers typically offer a dozen or more different DSP modes—from different concert halls to specific Hollywood soundstages.)

Power Up

Whether you're looking at separate power amplifiers or full-featured a/v receivers, there is one simple test that almost always tells you which unit puts out more, cleaner power. All you have to do is pick up the unit—the heavier unit typically is the better one! High-end amps and receivers typically have anti-resonant features that create an ultra-solid chassis and cabinet, as well as extra-large power supplies, capacitors, and heat sinks—all of which add weight to the unit. So, while it's not an absolute, in general more weight means better sound!

The four different surround processors available in today's a/v receivers include:

➤ **Dolby Digital.** This is a true 5.1-channel surround format, requiring five amplifiers (for front left, front center, front right, surround left, and surround right) plus a separate nonamplified feed for a subwoofer. All Dolby Digital processors will also decode Dolby Pro Logic soundtracks.

➤ **Dolby Digital EX.** This is a 6.1-channel version of the basic Dolby Digital system; the extra channel is a surround rear positioned between and behind the surround left and surround right channels. All Dolby Digital 6.1 processors will also decode Dolby Digital 5.1 and Dolby Pro Logic soundtracks.

➤ **Dolby Pro Logic.** This older surround format is still used in television broadcasts and prerecorded videocassettes, and is often the sole surround technology used in lower-end a/v receivers. This is actually a four-channel format (front left, front center, front right, and mono surround) that requires five amplifiers (the mono surround signal is fed to rear-left and rear-right speakers).

Power Up

Some users get into the bad habit of leaving their surround-sound processor activated all the time, even when they're playing nonsurround material. Any audiophile will tell you that stereo recordings are meant to be listened to in stereo, *not* in fake surround. Select the proper listening environment for the material—and *don't* try to create an all-surround environment where it doesn't exist!

➤ **DTS.** This 5.1-channel format competes with Dolby Digital, and requires the same five amplifiers plus subwoofer output. (There is also a newer DTS ES format, which—like Dolby Digital EX—has 6.1 channels.) Most high-end a/v receivers include both Dolby Digital and DTS decoding.

Cash for Connections

If you have a lot of source components—broadcast/cable, digital satellite, DVD, VCR, CD, hard disk recorder, WebTV, audio cassette, MiniDisc, and an old turntable from your college days—then you need a lot of inputs on your receiver. Count up the number of separate audio and audio/video inputs, and check the *types* of inputs to make sure you're maximizing the picture and sound quality from your newer components.

While not all receivers will have all the different types of inputs and outputs, you should look for the types of inputs and outputs detailed in the following table.

Audio/Video Receiver Inputs and Outputs

Type	Input/Output	Use
5.1	Input	From devices (such as some DVD players) with built-in Dolby Digital decoders; uses the other component's decoded signal as opposed to the receiver's built-in decoder
Audio (L/R)	Input	From audio and audio/video sources, including CD players, VCRs, and the like
Audio (L/R)	Output	To audio and audio/video recording devices
Coaxial digital	Input	Audio from DVD players and other digital sources

Type	Input/Output	Use
Coaxial digital	Output	Audio to MiniDisc, CD recorders, and other digital recording devices
Component video (Y, Pr, Pb)	Output	To higher-end televisions and other video displays; the highest-quality video output
Component video (Y, Pr, Pb)	Input	From DVD players and other high-quality video sources; the highest-quality video input
Composite video	Output	To VCRs, televisions, and other video displays
Composite video	Input	From VCRs and other video sources that don't have higher-quality S-Video outputs
Optical digital	Input	Audio from DVD players and other digital sources; also called Toslink inputs
Optical digital	Output	Audio to MiniDisc, CD recorders, and other digital recording devices
Phono	Input	Audio from a turntable (which outputs lower-voltage signals than other sources)
Preamp	Output	Low-voltage, unamplified audio to a power amplifier
RF	Input	Combined audio/video input from broadcast antennas, cable boxes, and other video sources without higher-quality component video or S-Video connections
RF	Output	Combined audio/video output to VCRs, televisions, and other video displays
Speaker	Output	Amplified audio to your front and rear speakers
Subwoofer	Output	Audio to your subwoofer; this is a non-amplified output, since subwoofers contain their own built-in amplifiers
S-Video	Input	Video from DVD players, VCRs, and other video sources; higher quality than component video
S-Video	Output	Video to televisions and other video displays; higher quality than component video

continues

Audio/Video Receiver Inputs and Outputs   (continued)

Type	Input/Output	Use
Tape monitor	Input/Output	Set of audio inputs and outputs that enables you to "loop" unamplified signals to and from an audio recorder; can also be used for connecting an equalizer, surround-sound decoder, or other external signal processing device

In addition, look for at least one set of front panel inputs, to facilitate the constant connecting and disconnecting of more temporary components, such as camcorders and video games.

Coins for Control

You'll use your a/v receiver's remote to control most of the operations of your home theater system. In fact, the better your receiver's remote, the more it can control.

There are three general types of remotes available with a/v receivers:

Power Up

If your receiver doesn't have a dedicated subwoofer output, you can still hook up a subwoofer to your system. Just connect it in-line between your receiver and your main stereo speakers; run one set of speaker wires from the receiver's speaker outputs to the subwoofer, and then run another set of speaker wires from the subwoofer to your main stereo speakers.

➤ Single manufacturer remotes that operate the a/v receiver and other components from the same manufacturer.

➤ Multibrand remotes, which come preprogrammed to operate components from other manufacturers.

➤ Programmable remotes (also called learning remotes), which you can manually program to operate other components. Some programmable remotes can also be programmed with multistep functions (also called macros), such as turning on a component and switching the receiver to that source, all with the push of a single button.

In addition, some a/v receivers display system status and other operations on your TV screen—even when you're performing nonvideo operations. As an alternative to on-screen displays, some remotes come with their own LCD screens to display system status and provide visual feedback. (To learn more about remote control options for your home theater system, turn to Chapter 22, "Take Charge: Controlling Your System.")

Shop Smart: What to Look For

When you're ready to purchase a new audio/video receiver (or separate components), set your budget and then consider the following:

➤ **Power.** In general, you're better off getting as much power as you can afford, within limits. Don't sweat 10–20 watt per channel differences between models, as the difference won't likely be noticeable. However, do look beyond simple power ratings, to compare total harmonic distortion levels—which typically have more effect on the actual sound than do power ratings.

➤ **Surround format.** Unless you're really on a budget, go for a unit with Dolby Digital 5.1 or Dolby Digital EX 6.1 decoding. (Any Dolby Digital processor will also decode Dolby Pro Logic programs.) Don't worry about DTS (it isn't that widely used), and don't get too enthralled with all the different DSP-simulated environments—most are gimmicky, some are plain unlistenable, and if you use the DSP settings at all, you'll probably find yourself settling on a single soundstage for all your listening.

➤ **Adjustability.** Look for all the different ways you can adjust the sound on your receiver. Look beyond simple bass and treble controls to multiband equalization, surround-sound delay, and other key adjustments—many of which are apt to be found on the remote control only, using on-screen displays.

➤ **Inputs and outputs.** This is key. Make sure there are enough—and the right kinds—of input and output jacks to connect all your different components. Also look for at least one front-panel audio/video connection, for camcorder and video game use.

Overload!

If you want to connect an equalizer to your system, you'll have to connect it through the tape monitor loop. However, you shouldn't use your equalizer if you're playing back Dolby Pro Logic programming, since equalizing a matrixed signal will throw off the frequency balance and your decoder's channel steering.

➤ **Remote control.** Once the receiver is installed, it just sits there. The thing you interface most with is the remote control. Make sure you like the way it feels in your hand, and understand the way it works. If you want to use a single remote to control multiple components, ask ahead of time if this unit has preprogrammed codes for your specific components—or if it can easily "learn" the codes from your other remotes.

➤ **Usability.** This is hard to measure, but it's quite important—how comfortable are you using this receiver? Are there *too many* controls and adjustments for you? Is the sequence for turning on and switching to a component fast and logical? Put simply, how does this receiver *feel* to you?

➤ **Sound.** Before you buy, listen. Does this model sound noticeably different or better than comparable models? Is the sound loud enough, clean enough, and smooth enough? Make sure you bring your own source material when comparing units—and compare different types of sources. If you're primarily a music lover, bring your favorite CDs and listen to the receiver in two-channel mode; if you like action films, bring a blockbuster DVD and turn up the volume.

Remember, try before you buy. It's difficult to buy something this important without giving it a test drive. Specs on paper are one thing, but actually listening to and using a receiver are necessary to determine if it's a good fit in your system.

The Least You Need to Know

➤ Every home theater system needs a preamplifier, digital signal processor, and amplifier, which can all be combined into a single audio/video receiver.

➤ You should look for a receiver that delivers at least 60 watts per channel— although 100 watts per channel is recommended for larger rooms or when playing more dynamic material.

➤ Unless you're on a strict budget, look for a receiver with a built-in Dolby Digital 5.1 or Dolby Digital EX 6.1 decoder—which will also process Dolby Pro Logic signals.

➤ Make sure your receiver has enough inputs and outputs for all your different components—and that the *types* of connections enable you to get the maximum performance from your components.

➤ If you want your receiver's remote to control other components in your system, make sure it's preprogrammed with those components operating codes, or that it can "learn" the codes from your other remote controls.

Chapter 16

Woofers and Tweeters and Horns, Oh My: Speaker Systems

In This Chapter

➤ How speakers work—and the different types of speakers available

➤ Determining what speakers you need

➤ Why reusing your existing speakers for home theater is problematic

➤ Why "rear" speakers should really be called "side" speakers

➤ What to look for when you're evaluating new speakers

You can have the best surround-sound processor in the world and run through the cleanest and most powerful amplifier, but your system will sound horrible if you use the wrong or poor-quality speakers. Choosing the right speakers is essential to creating the best possible home theater experience; if you have any spare money in your home theater budget, there's no better place to spend the bucks than in upgrading your system's speakers!

Sound in a Box: A Speaker Primer

While all of the components in your home theater system work together to deliver a signal to your speakers, it's your speakers that actually deliver the sound to your ears. If your speakers sound bad, the efforts of all your other components are wasted.

As you can see—and hear!—speakers are among the most important components of your home theater system. To help you choose the right speakers for your system, let's do a little homework and learn how speakers work.

Woofers and Tweeters: Understanding How Speakers Work

All speaker enclosures contain one or more *drivers*. Most speaker drivers consist of a voice coil connected to a diaphragm. The diaphragm, which might resemble a horn or a cone, moves in and out in accordance with the electrical impulses generated by the voice coil to produce sound.

Most speaker enclosures include at least two of these speaker drivers. The smaller driver is called a tweeter, and it's used to reproduce the highest frequencies—everything above 2,000 Hz or so. The larger driver is called a woofer, and it's used to reproduce the lower frequencies—everything below 2,000 Hz or so. Some enclosures have a third driver sized in between the tweeter and woofer, called a midrange driver, to better reproduce the frequencies where the tweeter and woofer meet.

As shown in the following figure, a speaker enclosure with two drivers is called a two-way speaker; one with a midrange driver is called a three-way. The circuitry used to split the signals between different drivers is called a crossover.

Product Specs

Very large speakers—like the ones you see at live concerts—may use horns instead of traditional tweeters. These **drivers**—which look just like large horns—deliver the type of very loud high-frequency sounds necessary to fill large concert halls and auditoriums.

A two-way speaker has a woofer and a tweeter; a three-way speaker adds a midrange driver.

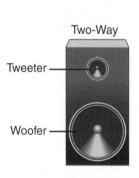

Two-Way

Tweeter

Woofer

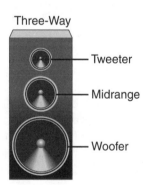

Three-Way

Tweeter

Midrange

Woofer

If all the drivers in a speaker are facing in the same direction, the speaker has a monopole design. If the drivers fire in different directions, the design is either bipole or dipole, discussed later in this chapter. You can use monopole speakers anywhere in your surround layout; bipoles and dipoles are suitable only for surround channels, as they produce a more diffused, non-directional sound.

Input/Output

When the drivers in your right and left speakers are moving in and out at the same time, your speakers are said to be "in phase"—which is what you want. When speakers are "out of phase"—when one speaker's driver is moving in while the other's is moving out—you'll hear significantly less bass and experience a weak center image in between your speakers.

To hook up your speakers in phase, make sure that the positive (+) and negative (–) leads on your speaker wire are connected the same way at the receiver and at the speaker. (Just pay attention to the markings on the wire itself, and connect the + to the + and the – to the –.) If you find that your speakers are out of phase, all you have to do is reverse the leads for one of your speakers (it doesn't matter which one) to bring the two speakers back into phase.

Bookshelf, Floor, and Wall: Understanding Speaker Enclosures

While all speakers contain some type and combination of woofer and tweeter, there are several different types of speaker enclosure. Which type of enclosure you choose depends on your room, the space you have, and your personal tastes.

The four primary types of speaker enclosures include

➤ **Floor-standing speakers.** These are speakers that are big enough to stand on the floor (either on their own, or with the help of speaker stands). Floor-standing speakers typically are larger than other types of speakers, reproduce a wider range of frequencies (including deep bass), and are quite efficient, producing more volume per watt. The downside of floor-standing speakers is that they take up valuable floor space, which may or may not be convenient for you.

Input/Output

Floor-standing speakers that include built-in powered subwoofers are called powered towers.

➤ **Bookshelf speakers.** If you're working with limited space (including space within an audio/video cabinet), bookshelf speakers can be a more attractive alternative to floor-standing models. With bookshelf speakers, you get smaller speakers that take up less space (and can be mounted on stands or on shelves), good performance, and (in most instances) a smaller price tag. Some bookshelf speakers don't have a lot of oomph on the low end, and benefit from being paired with a powered subwoofer.

➤ **In-wall speakers.** While built-in speakers have been used for decades in commercial applications, in recent years the performance of these smaller speakers has improved to the point where they're acceptable options for home theater use. With in-wall speakers you don't lose any floor space—the speakers mount flush to the wall or ceiling—and in many cases the grilles can be painted to match your room. The downside is that in-wall installation is more involved than setting up traditional speakers. As with bookshelf speakers, you probably want to augment total system performance by adding a subwoofer.

➤ **Subwoofer/satellite systems.** The latest rage, exemplified by systems from the Bose Corporation, is the combination of very small satellite speakers with a subwoofer. Thanks to advances in speaker design, these satellites—which can fit in the palm of your hand—produce surprisingly good performance. Satellite speakers are small enough that they can be mounted or placed just about anywhere; the larger subwoofer makes up for any lack of bass in the satellites themselves.

Power Up

For the best sound, you want the tweeters in your speakers to be placed at about ear level. If you have smaller floor-standing speakers, bookshelves, or satellites, you may need to place your speakers on stands to get them to the proper height.

Louder and More Efficient: Understanding Speaker Designs

The "color" (tonal characteristics) of a speaker is affected not only by its drivers and enclosure, but also by the general design of the speaker. Here are some of the more common speaker designs you can choose from:

➤ **Acoustic suspension.** This design completely seals the speaker enclosure to provide accurate, tight bass response. Acoustic-suspension speakers give up some degree of efficiency to provide this better bass, so they may require more amplifier power to play at the same volume level as comparable bass-reflex speakers.

➤ **Bass reflex.** This design uses a "tuned" opening in the enclosure—usually a round hole, sometimes called a port—to release some of the energy created by the movement of the woofer cone, which creates a louder bass response. Bass-reflex designs are more power efficient than acoustic-suspension designs—which means they sound louder, given the same amplifier power. However, the bass frequencies may sound a little less precise, or muddy. Still, if you have a low-powered amp or receiver, bass-reflex speakers may be a good choice for your system.

Power Up

Most manufacturers provide a recommended power rating for their speakers. However, just because you have a 100-watt-per-channel amplifier or receiver doesn't mean you need a speaker rated for 100 watts. Unless you run your speakers at abusive volume levels, a lower-rated speaker can be matched with a higher-power amplifier, no sweat. In fact, an amp or receiver with a high power rating is often safer for speakers than one with a lower power rating, since the lower-powered model may "clip" and produce distortion at high volume levels—which can cause damage to your tweeters.

➤ **Bipole.** Unlike a front-firing monopole (or direct-radiating) speaker, a bipole speaker generates equal amounts of sound both forward and backward. Bipoles reproduce the front and rear sounds in-phase, and are often used as rear or surround speakers.

➤ **Dipole.** This design is similar to a bipole speaker, in that sound is generated both forward and backward. With dipole speakers, however, the two sounds are reproduced out of phase. As with bipoles, dipole speakers are often used as surround speakers.

What Goes Where: Planning Your Home Theater Speaker Layout

A well-designed home theater system should consist of the six different speakers:

➤ Front-left and front-right speakers

➤ A single center-channel speaker

➤ Left and right surround speakers

➤ A powered subwoofer

All of these speakers work together to give dimensionality to movie soundtracks and put you in the middle of the action—as well as to reproduce any music you listen to from your system's audio sources.

The front speakers, of course, should be in front of you, in a plane aligned with your television screen. As shown in the following figure, the center speaker should be positioned at the same level as the left and right speakers, ideally just above or below the screen (so as to best "anchor" dialog with the picture).

As shown in the following figure, surround speakers should probably be mounted to the *side* of your listening position—*not* the rear. This is especially true if your system incorporates a Dolby Digital decoder; the 5.1 sound distinctly positions the surround-sound channels to the side of the listener. (Think about the last time you went to a movie theater—and remember all those speakers along the *sides* of the theater!)

Position your center speaker midway between your left and right speakers—and adjacent to your television screen.

On the other hand, your subwoofer can go anywhere—the sound it generates isn't directional. (Which means it's more felt than heard.) Some users put their subwoofers in a corner, or under a sofa, or behind a grille in an audio/video cabinet. You could even use your subwoofer as a coffee table, if you don't mind the speaker wire snaking across the middle of the room! (Note that positioning a subwoofer next to a wall causes additional sound radiation, which some listeners like; it produces a slightly more "boomy" sound.)

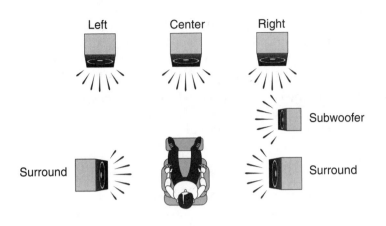

Surround speakers are best mounted to the side, not the rear.

Input/Output

Many speaker manufacturers, recognizing the huge demand for home theater, are now selling multiple speakers together in special "home theater" packages. These packages range from low-priced (and relatively low-performance) budget systems to some really great-sounding high-end systems. In addition, this is where you'll find the satellite/subwoofer systems pioneered by Bose and Polk Audio. You can also get prepackaged speakers in a variety of "home theater in a box" products, discussed in Chapter 20, "Quick and Easy Systems: Home Theater in a Box."

Left, Center, and Right: Selecting Front Speakers

The speakers you select for the front channels of your home theater system have to do double duty. Not only do they have to accurately reproduce dialog and sound effects from your favorite movies, they also have to reproduce the stereo music you listen to from your CDs and audio tapes. In fact, when you're evaluating front speakers, make sure you test them with both a movie and a CD!

Ideally, all three front speakers should be the same model from the same manufacturer. This is because dialog and action frequently move across the front soundstage, and any variation in speaker "color" will make the dialog and other sounds sound off as they move from one side to another.

If you already have left and right speakers and want to add a single center speaker, then try to find a center speaker that matches the general sound of your existing speakers. This is called voice matching; voices reproduced from the center speaker need to sound very similar to voices reproduced from the left and right speakers.

Whatever you do, don't skimp on the center speaker. When you're watching a movie, the center channel reproduces more than half of the total soundtrack information. A weak speaker in this position will definitely be noticed!

Power Up

Some so-called experts—primarily television manufacturers, in my experience—suggest that consumers can save a little money by using their television's built-in speakers as the center-channel speaker in their surround-sound system. While you *can* do this, you probably don't want to. The center speaker is the most important speaker in your entire setup, since that's where most of the dialog emanates, and the speakers found in most televisions—even higher-end models—typically aren't up to the task. In addition, for a smooth transition of sound across the front soundstage, you need all three front speakers to be identical in their tonal characteristics—which ideally means using the same model speaker for the center channel as you use for the left and right channels. In other words, turn off your TV's built-in speaker and go with a separate front-channel speaker!

To the Rear: Selecting Surround Speakers

If you have an older or lower-priced Dolby Pro Logic system, your rear speakers weren't that important—because the surround channel didn't carry much information aside from a little reverberation and some general surround effects. (Remember, with Dolby Pro Logic, both rear speakers were driven from the same mono signal.) With Dolby Digital 5.1, however, the two discrete surround channels can carry very precise information—which makes your choice of surround speakers more important than ever.

There are two strategies to choosing surround speakers. The first strategy is to go with a surround-specific speaker, typically a smaller speaker than you use for your front channels. The second (and my recommended) strategy is to use the same speaker model for your surrounds as you do for your front channels.

If you choose a different surround speaker, you should look at both bipoles and dipoles. Dipole speakers work best if you're mounting your surrounds to the side of the listener; bipoles are better if you're mounting your surrounds behind the listening position, as you would with a Dolby Pro Logic system.

Since all five channels receive the same bandwidth under Dolby Digital, a better solution is to use the same speakers for your surrounds as you do for your fronts. If this isn't feasible (for space or other concerns), then try to choose speakers that come close to matching your front speakers, tonally.

Whichever surround speakers you choose, remember that you want to create a seamless three-dimensional soundstage, where objects can move from front to back and side to side without their tonal characteristics changing dramatically.

Let's Get Ready to Rumble: Selecting a Subwoofer

While most larger floor-standing speakers (and even some bookshelf models!) deliver good bass response, even better bass is reproduced by a speaker dedicated to that job. That speaker is called a subwoofer, and it is responsible for reproducing frequencies in the 20–200 Hz range. The sound produced by a subwoofer is nondirectional, meaning you can't tell where it's coming from—so the subwoofer, which can sometimes be a little imposing, physically, can be placed anywhere in your home theater room.

Overload!

In addition, the ".1" part of the Dolby Digital 5.1 or Dolby Digital 6.1 specifications refers to the low frequency effects signal designed expressly to be sent to a subwoofer. If you have a Dolby Digital system, you must have a subwoofer to get the full digital theater experience.

Unlike other speakers, subwoofers are "powered" speakers—meaning that each subwoofer contains its own built-in amplifier. Your a/v receiver uses a line-level connection to send the signal to the subwoofer, where it is powered up and reproduced. Because of this, your subwoofer must be plugged into a power outlet, so consider that constraint when you're decided where to place it in your room!

Some consumers get confused by the "A" and "B" speaker connections on some receivers, and think (erroneously) that the B connections are for surround sound. This is wrong! B connections simply feed the left and right front-channel information to a second set of speakers, typically for listening in another room. For true surround sound, you need a receiver with rear-channel outputs—not just two sets of front-channel outputs!

Power Up

If you want to use a subwoofer to improve your system's low-bass response but your non-Dolby Digital receiver doesn't have a subwoofer output, don't fret. Just make sure that your subwoofer is equipped with speaker-level inputs, then connect your receiver's regular speaker outputs directly to the subwoofer—and then out from the subwoofer to the regular speaker. Your subwoofer's built-in crossover will keep the low bass frequencies for its own use, and route the midrange and high frequencies on to your right and left speakers.

Do You Really Need New Speakers for Home Theater?

If you already have an audio system in your living room, can you use your existing speakers for your home theater system—and just buy a new center speaker and surrounds? Many consumers do just that—even though the results are less than ideal.

The driving force in selecting speakers for a home theater system is achieving a good tonal balance between channels. Especially with Dolby Digital 5.1, the same sounds are likely to travel between all five speakers—and if one or more of your speakers sound different from the others, that sound in the movie will change as it moves back and forth between speakers. This can be annoying at best—and totally distracting at worst. After all, you want your speakers to be transparent—you're listening to the soundtrack, *not* to your speakers!

If you insist on reusing your existing speakers, at least shop for new speakers that sound as close as possible to the speakers you already have. In the best of circumstances, just buy more of the same model, if that model is still available. Whatever you do, don't buy speakers that sound wildly different from your existing models—if you have two bass-reflex speakers, for example, don't fill in the gaps with new acoustic-reflex models.

Ideally, though, you should start from scratch and buy a completely new speaker system, with all five speakers (the subwoofer excepted, of course) matching.

Shop Smart: What to Look For

Whether you're buying one speaker or six, here are some things to look (and listen!) for:

➤ **Flat sound.** When a speaker's sound is described as "flat," that's a good thing, as it means that the speaker can accurately reproduce a signal without adding any colorations of its own. You really don't want a speaker that sounds warm or cool or bright or deep—you don't want a speaker that has *any* sound of its own! You want a totally neutral speaker, so the original audio source comes through as intended, with no alterations.

➤ **Frequency response.** Of course, you must have a speaker that can accurately reproduce all frequencies fed into it. The wider the frequency response, the better.

➤ **Efficiency.** A more efficient speaker can reproduce louder sounds from the same power input. If you have a high-power amplifier or receiver, you don't have to worry much about efficiency; if you have a lower-power amp or receiver—or you're trying to fill a huge room—then look for more efficient models.

➤ **Video shielding.** For those speakers near your television—definitely your center speaker, and perhaps your front-left and -right speakers—make sure you're looking at models that are shielded. This shielding is actually for the benefit of your television, which can be affected by the impulses from the speaker magnets. If you put an unshielded speaker too close to a CRT, the tube's colors can be distorted.

➤ **Music or movies?** This is a tough one. If you're like most of us, you'll use your home theater system for movies *and* for music. Know, however, that speakers that sound great for movies might not sound so great when you're listening to specific types of music—and musical-sounding speakers might not deliver the *oomph* you like from movie soundtracks. The speakers you choose—especially the front-left and -right speakers—may end up being a compromise between what sounds good for music and what sounds good for movies. That's one reason I recommend performing listening tests with both audio and video source material—so you'll know how all types of programming sound.

By the way, when you're considering a new speaker system, realize that the room has a huge impact on any speaker's sound. How a speaker sounds in the dealer's showroom might be dramatically different from how it sounds in your living room. Ideally, you'll get the opportunity to test the speakers at home before you sign on the dotted line—or at least get generous return privileges in case the speakers you pick *don't* deliver when you get them home.

The Least You Need to Know

➤ For a true Dolby Digital 5.1 home theater, you'll need six speakers—front left, front center, front right, surround left, surround right, and a subwoofer. For Dolby Digital EX 6.1, you'll need to add a surround rear speaker between and behind the left and right surrounds.

➤ The center speaker is perhaps the most important speaker in your system, and should be voice-matched to the other two front speakers.

➤ All speakers should be positioned so their tweeters are at ear level, and surround speakers should be positioned to the side of the listening position.

➤ If you want to use existing speakers as part of your surround-sound system, make sure the new speakers you buy have similar tonal characteristics.

Chapter 17

Sound at the Speed of Light: CD Players and Recorders

In This Chapter

➤ The latest CD players and changers—including the new mega-CD jukeboxes

➤ How your DVD player can do double duty as a CD player

➤ How to record your own CDs

➤ SACD and DVD-A, the new ultra-high fidelity formats that are poised to re-place the CD format

For almost 20 years now, the standard for high-quality audio has been the compact disc. CDs store music digitally, and CD players use a low-powered laser to read the digital information from each disc. That digital bitstream is then converted to analog signals and fed to your preamp or receiver, and then to your speakers. The resulting sound is fantastic—much more accurate, in general, than what you were used to with vinyl LPs and audiocassettes.

While there are newer digital audio formats on the horizon—as you'll read later in this chapter—a CD player or changer remains an essential part of any audio or home theater system.

CD Players

Single-disc CD players range in price from $100 to $1,000. For most listeners, even the lowest-priced unit delivers superb sound; the higher-end units tend to include the eso-teric technologies that matter only to pure audiophiles. Look for a unit that contains the features you want, and that "feels" right to you; avoid lightweight or cheaply con-structed models. The reality is you can keep your CD player budget under $150 and still get a high-performance, well-constructed player.

CD Changers

If one CD is good, then five must be five times as good, right? That's the thinking behind CD changers, which let you load up five or more CDs for continuous or random play.

The most common type of changer is the five-disc carousel. These models load five CDs on a platter; while one is playing, you can switch out the other four.

For just a little more money—starting around $200—you can move up to a CD "jukebox," which lets you store up to 400 CDs in a massive carriage. With these units it's easy to store your entire CD collection in a single jukebox—and shuffle from disc to disc as often as you wish.

Many manufacturers let you chain several CD jukeboxes together—and control them all from a single remote control. If you have a really large CD collection, being able to select from up to 800 titles is a real joy!

Of course, remembering which CD is where in the jukebox can be a challenge. Some specialty manufacturers are addressing this problem by producing CD-management systems. My favorite system is TuneBase, from Escient. TuneBase lets you chain together up to three CD jukeboxes (for up to 1200-disc storage) and use the television in your home theater system to select which discs you want to play. Every time you insert a new CD in the jukebox, TuneBase dials up its own CD database and then downloads information about that disc (including cover graphics and song titles) into the TuneBase unit. As you can see from the following screen, you can then select discs by title, artist, song, or musical style—and create your own custom music station!

Use TuneBase to control your mega-CD collection— via remote control, using your television screen!

(Courtesy of Escient, Inc.)

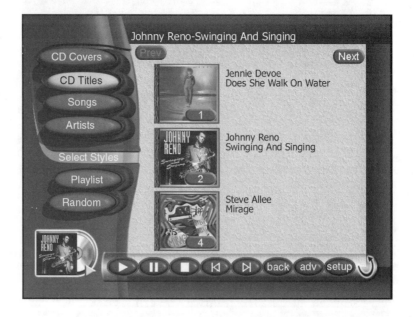

Since TuneBase is a fairly expensive ($3,000+) system, it might not be available at your local audio/video dealer. To learn more about TuneBase and the related PowerPlay product (for DVDs), visit Escient's Web site at www.escient.com.

CD Recorders

For years you were told that CDs were for playback only—you couldn't record your own. Well, that's changed ... and how!

Thanks to a new generation of lasers, the technology necessary to "burn" your own CDs is now within the price range of any home theater enthusiast. Audio CD recorders can be purchased for as little as $400—and CD recorders for your PC can be had for even less!

CD recorders record digitally on blank discs that can be played back on virtually any newer home, car, or portable CD player or changer. Your custom-recorded CDs will sound every bit as good as the CDs you buy at retail—and most CD recorders include digital inputs that let you record directly from any CD player with digital output at the full 44.1 kHz sampling rate.

You can record your own CDs in two different formats. The CD-R (CD-Recordable) format lets you record a disc once; blank CD-R discs are as cheap as blank audiocassettes, and can be played back on most regular CD players. The CR-RW (CD-Rewritable) format lets you record over and over to the same disc; blank CD-RW discs are higher priced, and can only play back on CD recorders or special players with CD-RW compatibility. For most consumers, CD-R will be your recording format of choice.

If you plan on doing a lot of CD recording, consider one of the dual-tray CD player/recorders. These machines include one tray for a playback CD, and one tray for the CD you want to record—and let you easily dub music from the one CD to the other. These dubbing decks can be found for less than $600.

Overload!

CD-R and CD-RW discs will not play back in most DVD players and changers. For a DVD player to read the CDs you record, it needs to have a second laser or lens specifically for CD-R playback, which most players *don't* have. In other words, if you record your own CDs, don't expect to play them back in a DVD player.

Input/Output

You can find two types of blank CDs—those for use with computer-based CD recorders and those for use with audio CD recorders. Look for those discs with the "Digital Audio" logo, since you can't use blank computer CDs in audio CD recorders.

Playing CDs in DVD Players

Here's something not everyone knows. All commercial compact discs will play in all DVD players and changers. (As noted previously, the CD-Rs you record yourself *won't* play in most DVD players.)

This means that you can use your DVD player to play your CD collection—and that you can get by, if necessary, with a single player in your home theater system for both DVDs and CDs!

Better CDs: DVD-Audio and SACD

As good as CDs are, there are some hard-core audiophiles that maintain that even the best CDs don't sound as good as the best analog recordings on vinyl LP. These comments have to do with the CD's digital sampling rate not being high enough to completely capture the original recording—and thus sounding less "warm" than the same music on LP. (These same audiophiles gloss over the obvious drawbacks of the LP format—not the least of which are the pops and crackles that come with normal disc wear.)

For these audiophiles—and, eventually, for the rest of us—the consumer electronics industry is working on not one, but two different high-performance audio formats. One of these formats will eventually replace the CD for music recordings, even though that day is probably several years away.

It's Super, Man: Introducing the Super Audio CD

From Sony and Philips, the two companies that developed the original CD, comes the new Super Audio CD—or just SACD for short. This new format is an enhancement of the original CD format, and is both forward- and backward-compatible with current CDs.

All SACD players are engineered to play back current-generation CDs as well as the new SACD discs. As to the discs, they'll be manufactured with either a single high-density layer, dual high-density layers (for longer pieces of music), or as hybrid discs that combine a high-density SACD with a normal CD. These hybrid discs will be playable on any CD player; the other types of discs will only be playable on the SACD players.

If you want to buy an SACD player today, you'll pay several thousand dollars—even though SACD discs will only cost in the $25 range. From all indications, SACD is aimed at enthusiasts and audiophiles, not the general public—and as such is unlikely to replace the CD format.

How does SACD sound? In a word: terrific. It delivers all the warmth and subtlety of the best analog recordings, with all the advantages of a digital format. The differences are noticeable, and should satisfy even the most discriminating audiophile.

A More Versatile Digital Disc: DVD-Audio

From Matsushita—and supported by most consumer electronics manufacturers—comes a new DVD-based audio format. DVD-Audio (DVD-A) uses the high-density storage of the DVD format for pure audio purposes, resulting in ultra-high fidelity music reproduction. While today's CDs use 44.1 kHz sampling, DVD-A can utilize eight different sampling frequencies, up to 192 kHz—and still deliver 74 minutes of music per disc. In terms of frequency response, it moves beyond CD's 5–20,000 Hz range (with 96 dB signal-to-noise ratio) to a theoretical 0–96,000 Hz bandwidth—with 144 dB S/N!

In addition, DVD-A is a multichannel format. For those of us who fondly remember the shining days of quadraphonic sound, DVD-A will bring back music that comes from all four (or more) speakers—promising to envelop the listener in full surround sound.

While combo DVD/DVD-A players are on the drawing boards from most manufacturers, no current DVD player will play back DVD-A discs. Which means if you're interested in DVD-A, you'll need to shell out $1,000 or so for a new DVD-A player.

Which Format Wins?

It's likely that only one of these two new formats will survive, and that five years from now the losing format will be relegated to the technology history books. If I were a betting man, I'd be broke by now, so I'm not going to put real money on this two-horse race—although I will offer some opinions.

From where I stand, the SACD format looks to be a niche format. It's only supported by a handful of manufacturers, it carries a price almost as high as its sampling rate, and the initial (two-channel) programming is targeted at enthusiasts and classical music aficionados. It's possible that SACD will be the Betamax of the digital audio world, but it's also possible that the format will have some sort of limited life to the ultra-high-end market.

DVD-A, on the other hand, looks ready to ride the wave of the DVD video format. If (or when) most new DVD players can play both DVD video and DVD-Audio discs, this format wins by default. And it's not a shabby format, either; the sound is noticeably better than the CD format, and the possible extra features (multichannel sound, on-screen graphics and lyrics, and so on) will have some appeal.

Of course, the best situation for us consumers would be a single deck that plays back everything—DVD, DVD-A, CD, SACD, and even CD-R and CD-RW. When that machine is manufactured—and it will be, mark my words—then the question of which high-end audio format "wins" becomes irrelevant.

As for now, unless you have golden ears and a platinum wallet, taking a wait-and-see attitude is recommended. Wait for prices to decrease—and program availability to increase—before you spend a lot of money supporting a new format.

163

Shop Smart: What to Look For

Assuming you want to stick with a traditional CD player (not one of the SACD or DVD-A models), here are some tips for choosing a new player:

➤ **DVD or CD?** Do you really need a CD player? After all, your DVD player can play all your commercial CDs, no problem. However, some CD players and changers include more CD-specific operations (track shuffle, random play, and so on) not found on all DVD players. Still, if you're short on space or money, it's perfectly okay to let your DVD player do double duty.

➤ **Player or changer?** Even if you're on a strict budget or seldom listen to music for more than a half-hour at a time, go with at least a five-disc changer. Heck, at today's prices, you might as well spring for a CD jukebox—they're just not that expensive!

➤ **Digital output.** The best sound comes from a CD player's digital outputs. So, if your receiver has a digital input—or if you plan on recording from your CD player to a CD or MiniDisc recorder—look for a unit with either an optical or coaxial output jack.

➤ **Check the specs.** While most listeners have trouble distinguishing one CD player from another during playback, it still doesn't hurt to check the specs from deck to deck. In particular, you can look at frequency response (the wider the better) and signal-to-noise ratio (the higher the better). In addition, for the very best performance, look for players with multibit digital-to-analog (D/A) converters, which reduce the number of errors when translating the digital information to an analog signal.

The Least You Need to Know

➤ CD players are an essential part of any home theater or audio system, and can be purchased for as little as $100.

➤ Multidisc CD changers are increasingly popular, from simple five-disc carousels to 400-disc jukeboxes.

➤ All DVD players can play all commercial CDs, so you can use your DVD player as a CD player if you want to.

➤ CD recorders let you make your own custom-recorded CDs, in one of two formats; the CD-R format is best suited for audio recording and playback.

➤ Super Audio CD (SACD) and DVD-Audio (DVD-A) are two competing formats for the playback of ultra-high fidelity audio; SACD players can play back standard CDs, while new DVD/DVD-A combo players will play back both video and audio DVDs.

Chapter 18

Make Your Own Kind of Music: Audio Recorders

In This Chapter

➤ Why an audiocassette recorder is still viable—and which noise reduction system is best

➤ Should you include a MiniDisc recorder in your system?

➤ The new generation of CD recorders

➤ The new MP3 format—why it's taking the Internet by storm

Playing back prerecorded music is great, but what if you want to create your own custom mixes? Or make a copy of your favorite CD to play in your car or portable device?

If you want to make your own kind of music, you'll need to add an audio recorder to your home theater system. As you'll learn in this chapter, you have several different types of recorders to choose from—from the traditional cassette recorder to the newest digital recorders.

The Old Standby: Cassette Recorders

The audiocassette deck is a staple in any home audio system. Even with the proliferation of compact disc audio, many people still listen to audiocassettes in their cars or when jogging. And nothing beats the convenience of recording your favorite songs on your own custom cassettes.

Today's cassette decks are better sounding, easier to use, and lower priced than ever before. The best decks include three heads (which let you compare what you're recording to the sourced material, in real time) and one or more types of Dolby noise reduction to reduce the amount of background noise and hiss on the tapes you record.

When you're comparing decks, look at the different types of noise reduction available. All noise reduction works via an "encode/decode" process, where both the recording deck and playback deck must have the same type of noise reduction for best results. So, make sure that your home deck has the same type of noise reduction as your car player or Walkman, or the tapes you record at home will sound overly bright when played back on other devices.

As shown in the following chart, here are the types of noise reduction you can find on the current generation of home audiocassette decks:

➤ Dolby B, which reduces high-frequency hiss by 8–10 dB; Dolby B is the de facto noise reduction standard, and is found in most car and portable cassette decks

➤ Dolby C, which works over a wider frequency range and reduces hiss by 15–18 dB; few car and portable cassette decks can play back Dolby C tapes

➤ Dolby S, which works over the full range of audible frequencies and reduces hiss by up to 24 dB in the higher frequencies and 10 dB in the lower frequencies; Dolby S tapes can be played back on any Dolby B-equipped deck

Comparing the signal-to-noise ratio of the various Dolby noise reduction systems.

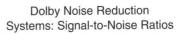

Dolby Noise Reduction Systems: Signal-to-Noise Ratios

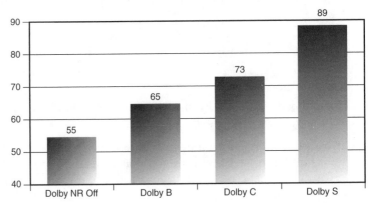

If you're looking for a new cassette deck, you should also compare each deck's frequency response (this will be different for different tape formulations; wider is better), signal-to-noise ratio (higher is better), and wow and flutter (a lower percentage is better). In addition, look for useful features such as automatic bias adjustment, auto-reverse, a time counter, and track indexing.

Sony's Digital Standard: MiniDisc Recorders

Audiocassettes record music in analog format; Sony's MiniDisc records music digitally. This format, which is pretty much a Sony-only thing, records up to 74 minutes of high-quality music on a tiny 2.5" disc—digitally.

Like a CD, a MiniDisc is a laser-read optical disc. While MiniDisc sound quality is not quite CD-quality, it is much better than recording with analog cassettes—and has virtually no noise, hiss, or wow and flutter. Thanks to its digital recording format, MiniDiscs also provide many CD-like playback features, including shuffle play and instantaneous track access.

MiniDisc is an ideal format for recording music from compact discs. Just connect a cable between your CD player's optical output jacks and the MiniDisc recorder's optical input jacks, and you're recording the straight digital bitstream. This process is made even easier if you use one of Sony's CD/MiniDisc combo player/recorders, which can be had for as little as $400. Standard MiniDisc recorders cost as little as $200.

The big downside to the MiniDisc is that it's a format that hasn't really caught on. Sony is pretty much the only manufacturer of MiniDisc equipment, and you won't find MiniDisc players in any automobiles. That said, it's high-quality digital recording at a low price; you just won't find a lot of other units that can play back any MiniDiscs you record.

The Best Way to Record from a CD— CD Recorders

As discussed back in Chapter 17, "Sound at the Speed of Light: CD Players and Recorders," you can now record your own CDs, using an affordable CD recorder. CD recorders can record in two different formats (CD-R and CD-RW), with CD-R discs playable on all newer CD players. (Neither CD-R nor CD-RW discs are playable on DVD decks, however.)

While CD recorders are a little more expensive than either audiocassette decks or MiniDisc recorders, $400 will get you your own in-house CD recording studio—with the best quality digital audio available!

Record from the Internet: MP3 Recorders

If you're a college student, I don't have to explain to you what MP3 is. If you're new to the format, however, there are a few things you need to know.

First, know that MP3 is the hottest thing to happen to recorded music in years. It's a music format popularized by college students, who download MP3-format music for free from the Internet. The MP3 format stores near-CD quality music in much less space than used by comparable CDs. A typical three-minute song in MP3 format only takes up 2Mb of disk space.

Although large record companies despise MP3 (they fear the threat of unauthorized copying), Internet users—particularly college students—love it and have wholeheartedly embraced the format. MP3 has quickly become the standard for music on the Web.

MP3 songs can be stored on a computer hard disk, on portable "memory sticks" that can be transferred from device to device, and on recordable CDs. While there are several portable MP3 players available today that use either CD-Rs or memory technology as a storage medium for the MP3 files, there aren't a lot of "home" MP3 players—or at least, not yet. Expect several major consumer electronics manufacturers to release MP3 decks, probably using CD-Rs as the storage medium and including built-in MP3 player software.

Input/Output

If you want to learn more about MP3, download MP3 files, find MP3 player software for your PC, or look for new MP3 hardware, here are the Web sites to check out:

- ➤ 2look4 (www.2look4.com)
- ➤ askMP3.com (askMP3.com)
- ➤ Audiofind (www.audiofind.com)
- ➤ DAILYMP3.COM (www.dailymp3.com)
- ➤ Dimension Music (www.dimensionmusic.com)
- ➤ Lycos Music MP3 Search (mp3.lycos.com)
- ➤ MP3 Place (www.mp3place.com)
- ➤ MP3.com (www.mp3.com)
- ➤ MP3now.com (www.mp3now.com)
- ➤ MultiAudio.net (www.multiaudio.net)
- ➤ Musicseek (www.musicseek.net)
- ➤ Napster (www.napster.com)
- ➤ Palavista Digital Music Metacrawler (www.palavista.com)

You can also find lots of MP3 files in various Usenet newsgroups. Look for groups in the alt.binaries.sounds.mp3 hierarchy.

Should you add an MP3 player to your home theater system? If you have a lot of MP3s you've downloaded from the Internet, it makes a lot of sense. Know, however, that the MP3 format is *near* CD quality—it isn't up to the standards of most audio/video enthusiasts. While MP3s sound okay when played through your computer's sound system, they are definitely lacking when played through your a/v receiver and home speakers.

The Least You Need to Know

➤ If you want to make recordings you can play back in your car or on your portable tape player, go with an audiocassette recorder—and use the Dolby B or Dolby S noise reduction.

➤ Unless you have a portable MiniDisc player or want to play back MiniDisc recordings through your home theater system, skip the MiniDisc format completely.

➤ If you want to make high-quality digital recordings, buy a CD recorder.

➤ If you have a lot of MP3 downloads that you'd like to play on your home theater system—and don't mind the inferior sound quality—look for a home MP3 player, or a way to connect a portable MP3 player to your home theater system.

Part 5

Everything But the Popcorn: Building Your Home Theater System

Enough background information—it's time to get your hands dirty and put together your own personal home theater system! Not sure which is the right kind of connection—composite video, S-video, or component video? Wondering how to put together a surround-sound system on the cheap? Thinking that it might be better to hire a pro to install your system? Read these chapters to learn how to plug things in and set them up—and find out just what kind of system you can buy on your budget!

Chapter 19

Get Ready: Prepare Your Room for Home Theater

In This Chapter

➤ What types of rooms work best for home theater

➤ How to best position your components and speakers within your room

➤ The jacks and receptacles you'll need before you start connecting your components

Before you unpack all your equipment boxes and start to run the roughly 374 miles of cables you'll need to connect all your audio/video components, you probably need to stop for a moment and consider the room you'll be using for your home theater system. Is the room ideally suited for a home theater? Are there things you can do to the room to improve its acoustic or viewing characteristics? What needs to be prepared before you set up your system components?

This chapter walks you through some useful preparation you can—and should—do before you start building your home theater. Follow the advice here, and you'll make the final setup a little easier—and make your room a better place to watch your favorite movies!

Space, the Final Frontier: Creating the Ideal Home Theater Room

Unless you design your house from scratch with home theater in mind, chances are the room you pick to house your system will be somewhat less than ideal for movie-viewing and music-listening activities. What makes for a good home theater room? Here are some things to look for:

➤ Look for a relatively enclosed space; rooms without defined walls (rooms that lead seamlessly into other rooms) not only lack surfaces on which to mount speakers, but also "leak" a tremendous amount of sound. Think of it this way— if your home theater area lacks a full rear wall (for example), your system will be trying to fill the entire area beyond your specific listening space with sound. And the larger area you try to fill, the more power you need. It's easier to fill a smaller space than it is a larger one.

➤ Try to avoid spaces that are perfectly square, or that have one dimension exactly twice another. These types of spaces can produce unwanted resonances that can muddy your system's sound.

➤ If possible, avoid too many hard surfaces. Hard surfaces reflect sound, and too many reflections make it difficult to sort out positioning within the home theater sound field. Remember the last concert you saw in a big stadium? Those kinds of echoes, on a smaller scale, are created if your walls, ceilings, and floor are all very hard and reflective. (A little carpet, a few rugs, and some nice drapes go a long way toward reducing this problem.)

➤ Look out for too much light. Direct light sources can reflect off the TV screen— or affect your peripheral vision—and interfere with your viewing. Turn on all the lights in your room and then stare into a blank screen; if you see any lights reflected back at you, turn them off or move them. You'll probably also want to pull the drapes before you watch a movie; dimming the lights (even those that don't reflect off the TV screen) is also a good idea. The darker the room, the more your vision can focus on the activity on the TV screen.

➤ Don't put too much white around your screen. Have you ever noticed how television manufacturers surround the picture tube with a dark bezel—or how movie theaters put dark curtains on either side of the screen? That's because too much contrast around the picture is hard on your eyes. You can experiment with this yourself; surround your TV screen with an all-white material, and then compare that experience to one where you surround the screen with an all-black material. A darker "frame" around your screen is better.

➤ When you're ready to fire up your system, be conscious of extraneous noises. You may be used to the noise made by the pump in your fish tank, but it can detract from your enjoyment of watching a quiet movie or listening to a soft

CD. While it's practically impossible to totally soundproof a normal living room, use your ears to isolate and eliminate unnecessary sources of sound. (This may also mean not running the dishwasher or washing machine while you're using the home theater!)

➤ Make sure the room is big enough (or small enough!) for your video display. A screen that's too big can overwhelm a small room, just as a small screen can get lost in an oversized space. To review the guidelines for sizing your display, see Chapter 4, "Pick a Picture: Choose the Right TV for Your System."

➤ Make sure the home theater experience is good for everyone in the room. Granted, in a small room there's really only one ideal viewing and listening position. (You have more flexibility in a larger room, as the viewing angle widens and the surround sound becomes a bit more diffuse.) Check out the sound and picture from multiple sitting positions, and be aware of how a projection TV picture gets darker as you get more off-angle, and how the surround sound loses its positioning as you move from the exact center of the sound field. If necessary, reposition your furniture to facilitate better viewing and listening—or reposition your speakers and TV to create a more tolerant space.

Input/Output

If your room isn't perfect, there are a few things you can do.

If you're having a problem with reflected sound, which typically manifests itself in the form of unwanted echoes and reverberation, throw up some more drapes or soft wall coverings; even a few big pillows thrown in the corner can absorb some of the reflections. You may also need to reposition any mirrors or large glass-front pictures hanging on your walls, as these can be sources of isolated reflections. You should also take great pains to *not* place your speakers near corners, and maybe even move them a few inches away from the wall.

If you're having a problem with reflected light, your choices are simple—move the light, or turn it off. If the unwanted light source is a window, try closing the drapes, or buying heavier (and darker) drapes.

Bottom line: You'll probably need to experiment with the placement of things to create the best possible viewing and listening experience—and remember that changing one element, even just a little, can change the effect of other elements in your room.

Here, There, and Everywhere: Positioning Your System

As you plan your home theater layout, you'll need to position your video display, speakers, and furniture carefully to create the best possible viewing and listening experience. This is made easier if your room is somewhat symmetrical; asymmetrical spaces (or cathedral ceilings with an off-center peak) can play havoc with the way sound reflects off the walls to the various listening positions.

In general, you want to center your seating area between the side walls on which you mount your surround speakers. The distance from your viewing screen to the center of your seating area should be roughly three times the diagonal measure of your TV. (If you have a 36" TV, your seating area should be about nine feet away from the screen.)

The positioning of your speakers is also important. Ideally, you want each of the five front and surround speakers to be positioned at or near the same height, to facilitate positioning of elements that move around the theater sound field. If this is impractical, focus on the front axis first, and make sure your left and right front speakers are at the same height. Then work with your center speaker, and position it so that its midrange speaker or tweeter is no more than 12" above or below the midrange or tweeter of the left and right speakers. Then you can work with the surround speakers, and try to get them as close as possible to the same height.

What's the right height for your system's speakers? You can go about this a couple of different ways. One way is to position your center speaker first—it should be positioned either directly above or directly below your TV screen—and then match the other speakers to this height. Alternately, you can try to position *all* your speakers so they're roughly at ear level. (That's ear level while you're sitting down, of course!)

When you're positioning your speakers, remember that the closer a speaker is placed to intersecting room surfaces—a corner, the wall and ceiling, or the wall and floor—the stronger its bass output. This effect can result in overpowering or muddy bass, so unless you deliberately want a bass boost, keep your speakers away from corners.

Your subwoofer, however, might benefit from corner placement. A subwoofer is nondirectional, so where you put it is unimportant in terms of positioning the sound field. Placing the subwoofer in a corner or under a stairway, however, can add a little extra oomph to your system's low end, and should be considered.

Power Up

Speaking of height, your video display should be positioned more or less at eye level. That might mean raising a low-sitting rear projection set, or getting a taller stand for a direct-view monitor. If your display *isn't* at eye level, you risk some off-axis effects (in the form of darkened or distorted picture), especially with projection models.

Plugged In and Ready to Go: Assembling All the Connections

Now that you've examined and worked around your room's acoustics, you're ready to start setting up your system—right? Well, hold off for just a minute longer as we consider the kinds of outlets and receptacles you'll need to get everything plugged in and powered up.

In most homes, any given wall has a single power receptacle with two outlets. Given that your system will include a half-dozen or more components that all need their own power, this simply won't suffice. You'll need to supplement the standard power outlet with a multiple-outlet power strip—preferably one that also functions as a surge suppressor. Depending on the number of components in your system, you may have to gang two of these strips together to provide an adequate number of power connections.

You'll also want to make sure your antenna, satellite dish, or cable system runs into the area where you'll be positioning your TV and other components. The last thing you want is to string an ugly piece of coax cable from one wall to another; it's best to have your cable guy or other installer run the proper connections to the proper place within your wall (or under your floor, if you have a basement or crawl space) beforehand.

Finally, make sure there's a phone jack behind your system cabinet. Most folks don't think about this, but several different components—in particular, digital satellite receivers, hard disk personal video recorders, and WebTV boxes—all dial into their specific services on at least a daily basis. If you have more than one of these devices, you'll probably have to purchase one of those adapters that lets you plug two or three phones into a single jack, so you can get all your equipment jacked into the phone line.

Overload!

Every piece of electronic gear you own *is* susceptible to power line surges and—in the worst possible case—lightning strikes. You can minimize the potential for damage by plugging each piece of equipment into a surge suppressor strip, which will help protect your system from damage. (You should also look for a surge suppressor with RF and phone connections—power surges can also come through your antenna, cable, or phone line!)

As to running wires to your surround speakers—you're on your own with this one! It's easy enough to run speaker wire under the carpet, or feed it up through a basement or crawl space, or down from the attic. When you get into feeding the wire through the wall and out again, you're into a lot of work—which is probably necessary, but a chore nonetheless.

Finally, if all this positioning and cabling and calibrating make you nervous, bite the bullet and call a professional installer. They do this sort of thing for a living, have all the proper tools, and know all sorts of shortcuts and workarounds that you'll never stumble across! (For more information on custom installers, see Chapter 24, "Home Beautiful: Installing a Custom System.")

The Least You Need to Know

➤ You should carefully choose the space for your home theater system to avoid unnecessary sound and light reflections, and to maximize the viewing and listening "sweet spot."

➤ Make sure that your home theater room is dark enough for enjoyable viewing, and quiet enough for enjoyable listening.

➤ Position your seating area midway between your two surround speakers (which should be mounted on the sides of your room, not the back!), and three times your TV screen's diagonal measurement from the front of the screen.

➤ Make sure you have the proper jacks and receptacles where you'll be positioning your TV and components; this includes a half-dozen ormore power outlets (via a power strip or surge suppressor), antenna/cable/satellite feed, and phone jack.

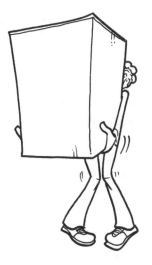

Chapter 20

Quick and Easy Systems: Home Theater in a Box

In This Chapter

➤ How home theater in a box systems let you build a surround-sound system for under $500

➤ Which home theater in a box delivers the best bang for the buck

➤ Why you should consider purchasing a packaged set of home theater speakers for your system

Throughout this book we've examined all types of audio/video components, with the goal of constructing a home theater system one piece at a time. There are two problems with this approach: It's complicated, and it can be costly. (For the ultimate in complexity and cost, look at the million-dollar system highlighted in Chapter 24, "Home Beautiful: Installing a Custom System.")

A simpler—and, in most cases, less expensive—solution is to buy all your home theater components as a package. This package—fondly called "home theater in a box"—can get you up and running with a surround-sound system for as little as $400!

One Box, Lotsa Stuff

Home theater in a box (HTIB) is the generic name for prepackaged systems that include an audio/video receiver and surround-sound speakers. These systems, while not delivering exactly the highest-quality audio available, do include all the components you need to build the audio part of your home theater system.

What's in the Box?

HTIB systems are available from Aiwa, Kenwood, Pioneer, Sony, and other manufacturers, and are typically priced in the $400–$800 range; the most popular models fall around $500. For this price, here's what you'll get:

➤ Audio/video receiver with 80–100 watts/channel (but with reduced frequency response and relatively high signal-to-noise ratio), surround-sound processor (typically Dolby Pro Logic, although some models include Dolby Digital 5.1), three video inputs (typically component video, although some models feature S-Video inputs), four or more audio inputs, video monitor output (typically composite video, but some models feature an S-Video output), and remote control

➤ Front-left and front-right speakers

➤ Center channel speaker

➤ Two surround speakers (typically smaller than the front speakers)

➤ Subwoofer (passive in lower-end systems, powered in higher-end systems)

Overload!

Note that most HTIB manufacturers rate their systems' power by *combining* the power from all channels. So, if the system delivers 80 watts per channel across 5 channels, they'll rate this as a 400-watt system. (More than a little misleading, in my opinion.) Also know that while these systems may carry similar power ratings to separate receivers costing in the $500–$1,000 range, the HTIB power is delivered with a narrower frequency response—typically 40Hz–20kHz vs. the better 20Hz–20kHz, which delivers a noticeably weaker low end. The signal-to-noise ratio total harmonic distortion of the HTIB units is also noticeably higher than that of separate a/v receivers.

As you move up in price, you'll typically get slightly more (and cleaner) power, better surround-sound processing (Dolby Digital), S-Video inputs and outputs, and better speakers (especially in the subwoofer). Most of these packages also make hookup relatively easy, using color-coordinated speaker cables for each channel.

Smart Shopping: What to Look For

So, what should you look for if your budget leads you to a home theater in a box system? Surprisingly, there are some significant differences between models at similar price points, so keep your eyes peeled for the following:

➤ **S-Video inputs and outputs.** S-Video delivers noticeably better picture quality than the more common composite video connections.

➤ **Dolby Digital surround sound.** Most HTIB units come with the older Dolby Pro Logic system; if you can find a package with the better Dolby Digital 5.1 surround, go for it.

➤ **Digital sound processing modes.** Some models include several DSP-simulated surround modes. I wouldn't consider DSP-simulated surround as a necessary feature; given the choice, I'd trade off for one of the more performance-oriented features.

➤ **Cleaner sound.** All these units will deliver power in the 80–100 watt per channel range. Seek out detailed system specs to find a unit that has a wider frequency response and lower signal-to-noise (S/N) ratio and lower total harmonic distortion (THD).

➤ **Powered subwoofer.** The bigger and the more powerful the subwoofer, the better.

Input/Output

Home theater in a box systems are convenient, but most audiophiles and home theater enthusiasts tend to dismiss these packages as being of inferior quality for true home theater reproduction—and, to be upfront about it, I wouldn't try to build my own personal system around such a package. Let's face it—you're not going to get the same sound quality from $500 worth of equipment as you will from a separate receiver and speakers costing $2,000 or more.

However, HTIB systems are viable alternatives for consumers on a budget who still want some semblance of the home theater experience. Given the only reasonable alternative—relying on your TV's built-in speakers—HTIB systems deliver superior performance, plus true surround-sound reproduction. Granted, these aren't high-end systems, but they're better than having no system at all!

You can also look for bigger speakers, but bigger speakers don't necessarily deliver better sound. It's better to just listen to the system and determine for yourself which one delivers the better sound.

Make a Match: Home Theater Speaker Systems

Similar to home theater in a box systems are home theater speaker packages. These are matching sets of speakers—including front speakers, surround speakers, and a subwoofer—packaged together by a single manufacturer for a quick and easy surround-sound solution.

Home theater speaker systems are actually pretty good deals, and should be considered for inclusion in any home theater system with a budget of $5,000 or less. These systems range in price from $500 to $2,500—which makes it obvious that you can choose from a wide range of features and performance.

At the low end of this range are systems from Bose, Polk Audio, Sony, and similar manufacturers. These systems typically match smaller "satellite" speakers with a subwoofer to handle the bass.

Move to the higher end of this range and you find systems from Polk Audio, Definitive Technology, and others that include full-size speakers all around. These systems typically include high-powered subwoofers, as well.

There are several advantages to going with a home theater speaker package instead of speakers purchased separately. First, you can be reasonably assured that the speakers in a package are well matched and will deliver pretty good surround sound. Second, it's a lot more convenient to buy one product instead of six—and maybe a little easier to hook up, as well. Third, you'll probably get a little bit of a price break by buying all these speakers together in a package, as opposed to purchasing them individually.

The bottom line: Packaged home theater speaker systems simplify the selection of speakers for your home theater system!

The Least You Need to Know

➤ Home theater in a box systems package a low-end audio/video receiver with a set of surround-sound speakers, and sell in the $400–$800 price range.

➤ If your budget dictates a home theater in a box system, look for one with Dolby Digital 5.1 surround and S-Video inputs and outputs.

➤ If you can afford a little bit more money, you might want to consider a home theater speaker system, which packages six matching speakers from the same manufacturer.

Chapter 21

Plug It In: Which Cable Goes Where

In This Chapter

➤ Different types of audio and video connections, including composite video, component video, and S-Video

➤ Which connections you should use for your specific components

➤ The best way to connect all your components to create a complete home theater system

Choosing the components for your home theater system is a piece of cake. The hard part comes when you have to hook them all up—and make them all work together! Dealing with the spaghetti-like tangle of cables and trying to figure out which plug to connect to which jack (when you have something like 253 different jacks on the back of a typical audio/video receiver) can reduce even the most experienced home theater installer to a quivering mass of human flesh.

It's not easy, as you well know!

That's why you need this chapter. Forget the rest of this book—read the following pages carefully, over and over again, until you recite from memory the different types of audio and video connections, and which ones to use when. (Bonus points if you can describe the difference between composite and component video, in 100 words or less!)

You'll get through this ordeal, trust me—and if you don't, you can always call a professional installer to do the job for you!

You Say Component, I Say Composite: A Connection Primer

Before there was home theater, you only had to deal with connecting a coax cable to your TV, plugging a left/right audio cable between your turntable and your receiver, and running speaker wire to all your speakers (all two of them, that is). Now you have to worry about five or six speakers, plus all sorts of audio and video components that offer a multitude of connection options.

Before you try plugging anything in, it's probably a good idea to understand all these different types of connections—and when to use which ones.

RF (Coax)

All television sets retain the standard coaxial connection you've grown to love over the years. This connector feeds an RF (radio frequency) signal directly to your set's tuner; this signal carries both audio and video information, all squooshed together, and delivers the lowest-quality video signal of all possible connections. RF doesn't do a great job in separating chrominance and luminance, and results in a noticeably less-sharp picture with poor color separation. A typical RF connection uses 75-ohm coaxial cable with F-fittings on either end.

Connect your broadcast antenna or cable box via an RF input.

RF connections are used primarily for broadcast television (fed from an antenna) and cable (typically fed from a cable box). Some video components (such as VCRs) include RF output, which can be connected to the RF input on your TV or a/v receiver; it's better to bypass this connection in favor of a composite video or S-Video connection, where available.

Composite Video

The first step up from an RF connection is a composite video connection. Unlike the RF connection, composite video delivers only video signals; audio signals are transmitted via separate line audio connections (described later in this chapter). The composite video signal, however, contains both chrominance (color) and luminance (brightness) information; more advanced connections (such as S-Video and component video) separate the brightness from the color.

Use the composite video jack to connect your VCR.

A composite video connection uses a standard RCA plug and jack, and delivers noticeably sharper pictures than a standard RF connection. Most video components feature composite video outputs (typically labeled just "video"), and most TVs and a/v receivers feature a ton of composite video inputs.

S-Video

Even better than composite video is an S-Video connection. An S-Video connection—which uses a four-prong plug and jack—separates the luminance (brightness) and chrominance (color) signals; in comparison, these signals are combined in a composite video connection. By separating these signals, S-Video delivers a sharper picture, improved color accuracy, and reduced distortion.

When available, use S-Video connections for sharper pictures.

Component Video

An arguably better video connection than S-Video is component video. Component video not only separates luminance from chrominance (as does S-Video) but also breaks down the chrominance (color) information into its two main color difference signals, using a set of three plugs and jacks, typically labeled Y (for luminance or brightness information), Pr (for red chrominance or color information), and Pb (for blue chrominance or color information). Component video delivers extremely high-quality picture signals, with improved color accuracy and reduced color bleeding.

Component video delivers the best video signals, period.

Power Up

Sometimes the labeling for component video replaces the Pr and Pb with R-Y and B-Y.

Component video is typically connected via 75-ohm coax cable with RCA-type jacks on either end. Not all components feature component video outputs, and only high-end televisions have component video inputs. Few a/v receivers feature component video inputs and outputs, meaning that you'll need to connect your component video-equipped components directly to your component video-equipped TV.

Input/Output

Is component video worth the hassle? Maybe not.

First, for component video to deliver its optimal picture quality, your television must be perfectly adjusted—and this includes the convergence, especially critical on projection televisions. Since most TVs aren't professionally calibrated, they won't deliver the full potential of component video.

In addition, adding a component video source to your system introduces an additional layer of operational complexity. The video levels required for component sources are typically very different from those required for S-Video and composite video sources, which means you'll need to adjust your TV's contrast, brightness, color, and tint controls every time you switch from a component video source to another source.

Finally, few a/v receivers incorporate component video inputs and outputs—which means you probably can't use your receiver to switch your component video source. You'll end up connecting your component video source directly to your TV, which means you'll have to switch your TV from one auxiliary input to another when you want to watch your component video source.

So, should you use the component video outputs on your new DVD player or other video source? The best way to decide is to hook up both the component video and the S-Video outputs, then switch between the two. If there's a big enough difference, the hassle might be worth it; if you can't see much of a difference, you might want to stick with the easier-to-use and more-flexible S-Video connections.

RGB Video

Even better than component video is an RGB connection, which goes beyond component video in separating three different chrominance signals (red, blue, and green). Even though this is the default connection for computer monitors, only a few consumer electronics products feature this type of connection.

RGB inputs are used to connect personal computers and some HDTV tuners.

By separating the red (R), green (G), and blue (B) signals, an RGB connection delivers the best possible picture quality, with superior color separation and picture sharpness. While RGB isn't widely used in audio/video components, some manufacturers are using RGB to connect HDTV tuners and components to HDTV or digital-ready televisions.

Line Audio

Most audio components you've ever owned have been connected via line audio connections. These connections deliver line-level right and left audio signals from a component to a preamplifier or receiver. Line audio connections use the same RCA jacks as used by composite video connections.

Most of your audio connections will be via line audio inputs.

There's nothing at all wrong with using line audio connections. Note, however, that the signals transmitted via line audio are analog; if you have a digital source (such as a DVD player) you may want to use the digital audio connection, which transfers a digital signal from one component to another.

5.1 Audio

If you have a DVD player with a built-in Dolby Digital decoder, you'll find a set of RCA jacks labeled "5.1 audio." These analog connections feed the output from the

Dolby Digital decoder to similar inputs on the back of Dolby Digital-ready receivers—that is, receivers that can switch and amplify the 5.1 signals, but don't include built-in decoders of their own.

Use the 5.1 audio connection to run signals from an outboard Dolby Digital decoder to a Dolby Digital-ready receiver.

You connect the 5.1 audio connections using standard audio cables equipped with RCA jacks. Of course, if your receiver has its own Dolby Digital decoders, you can ignore these jacks completely.

Digital Audio

A better way to connect digital components—such as DVD players or high-end CD players—is through the digital audio connection. This connection feeds the entire digital bitstream from one component to another, and is especially useful for making mirror-image MiniDisc or CD-R recordings from digital sources.

There are two types of digital connections available—coax and optical. The digital coax connection uses the same 75-ohm coaxial cable as used to connect your antenna or cable to your TV, but with an RCA-type connector; the optical digital connection uses a fiber-optic cable. Under most conditions both coax and optical perform equally well. Under some rare circumstances, however, long coax cables can pick up RF interference; this is not a problem with the more expensive optical cables.

Digital audio connections deliver the digital bitstream from digital audio components (such as DVD players); some components offer the choice of either optical or coax connections.

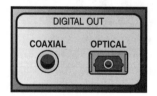

Input/Output

If you're still not sure what connections to use, you're not alone. Let's look at all the available connections, in order of quality and preference.

For connecting video, here are the different types of connections, in descending order of quality:

1. RGB video
2. Component video
3. S-Video
4. Composite video
5. RF

For connecting audio, here are the different types of connections, in descending order of quality:

1. Digital (optical)
2. Digital (coax)
3. Line audio

Speaker Connections

When everything else is hooked up, it's time to connect your speakers to your receiver.

There are a number of different types of connections used on both the receiver and the speaker end of things. You could run into plain screws or terminal posts (which require bare ends or spades on your speaker wire), various types of plugs and jacks, or so-called "banana" connectors (my personal favorite speaker connectors!). Just make sure you use a high-grade speaker wire—and the lower the gauge the better! (For example, 10 gauge wire is better than 16 gauge.)

Overload!

Make sure that your speakers are all hooked up in phase by connecting the positive (+) and negative (–) leads on your speaker wire the same way at both ends (at the receiver and at the speaker). If you find that your speakers are out of phase, you can bring them back in phase by reversing the leads for one of the speakers (it doesn't matter which one).

Subwoofer Connections

After your front and surround speakers are connected, the only thing left is your subwoofer. Subwoofers are powered speakers, which means that they include their own built-in amplifiers. As such, the proper way to connect a subwoofer is with the dedicated subwoofer line audio output on your receiver. (All Dolby Digital 5.1 receivers have a separate subwoofer output—it's the ".1" in the 5.1.)

If your receiver doesn't have a separate subwoofer output, you can still hook up your subwoofer to operate "passively" with your other speakers. Assuming that your subwoofer is equipped with speaker-level inputs (most are), connect your receiver's regular speaker outputs directly to the subwoofer—and then out from the subwoofer to your regular speakers. Your subwoofer's built-in crossover will keep the low bass frequencies for its own use, and route the midrange and high frequencies on to your right and left speakers.

When you don't have a separate subwoofer output, connect the subwoofer in between your other speakers.

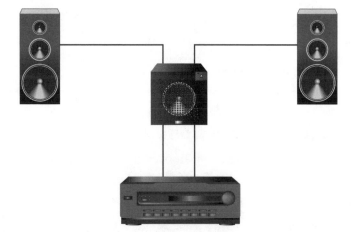

A Selection of Connections: The Best Ways to Hook Up Your Home Theater Components

Now that we have all that connection coverage out of the way, let's get down to the nitty-gritty of hooking up your home theater system.

The following sections will show some general connection diagrams for the most typical types of systems. Note, however, that every system is different; the types of components you have and their connection capabilities will determine the precise setup you use.

Know, however, that the easiest and best setups come when you have an audio/video receiver at the center of your home theater universe. The setups get even easier if your a/v receiver has more than enough video inputs for the number of video sources in your system—and when the receiver uses S-Video, component video, and digital audio connections.

The Preferred Connection: Feed Your Receiver

The best home theater systems feed every audio and video source into a single audio/video receiver, which then feeds its output direct to your television and your speakers. You can then use your a/v receiver as a sophisticated switching device; whichever input you select on your receiver goes directly to your TV and speakers.

The following diagram shows how a receiver-centered system is connected, and the following table details the recommended connections for each component.

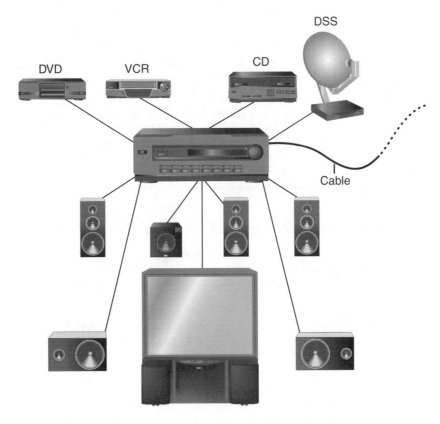

A typical home theater setup—everything feeds into the a/v receiver.

Recommended Component Connections for a Receiver-Centered System

Component	Recommended Connections
DVD player	Component video out on player to component video in on receiver (alternately, use S-Video output and input jacks); digital audio out on player to digital audio in on receiver (alternately use right and left line audio output and input jacks)
Digital satellite receiver	S-Video out on satellite receiver to S-Video in on a/v receiver; left and right line audio out on satellite receiver to left and right line audio in on a/v receiver (alternately, use digital output and input jacks, if available)
VCR	Composite video out on VCR to composite video in on receiver; left and right line audio out on VCR to left and right line audio in on receiver
CD player	Digital out from CD to digital in on receiver (if digital isn't available, use left and right line audio connections)
Antenna or cable	Connect to RF input on receiver (alternately connect directly to RF input on TV)
Television	Connect *all* of the following: RF out on receiver to RF in on TV, component video out on receiver to component video in on TV, S-Video out on receiver to S-Video in on TV, composite video out on receiver to composite video in on TV, and left and right line audio out on receiver to left and right line audio in on TV

The Number-Two Choice: Let Your TV Do the Switching

If you don't have an audio/video receiver, then you have to run all your components to your TV. Most higher-end televisions will have multiple audio and video inputs, so you should be able to switch between antenna/cable and a small handful of other video sources without a lot of hassle.

The following figure shows how a TV-centered system is connected, and the following table details the recommended connections for each component.

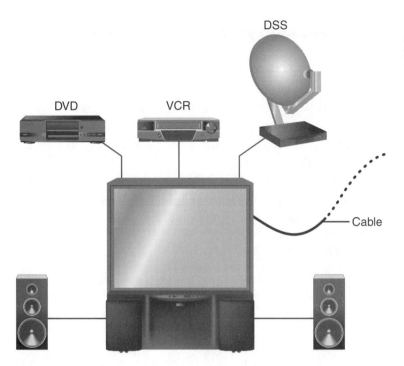

An installation that uses the TV to switch between video sources.

Recommended Component Connections for a TV-Centered System

Component	Recommended Connections
Antenna or cable	Connect to RF input on TV
Digital satellite receiver	S-Video out on satellite receiver to S-Video in on TV (alternately, use composite video jacks); left and right line audio out on satellite receiver to left and right line audio in on TV (alternately, use digital output and input jacks, if available)
DVD player	Component video out on player to component video in on TV (alternately, use S-Video or composite video connections); left and right line audio out from player to left and right audio in on TV
VCR	Composite video out on VCR to composite video in on TV (alternately use RF connections); left and right line audio out on VCR to left and right line audio in on TV

The Fallback Connection: Everything in a Series

What do you do when you just don't have enough input jacks on either your TV or your a/v receiver to connect all your components? If this is the case in your home theater system, you can either dump some components (no way!), buy an expensive switching device, or start chaining some of your components together.

When you chain components together, the components in the middle (when not turned on themselves) pass through the signals from the component previous in the chain. Not all components can (or should) be chained; the best candidates for screening are those components that can use RF inputs and outputs.

For example, a very common connection chains your antenna/cable connection through your VCR to your TV, all using RF connections. When your VCR is turned off, your TV receives the antenna/cable signal as passed through the VCR; when the VCR is turned on and playing a tape, your TV receives the VCR signal, not the antenna/cable signal.

Input/Output

When choosing cables and speaker wires, you're faced with a large number of options. Should you go with an expensive cable, or one of the cheaper cables?

In general, the better cables—those with gold connectors and extra insulation or shielding—will perform slightly better than the cheaper cables, especially with the more sophisticated types of connections, such as S-Video, component video, and digital audio. However, the difference is minimal and won't be noticed by a lot of users.

When it comes to speaker wire, there is a noticeable difference between the thin "zip cord" wire and the heavier-gauge wire sold by Monster Cable and others. However, you can definitely go overboard when it comes to this heavier wire; while some "golden-eared" audiophiles claim to hear sonic differences with ultra high-end wire, most listeners don't hear a thing.

The more productive element to consider is the length of your cables and wires. Too-long cable and wire runs increase the possibility of signal leakage and degradation, as well as interference from outside sources. Keep your cables and wires as short as possible—leave just enough extra to comfortably pull out your components to access the rear panels. Do *not* cut your cables and wires several feet longer than necessary, and then leave the excess wadded up or rolled up behind your system!

Other chaining connections can include

➤ Digital satellite receiver to VCR to TV.

➤ Antenna/cable to digital satellite receiver to VCR to TV.

➤ Antenna/cable to digital satellite receiver to TV.

➤ Antenna/cable to personal video recorder to TV.

➤ Digital satellite receiver to personal video recorder to TV.

➤ Antenna/cable to digital satellite receiver to personal video recorder to TV.

The following figure shows some of this chaining.

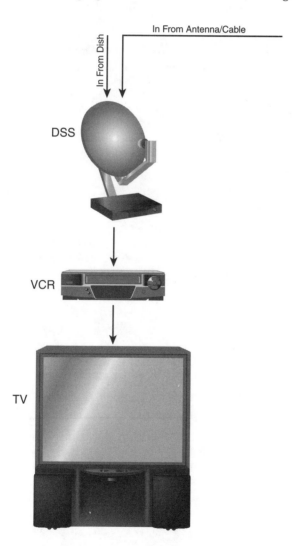

When you don't have enough inputs, connect everything in a series.

Instead of running your antenna or cable signal through a series of components (through your VCR to your TV, for example), use a signal splitter to split the signal and run separate feeds to each component. This should reduce signal loss and eliminate the need to use the TV/VCR switches on your equipment.

The Least You Need to Know

➤ The traditional RF connection combines all video and audio signals, and delivers the lowest-quality picture.

➤ Composite video separates the video signals from the audio, and delivers a better picture than RF.

➤ S-Video separates the luminance (brightness) from the chrominance (color) in the video signal, and delivers an even sharper picture than composite video.

➤ Component video separates the color information into red and blue components, and delivers a slightly more accurate picture than S-Video.

➤ RGB video, while not widely used, separates the color information into three components (red, blue, and green) and thus theoretically delivers the best possible picture.

➤ When connecting the components in your system, use the highest-level connections available; for example, if you have a choice between composite video and S-Video, use the S-Video jacks.

➤ The recommended way to connect all the components in your system is to run everything through your audio/video receiver and then connect your receiver to your TV and speakers; you can then use your receiver to switch between all available inputs.

Chapter 22

Take Charge: Controlling Your System

In This Chapter

➤ How to reduce the clutter of remote controls taking up space on your coffee table

➤ The many different types of remote controls—from standard remotes to custom remote control systems

➤ The differences between universal, learning, and programmable remotes

➤ Which type of remote control is best for your needs

Controlling a home theater system is only slightly less complex than piloting the space shuttle. You use one remote to turn on your a/v receiver and switch to a specific input, another remote to turn on your TV and switch to the appropriate input, then yet another remote to turn on and operate your DVD player. If you want to switch to your VCR, one more remote control enters the picture. It's a pain.

It's also pretty much impossible to explain to any visitors you might have—although I've found young children tend to pick it up pretty easily. For everybody else, however, just try explaining that these buttons on this remote adjust the volume, while those buttons on that other remote change the channel. It's too confusing!

There are solutions to this remote control conundrum—which is what this chapter is all about!

Point and Click: Understanding the Different Types of Remotes

Here's your choice: You can live with all the different remotes that came with each of your system's components, or you can buy a new remote that can control all or some of your system all by itself. Sound like an easy choice? Think again; each option comes with its own unique benefits and disadvantages.

Input/Output

One common accessory these days is the **infrared blaster.** This is a small device that attaches to the front of one component and the back of another, and sends infrared remote control signals from the second unit to control the operation of the first.

Infrared blasters are used when one component needs to control another. For example, if you want your digital satellite receiver to control your VCR (to tape a program when you're away), you attach the satellite receiver's infrared blaster to the front of your VCR. The receiver then sends the proper remote control signals to turn on the VCR and initiate recording, just as if you were sending the signals from a standard remote control.

The problem comes when you have multiple components wanting to control the same component. For example, if your cable system uses a cable box, you might end up with three different infrared blasters hanging over the front of the cable box—one each from your VCR, WebTV box, and personal video recorder. In cases like this, your only alternative is to live with the clutter; there's no way to combine blasters from different components.

Deciding which remote to use is further complicated by the fact that there are no fewer than *six* different types of remote control to choose from! In increasing order of complexity (and control—and price!), here's what's available:

➤ **Standard** remote controls are the units that come with each component

➤ **Single-brand** remote controls are units that come standard with one component but also control other components by the same manufacturer

➤ **Universal** remote controls come preprogrammed with operating codes for lots of different components from different manufacturers

➤ **Learning** remotes "dock" with your existing remotes and "learn" their operating codes

➤ **Programmable** remotes include some combination or preprogrammed codes and learning capabilities, but then let you program in your own multiple-step functions (via automated *macros*) and configure your own remote control interface on a built-in LCD screen

➤ **Custom** remote control systems are expensive systems that can be programmed to control your entire home theater system (or, in some cases, your home automation system) via a custom controller interface; these systems are typically sold and programmed by custom installation specialists

Know that some remotes blend features from these different general types. For example, it's not unusual to find learning remotes that include universal codes, or programmable remotes that include both universal and learning functions.

The following table compares these six different types of remotes; each type is then discussed in the following sections.

Product Specs

A **macro** is a set of instructions or operations that have been automated; the macro (and the associated operations) is typically run with the push of a single button on the remote.

Types of Remote Controls

Features/ Operations	Standard	Single-Brand	Universal	Learning	Program-mable	Custom
Operates multiple components	No	Yes	Yes	Yes	Yes	Yes
Operates multiple brands	No	No	Yes	Yes	Yes	Yes
Preprogrammed operation codes	No	Some	Yes	Some	Yes	Yes
"Learns" from other remotes	No	No	No	Yes	No	No
Correct source labeling	N/A	Yes	No	No	Yes	Yes
Programmable macros	No	No	No	Some	Yes	Yes
One-touch system turn-on	No	No	No	No	Some	Yes
Automated input/mode selection	No	No	No	No	Some	Yes
Programmable touchscreen	No	No	No	Some	Yes	Some
Typical price	Included	Included	$25	$25	$250	$1,000+

Power Up

Before you decide to replace a standard remote with a universal or learning remote, take a closer look at the remote control itself—and its instruction manual. It's quite possible that your old remote can also operate other components, either through universal codes or learning capabilities. (This is even more likely if the remote control came with your high-end TV or a/v receiver.) You may not need to buy a new remote after all!

Gotta Use 'Em All: Standard Remotes

Virtually every component you buy for your home theater system comes with its own standard remote. This remote is custom-built for your component; it includes just the right buttons to operate all the component's key functions.

The advantage of using a standard remote is that it is perfectly suited to operate that one component. You'll never find another remote—not even the expensive programmable and custom types—that adequately duplicate the operation of a good standard remote. (The best example of this is the jog dial found on some DVD, CD, laserdisc, and VCR remotes; you can't duplicate a dial with a pushbutton, no matter how hard you try!)

The disadvantage of using standard remotes is that they start piling up. In a typical home theater system, you'll end up with a half-dozen or more standard remotes, which not only clutters the coffee table (where do you put the coffee?) but requires you to juggle multiple remotes to perform the simplest operations.

Rewarding Brand-Loyal Consumers: Multiple-Component, Single-Brand Remotes

Some manufacturers preprogram their remote controls to operate other components that they manufacture. So, if you have a Sony a/v receiver, chances are it can also operate Sony TVs, VCRs, DVD players, and CD players. Chances are it *won't* operate equipment from other manufacturers; for that you need a universal or a learning remote.

The advantage of using a single-brand remote is that if you have multiple components from the same manufacturer, you can probably eliminate some remote duplication. The disadvantage comes if all your components aren't of the same brand; your single-brand remote won't operate them.

Punch In the Codes: Universal Remotes

Universal remotes—such as the popular All-In-One units—contain preprogrammed infrared codes for most popular types and brands of equipment. All you have to do is punch in the code of the unit you want to control, and the universal remote automatically transmits the proper codes for that component. Most universal remotes contain codes for some combination of the most popular brands, the most popular components, and the most recent models.

There are several advantages to using a universal remote. First, it's easy to get the remote up and running for a particular component; just punch in a three- or four-digit code. Second, if you have relatively standard equipment, chances are this one remote is preprogrammed with the proper codes, so you can use it to control multiple components.

The disadvantage to using a universal remote is that it typically isn't programmed for older or nonstandard equipment. So, if you have a 10-year-old VCR or a high-end component only available from specialty retailers, it's likely the remote won't recognize the equipment. In addition, the buttons on universal remotes are somewhat generic—you'll probably find some functions available on a particular component *aren't* available with a universal remote.

Power Up

Most universal remotes come with a code sheet that lists *most* of the codes available for that remote. In many cases, the remote can control even more components than are listed, since new codes are being added every day. If you can't find a code for a particular component, call the remote's manufacturer for an updated code list; in some cases, you may even be able to send your unit back to the factory to be reprogrammed with additional built-in codes.

Do a Brain Dump: Learning Remotes

Learning remotes don't rely on preprogrammed codes to operate different components. Instead, a learning remote "learns" the codes directly from the component's standard remote control.

This typically works by placing the two remotes head-to-head, putting the learning remote into learning mode, pressing a button for an operation on the standard remote, and then pressing the button you want to use for that operation on the learning remote. The learning remote learns that operation, then you move to the next operation.

This is a time-consuming process, but it lets you add functions from almost any remote to your learning remote. If you have an older or nonstandard component, this may be your only option in terms of consolidating remotes.

The advantage of a learning remote is its ability to replace virtually any remote you have. The disadvantage is that it takes a lot of time to transfer all the operations from one remote to another; it's also possible that if you try to learn too many commands, you'll exceed the learning remote's built-in memory.

Teach a New Dog Old Tricks: Programmable Remotes

Taking learning remotes a step further are remote controls that include an LCD screen in place of the standard complement of buttons. Not only can you program this type of remote with the commands from another remote (either via universal codes or learning functionality), you can also program a custom interface on the LCD screen for each component operated by that remote.

Programmable remotes also let you record your own macros to automate multistep operations. Say you normally turn on your receiver, turn on your TV, turn on your DVD player, switch the receiver to DVD input, and then press Play on the DVD to start playing a movie. With a programmable remote, you can automate all those steps into a single button.

These types of remotes cost a bit more than universal or learning remotes—typically in the $200–$400 range. Within that range, though, you have a number of choices.

Product Specs

A remote control with **two-way operation** not only sends signals to a component, but also receives signals from the component. For example, a two-way remote might send a signal to play a CD in your CD player, but then receive a signal from the player about the CD currently being played; the remote control's LCD screen might then display the name of the CD and its artist. Two-way operation can be found on any type of remote, from standard to custom, but needs an LCD screen on the remote to display the two-way information.

For example, the popular Sony AV-2100 is a learning remote with two-way operation that displays a set of "buttons" for various operations on its LCD screen. You can program any button for any specific operation, as well as assign a specific label to any button. It also features *two-way operation*, in that it receives feedback of various sorts from specific components.

Even more advanced than the Sony is the Philips Pronto, shown in the figure on the next page. In terms of size and form factor, the Pronto resembles nothing else so much as the Palm Pilot PDA; it features a powerful graphical operating system that lets you customize one or more individual screens for each component in your system. You can add, delete, and arrange panels, buttons, and devices on the LCD screen; you can also change fonts and import graphics. For example, you could create a specific page on the Pronto dedicated to your favorite TV channels, using the network logos for identification.

The most advanced programming operations are accomplished when you connect the Pronto unit to a personal computer and the Internet. Using the Windows-based ProntoEdit software, you can create your own graphical screens, trade screens with other users, and download updates to the Pronto hardware itself from the Philips Web site.

Program each screen of the Pronto for each of your components.

(Courtesy of Philips Consumer Electronics Company)

Similar in concept to the Pronto is the Take Control by Harman/Kardon, developed in association with Microsoft. You can program the Take Control via universal codes, learning functionality, or via your Windows-based computer. When you use the Take Control software and Web site, the unit's touchscreen buttons can be arranged, reprogrammed, and renamed to reflect your own personal preferences.

The advantage of a programmable remote is that you can totally customize it not only for your particular equipment, but also for your own personal way of using it. The disadvantage is that these units are expensive and difficult to program; it's easy to spend more time fiddling with your custom interface than you actually spend using the remote itself!

Power Up

An entire subculture has developed among hard-core Pronto users. One of the best places to find codes, macros, graphics, and other information for the Pronto is the Remote Central Web site, at www.remotecentral.com. Remote Central is also a good source in general for information about advanced remote controls—check it out!

Total Control: Custom Remote Control Systems

The most advanced remote controls are complete systems, typically set up and configured by a professional installer, that are programmed for your specific home theater system. These systems go beyond simple sending of infrared signals to total control of all your system components.

A custom remote system typically consists of two main parts: the system controller and the control processor. The system controller is the remote control unit, consisting of a set of buttons or a personalized touchscreen; this device can be either wired or wireless. The control processor receives the signals from the system controller, routes them to the appropriate components, and monitors feedback from the components regarding their current operating status; all your components are connected to the processor, and thus controlled through the processor.

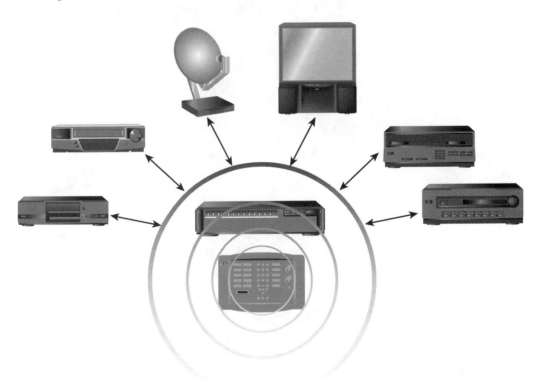

Custom remote control systems send all signals from the system controller to the control processor—and then to your individual components.

One of the more popular—and lowest-priced—custom remote control systems is the IntelliControl system from Niles Audio, shown in the following figure. The IntelliControl system controller is one of the simplest and easiest-to-use units available. Your custom installer will program the individual buttons on the controller to correspond to specific operations for each of your system's components. For example, the TV button might be programmed to turn on your projection television, switch to the broadcast tuner, then turn on your a/v receiver and switch to the TV input.

The Niles IntelliControl system; you press a button on the remote, and the Main System Unit sends the appropriate codes to specific components in your system.

(Courtesy of Niles Audio Corporation)

The IntelliControl control processor (what Niles calls the Main System Unit) sits behind the scenes and monitors each component's operating status, via video and 12-volt "synching" connections. After receiving a command from the remote control unit, it then sends the appropriate series of commands to the appropriate components.

At a base price of $1,200 (before programming charges), the IntelliControl system is within the reach of many home theater enthusiasts—although you can increase the price by adding additional controllers and rooms (or "zones") to the system. Other manufacturers offering systems in this price range include Elan and Lexicon.

Product Specs

Infrared remotes operate via a beam of infrared light; the component must be in line of sight with the remote unit in order to receive the signals. **RF (radio frequency) remotes** operate via radio waves, and can transmit through walls and cabinet doors.

Input/Output

Only a custom remote controller can perfectly control all your components. This is because most other remotes dramatically simplify the operation of your core components.

The best example of this is the simple on and off operation. Most components have one internal code to turn the unit on, and a separate code to turn the unit off. However, the typical infrared code is a simple "toggle" code; this single code is used to turn the unit both on and off. Think about it; the remote control has an "On/Off" button, not separate "On" and "Off" buttons. Press the On/Off button once and you turn the unit on; press it again and the unit turns off.

However, most complex operations require components to be in a certain state before the operation can be executed. Take the example of turning on a TV and switching to an auxiliary input. The remote sends one code to turn the TV on, and a second to switch input modes. This requires the TV to be in the "off" mode before the operation can be completed. What happens, though, if the TV *is on* when you execute this operation? A normal remote sends the single "on/off" code, which turns the TV *off*—and then tries to switch inputs!

The only way around this type of situation is to access the component's separate internal on and off codes, which most remote controls typically don't do—they simply mimic the transmission codes from the components standard remote—and to monitor the status of the component, accordingly. To properly perform this type of operation, you have to move to one of the custom controller systems that use a separate control processor unit to access your components' internal codes and monitor their operating modes. This capability is one of the best reasons to bite the bullet and spend the bucks on a custom control system.

Move up to the $3,000 range and you get into high-end systems capable of controlling not just your home theater system, but the automation of your entire house. These systems—from Crestron, AMX, and others—require sophisticated programming to operate virtually any electronic device in your house, from anywhere in your house. Some high-end installations place a full-color touchscreen in every room (typically mounted in the wall); these touchscreens can be used to control the system, or to monitor security cameras or the entertainment being shown on the main home theater screen! You can even have several different remote controls in the same room—you might have a complex touchscreen for whole-house control, and a simple six-button remote that your babysitter can use. (See Chapter 24, "Home Beautiful: Installing a Custom System," for more information about whole-house systems.)

The advantage of a custom remote system is the capability of controlling any combination of devices anywhere in your house. The disadvantage, of course, is cost and effort—you'll definitely need the services of a professional installer to get one of these puppies up and running!

Get Control of Your Remotes: Choosing the Right Remote for Your System

Okay, now you're smarter about the different types of remote control units. Which type (or types) of remote control(s) should you select for your home theater system? Here are some guidelines to follow:

➤ If you don't want to lose any functionality of your components, stick with the standard remotes—and get used to juggling a half-dozen hand units!

➤ If all your components come from the same manufacturer, use a single-brand remote to eliminate some of the duplicate remotes.

➤ If you want to eliminate some of your remote control clutter and have relatively new and relatively standard components, check out one of the many popular universal remote controls.

➤ If you want to eliminate some of your remote control clutter and you have older or less common components, try a learning remote.

➤ If you want to totally personalize your remote for the components in your system—and don't mind spending the time to do the programming yourself—check out the Philips Pronto or other programmable remotes.

➤ If you have a sophisticated system and want a totally customized control interface, contact your custom installation specialist for a custom remote control system.

The Least You Need to Know

➤ Standard remotes come with each of your components, but don't operate any other components.

➤ Single-brand remotes operate multiple components from the same manufacturer.

➤ Universal remotes come preprogrammed with operating codes for most popular components; you can program a universal remote to operate two to four different components by punching in the codes for those components.

➤ Learning remotes "learn" commands directly from other remote control units; each command has to be learned separately.

➤ Programmable remotes enable you to program your own custom interface—and multistep macros—into their LCD screens.

➤ Custom remote control systems require professional installation and programming, but are capable of controlling your entire system—including, in some cases, a home automation system—via a totally customized control interface.

Chapter 23

What to Do When It Doesn't Work: Troubleshooting System Problems

---

In This Chapter

➤ How to troubleshoot problems in your home theater system

➤ What causes most home theater problems (hint: look in the mirror!)

➤ What to look for if your power is weak, your sound is silent, or your picture isn't perfect

---

Once you have your home theater system hooked up and in place, it's time to settle back and watch a movie. That's if, of course, everything works properly!

If something doesn't work right in your new home theater system, there's no reason to panic. Most difficulties are caused by something you did wrong—in particular, by something that isn't hooked up or connected properly. The good news is that this kind of problem is easy to fix, particularly if you follow the troubleshooting tips presented in this chapter!

Finding your problem is all about troubleshooting, by the way—and all troubleshooting is about detective work. You have to perform a series of tests that track down where the problem is originating, which can be problematic when you have three or more components interacting for any given operation in your home theater system. Diligent detective work, however, can pay off big time; once you've isolated the problem, you'll soon discover whether you can fix it yourself, or need to call in a pro!

Power Up

This may be a little self-serving (and not completely relevant), but if you ever encounter problems with your personal computer, you might want to check out another book I've written called *The Complete Idiot's Guide to Fixing Your @#$! PC*. It's all about troubleshooting PC problems—and can help you out of a jam if your computer is causing you fits!

Overload!

Whatever you do, *don't* open up the equipment's case! Not only will popping the lid void your warranty, it can also get you in some pretty deep doo-doo. Many components run quite a bit of current through their circuits, and you can get a nasty shock if you touch the wrong part—especially when you're dealing with televisions, receivers, and power amplifiers!

He's Dead, Jim: Pondering Power Problems

You turn on a component, and nothing happens—no sound, no picture, no lights, no nothing. What do you do now?

The answer to this question depends on exactly what is dead—is it your entire system, or just a single component? While the likely cause is similar (something's either not plugged in or has blown a fuse), you'll need to troubleshoot each separately.

Your Entire System Is Dead

If nothing works—not your TV, not your receiver, not your VCR or DVD player—then it's likely that your problem is bigger than any single component.

Are all your components plugged into the same wall receptacle? Make sure that receptacle is turned on (translation: flip the wall switch!) and has power. Now head out to your garage and check the circuit breaker or fuse for that wall socket; you may have plugged in so much stuff that you blew a fuse!

Are all your components plugged into the same power strip or surge suppressor? If so, check the strip or suppressor to see if it's plugged in and turned on. You might try bypassing the power strip and plugging one of your components directly into the wall receptacle; if this works, then you may have a bad power strip. (It happens.)

In some systems, multiple components are plugged into a single component. For example, you may have the power cords of your DVD player and CD player plugged directly into the back of your a/v receiver, so that they turn on and off automatically when you power your receiver up or down. If this is the case, any power problems with your receiver will also cause your other components not to power up. Try bypassing the receiver and plugging your components directly into the wall receptacle; if they now work—and your receiver is still dead—then you have a receiver problem.

A Specific Component Is Dead

The first thing to check when everything else in your system works is the power connection for that specific component. Is it plugged in? To a live receptacle? To a good power strip? Try replugging the unit into a different receptacle; you may have picked a bad receptacle, or one that wasn't turned on.

Is the power cable for this component plugged into the back of another component? This sort of component power switching is normal, but can cause problems if (1) the source component—typically a receiver—is either dead or has a bad power output, or (2) the source component isn't operated properly. That is, you won't get power from a DVD player hooked into a receiver if the receiver isn't turned on (or, in some cases, switched to DVD input)!

If you're trying to turn on the component using your remote control, try turning the unit on direct from the front panel instead. You could have a bad remote, or the remote could be accidentally set for a different type of component, or (if you have a learning or custom remote), your preprogrammed codes might not be working properly.

If you've eliminated all these causes, you probably have a problem with the equipment itself. If there's a fuse or circuit breaker on the back of the unit, try replacing the fuse or resetting the circuit breaker; sometimes brief power surges can cause these protective devices to blow. If this doesn't solve your problem, it's time to call an authorized service center.

Your Remote Control Doesn't Work

If your remote control doesn't operate any of the components in your system, there are a few things to check. First, make sure the remote has batteries installed, and that the batteries are fully charged. (When in doubt, just stick in a new set of AAs, okay?) Also, make sure that the batteries are installed properly; don't mix up your negative and positive terminals!

Next, make sure that the infrared signal from your remote is actually reaching your components. If your components are behind a closed door—or even a glass door—the infrared light generated by the remote might not be received properly. Also, check the other light sources in your room; I've had very bright sunlight at just the right angle interfere with the infrared from my remote.

Finally, make sure your remote is switched and programmed properly for your components. If you have a learning remote, make sure it isn't accidentally switched to "learn" mode. If you have a universal remote, make sure someone (read: your kids!) hasn't accidentally punched in the wrong codes.

I Can't Hear You: Solving Sound Problems

You can have audio problems with any one of your components; even video sources have sound problems! When you're having trouble with the sound from any part of your system, consult these troubleshooting tips.

Your System Has Power, But No Sound

The first question to ask is are you *sure* your entire system has no sound? Have you tried a different component—maybe it's just your DVD player that is silent, and your TV has plenty of sound. If you can isolate the problem to a particular component, all the better.

If nothing in your system produces audio, check some obvious things. Is your receiver turned on? Is it muted? (There's no sound when the mute button is pushed, you know.)

Now you need to check whether the problem is in your receiver or in your speakers. Plug a pair of headphones into your receiver; if they work, chances are it's somewhere in the speaker hookup. If you get no sound through your headphones, either, then you probably need to have your receiver looked at.

One Speaker or Channel Is Dead

The biggest cause of "no sound in one channel" problems is a bad speaker hookup. Check the speaker connections at both ends for the bad channel—at your receiver and at each speaker. Then check the connection in between, since a frayed or broken wire can cut out all sound to that speaker.

If the speaker connections appear good, then try switching speakers—hook your left speaker to the right channel of your receiver, and vice versa. If the same speaker stays dead, you have a speaker problem; if the dead channel switches sides, you have a receiver problem.

This all assumes, of course, that that channel is dead for all video and audio sources. If it's only one source with a missing channel, then check the audio cables between that component and your receiver. Make sure that right out is connected to right in, and that left out is connected to left in. If everything looks okay, try connecting that component to a different input on your receiver; your receiver could have a bad input jack. Then try running a new cable in between the component and the receiver; the cable itself could be bad. You can also try connecting a different component to that set of inputs on your receiver; if another component works okay, then the problem is in your original component.

If that particular component keeps generating a bad channel, then you have a problem with the component, and should have it looked at by a qualified technician.

A Specific Component Has Power, But No Sound

You turn on your CD player, press Play, see the little minute counter start counting, but hear nothing. You must have a problem in your CD player, right?

Perhaps, but not necessarily. First, you should check the obvious—make sure your receiver is turned on, not muted, and switched to the input for that component. Next, check to see if other components have sound; if not, you have a bigger problem.

Now it's time to check the connections between this component and your receiver. Make sure your cable is running from the right and left audio *out* jacks on your component to the audio *in* jacks on your receiver. (Also make sure the cable is running to the jacks you *think* they're running to; you won't get sound from your "CD" selection if you actually have your CD hooked up to your "DVD" inputs!) Make sure the cable is well connected and intact from end to end; you probably should also try replacing the cable, in case there's a loose connection somewhere in the middle.

If you have another receiver or amplifier sitting around the house, try connecting the component to that device. If it suddenly starts to work, you know the problem is somewhere in your old cabling or in your receiver. If the component still is missing one or more channels of sound, then the problem is in the component—which should be examined by a competent technician.

You Have a Buzz in Your Audio

When you have a buzz or a hum in your sound, chances are you have a grounding problem. This type of problem can be extremely difficult to track down, but here are a few things to try:

➤ Try reversing your receiver's power plug in the power receptacle. Then try reversing the plugs for all the other components in your system. (Not all plugs can be reversed, since one prong of the plug is often larger than the other, to prevent improper grounding.)

➤ If one or more of your components uses a three-prong power plug, make sure that you haven't defeated the third prong (which is used for grounding) by clipping it off or plugging it into a so-called three-prong adapter (which lets you plug a three-prong plug into a two-prong jack).

➤ Try plugging your components into a power strip or surge suppressor, instead of directly into a wall receptacle.

➤ If your receiver (or any of your components) has a grounding screw or plug on the back panel, run a wire from this screw to the center screw in your wall receptacle. This will ground your unit.

➤ Make sure all the cables leading into your receiver are firmly connected; also make sure no two cables are touching each other. (The same goes for the wires leading to your speakers.)

213

➤ Try shifting one or more components from one input jack to another on the back of your receiver.

What's particularly vexing about grounding problems is that a grounding problem with one component can actually produce a hum in a totally different component! You'll have to make sure that your entire system is connected and grounded properly to track down this problem!

Overload!

Turntables operate at a different impedance level than do any other components in your system, and the turntable input jacks on the back of your receiver are calibrated for that different impedance. If you plug another component into the turntable input, you could end up with all manner of buzz and hum problems—so don't do it!

Your Sound Is Bad (Tinny, No Bass, No Treble, Etc.)

When the sound is there but not quite right, the first things to check are your bass and treble controls. (If you're not sure how to adjust these controls, just center them—that's a relatively "flat" setting that should sound okay.) If your system includes a graphic equalizer (and few do, these days), check the settings there, as well. (Again, flat is good.)

The next things to check are your speakers. If you've suddenly lost bass, check to see if your subwoofer is operating properly. (Because a subwoofer is self-powered— it contains its own built-in power amplifier—that built-in amplifier can go bad, knocking out the entire speaker. I know; it happened to me!) If the bad sound can be isolated to a single channel, it's possible that speaker's woofer or tweeter might be blown. To check this, simply swap speakers; if the bad sound follows the speaker to a different channel, you have a speaker problem.

It's also possible that a poorly chosen surround-sound setting can create imperfect sound. Turning on the Dolby Pro Logic decoder for a program that wasn't recorded in Dolby Surround—like an old movie or local program recorded in mono—can actually result in rolled-off highs and a lack of crispness. For that matter, using a surround-sound mode on normal stereo audio programming can produce undesirable effects. Miller's Rule is simple—if you have a mono or stereo source, turn off the surround sound (including any simulated DSP modes)!

A Specific CD Won't Play in Your DVD Player

If your DVD player won't play a specific audio CD, chances are that CD is actually a CD-R or CD-RW—that is, a recordable or rewritable compact disc. DVD players won't play CDs you've recorded yourself, so this is probably your problem.

In addition, some early or lower-end DVD players may have problems playing some very old CDs. (It isn't the age of the CD that's important, it's more when it was pressed—and the technology used at the time.) If you have a lot of problems like this, consider investing in a dedicated CD player—which should play all these different types of CDs without any problems!

A Specific CD Skips or Won't Play

If you have a normal CD that skips or won't play in your CD player, then you probably have a defective or damaged disc. Check the disc for scratches or blemishes; you should even try cleaning the surface of the disc with a soft towel or CD cleaning kit. (The playing surface of the disc is the bottom side, by the way, opposite the label.) If the disc still won't play, you should probably throw it out. If you run into a lot of discs with the same problem, consider taking your CD player in for maintenance; the laser assembly might be dirty, out of alignment, or damaged.

An Audiocassette You Recorded Plays Back with Poor Sound

The most common cause of this problem is trying to play back a cassette recorded with one type of Dolby noise reduction on a deck with different noise reduction. For example, playing a Dolby C tape on a Dolby B deck will result in an overly bright and harsh sound; playing back a tape not recorded with noise reduction on a deck with Dolby noise reduction enabled will result in an overly flat and dull sound.

If you're sure the noise reduction matches between recording and playback, then you may be using a tape with a bias formulation that doesn't match your playback deck. For example, playing a metal bias tape on a deck that can't handle metal bias will result in overly bright sound.

It's also possible that the tape is old or worn. Old tapes tend to lose their highs, and sometimes are prone to excessive wow and flutter. This is definitely the problem if the tape sounds slow or warbly. (Of course, if all your tapes sound this way, then it's time to get your deck serviced—it probably has an old or worn belt or drive assembly.)

There's No Sound Coming from Your Rear Speakers

Just because you have a surround-sound system is no guarantee that you'll always hear sound from your rear speakers. In fact, your surround speakers will be the least-used components of your entire home theater system!

Many program sources aren't recorded in surround sound—and if there's no surround there, there's nothing to hear from the rear. Even if you're listening to a surround-sound movie or television show, the surround channels are very seldom constantly in use; quiet or simple parts of the movie might use the front channels only.

Of course, it's also possible that you forgot to turn on the surround sound on your receiver, or that the rear speakers are disconnected or bad. If you never hear sound from these speakers, these are things to check out.

Out of Sight: Verifying Video Problems

When the picture isn't right on your video display device, it's either some sort of system problem or you forgot to put on your eyeglasses. Assuming your prescription is up-to-date and your lenses aren't fogged, the following sections show you how to troubleshoot problems with the video part of your home theater system.

There's No Picture on Your TV

First off: Is your TV plugged in and turned on? Does it have sound—just no picture? If everything appears to be working properly, check to see if the no-picture condition exists with every video source. If your cable has a picture and your DVD player doesn't, your problem is with your DVD player or its connections; if your DVD works but your cable doesn't, it's time to call your cable guy.

Next thing to check is the connection between your audio/video receiver and your TV. If you're using your a/v receiver to switch video sources (and you probably are), then a bad or improper connection between your receiver (or a problem with your receiver, period) can cause a no-picture problem.

While you're at it, just confirm that your receiver is turned on and working properly; if you run video through your receiver, your TV won't receive any signals when the receiver is turned off. Also check the types of connections you're using; since you can't upconvert signals to a higher-resolution video source, don't expect to receive broadcast or cable signals if you've only run an S-Video connection from your receiver. (See Chapter 21, "Plug It In: Which Cable Goes Where," for more details on which types of connections flow through and which don't.)

It also doesn't hurt to check your set's brightness and contrast controls. If the brightness is turned all the way down, you'll see a very dark (read: totally absent!) picture.

If you rule out source and adjustment problems, then you probably have problems with your television. Call a repairman and find out what's really going on!

There's No Picture from a Specific Component

If a specific component is turned on and playing but delivers no picture, the first thing to check are the connections. If the component is fed through your a/v receiver, try connecting it direct to your TV; if it works this way, you either have a bad connection to or from the receiver, or have something switched wrong on the receiver end. Remember that you can't upconvert signals through a receiver; for example, if you connect your component to the receiver via composite video, that signal won't feed to your TV via S-Video. The best solution to this sort of problem is to connect every type of output from your receiver to your TV—RF, composite video, S-Video, and (if both your receiver and TV support it) component video.

One other thing to try is a different type of connection. If you're trying to connect your component via component video (and it doesn't work), try S-Video; if that doesn't work, try composite video or plain RF—and make sure your TV is switched properly for the different inputs!

Finally—and assuming that your TV delivers video from other components connected to the same jacks—it's possible that you have a bad video output section in your component. If this is the case, it's time to visit the repair shop.

Your TV's Picture Is Grainy (or Blurry or Fuzzy)

A fuzzy or grainy or blurry picture can be caused by a number of factors. First, there may be a bad or loose cable somewhere in between the signal source and your TV; loose coax connections are particular suspects in this sort of problem. Second, the video source itself may be generating a bad signal; your antenna may need to be readjusted, or you may need a visit from your friendly cable guy.

It's also possible that you've tried to split a cable or antenna signal, and the signal was simply too weak to split without adverse results. Disconnect all the splitters and extra cables and run a cable directly from the cable or antenna jack to your television; if this improves things, you may need to add a signal amplifier before you return to your previous hookup.

Also realize that different sources output pictures with different resolutions. It's common to think that something is wrong with your VCR the first time you watch a tape after you've hooked up a new DVD player; since DVD picture is twice as sharp as that of a VHS tape, you'll find it difficult to go back to VHS after watching DVD!

The Picture from Your Satellite Fades or Drops Out Completely

When your satellite picture starts to fade, it's because (1) something is getting in between your dish and the satellite, or (2) your satellite isn't pointing in the right direction. If the fade occurs during a rainstorm or snowstorm, you have rain fade, where moisture in the air interrupts the satellite signal. (This can happen even if it isn't raining on you at this moment; remember, your dish doesn't point straight overhead, so any big storms south of you can also interfere with the signal.) If the fade occurs on a sunny day—and your satellite signal stays dead—then something happened to knock your dish out of alignment. Check your system's signal strength (typically accessed through the setup menu on your satellite receiver); if it's too weak to work, you'll need to get out your tools and realign your dish.

If your dish appears to be aligned correctly but you still have signal strength problems, then you could have a bad LNB. (LNBs can be knocked out by thunderstorms, or just go bad like any electronic device.) It's also possible that the cable between your dish and your receiver is bad or worn or disconnected; check all your connections and try running a new cable if you think this is the problem.

Finally, during certain times of the year, sunspots can interfere with the broadcast of satellite signals. Check with your satellite provider to see if this could be causing your current problems.

A Specific DVD Won't Play in Your DVD Player

If you try to play a DVD from another country in your DVD player or changer, it probably won't play. This is because the DVD industry encodes each disc with a specific region code, and sells DVD players within that region that can only play discs with the right code. So, if you try to play a Japanese disc in your U.S. DVD player, it won't work. (The only solution to this is to purchase a so-called "code-free" DVD player—which will be more expensive and harder to find than a normal player.)

A Specific DVD or Laserdisc Skips or Won't Play

DVDs and laserdiscs are just like CDs—if the disc is scratched or damaged, the laser in your player will have trouble reading the information on the disc, resulting in skipping and sometimes not playing at all. You can try cleaning the disc (with a soft cloth), but it's almost impossible to remove scratches or blemishes from a disc. If you run into a lot of discs with the same problem, consider taking your DVD or laserdisc player in for maintenance; the laser assembly might be dirty, out of alignment, or damaged.

A Videocassette Doesn't Play Back Properly in Your VCR

VCRs are notoriously intolerant of bad or damaged tapes. If you see a lot of noise in a tape, you could have an old or damaged cassette—or your VCR's heads might be out of alignment. This can also be the cause if you see a constant horizontal line in the picture when playing back a tape; your deck's tracking might be out of synch with the tape's tracking information—or the tape itself might be creased or otherwise damaged. You can try adjusting your VCR's tracking control manually; this may be either a knob on the front of the deck or an on-screen menu control.

If you only have problems with a few old or rental tapes, figure the problem is with your tapes, not your VCR. If you have problems on a lot of tapes—including brand-new tapes, and tapes you record yourself—then it's time to take in your VCR for head cleaning and other maintenance, or consider buying a brand-new deck.

Once you get a new deck, you could run into a different but related problem. If you recorded tapes on an old VCR that was out of alignment, those tapes (recorded out of alignment) might not play properly on your new, properly aligned deck. There's not much to do about this, unless you want to keep your old deck around just to play back your poorly recorded tapes.

The Picture on Your TV Appears Distorted Horizontally or Vertically

If you have a 16:9 ratio television—or a regular 4:3 television that's digital-ready—there's probably an adjustment somewhere in the set's menus for normal or wide-screen display. (It's also possible that this switch is on your HDTV tuner, or your satellite receiver.)

If you set this switch incorrectly, you may end up stretching or squishing some program material—imagine smooshing a wide-screen movie from the sides to fit a normal-ratio screen, or stretching a normal picture to fill the entire wide-screen area. In any case, carefully and methodically go through your instruction manual and your setup menus until you identify the setting (which is often hidden or otherwise obscure) and switch it to the correct position.

Calling for Help

On that rare occasion that you have an actual, honest-to-goodness equipment problem, you need to call in some professional help. If you purchased your system from a custom installation firm, they should be your first line of defense; call your installer and ask them to come out and evaluate the problem. In most cases, the custom installer will remove the malfunctioning component and handle the service for you; some installers will even loan you a replacement component to use until yours is fixed.

If you put together your system yourself, you're responsible for arranging service. Contact your dealer or the component's manufacturer to find out where to take the component for service; in some instances, you may need to send the component back to the manufacturer for in-warranty service. (This is a good reason to hold onto all your boxes, by the way; it's easier to ship a component in its original box than it is to try to pack it from scratch yourself!)

Before you call the manufacturer's customer support line, there are a few things you need to prepare—and a few points to keep in mind:

➤ **Do some troubleshooting beforehand.** Don't just call the line up without doing a little homework. Go through the troubleshooting tips listed in this chapter, then read the product's manual for additional advice. You don't want to waste the customer support person's time (or your own!) if all you need to do is reconnect a wire or install a new set of batteries.

➤ **Exhaust all other means.** Before you put yourself through customer support hell, check a few other places for possible information. Your dealer is a good place to start, as is the Web site of your equipment's manufacturer. Many manufacturers offer complete manuals, FAQs (lists of frequently asked questions), and other helpful stuff online.

➤ **Have your model number and serial number handy.** For the customer support person to answer your questions, he or she has to know what you're talking about. You can get both the model and serial numbers off the back or bottom of your unit, off the unit's box, or (in some cases) off your store receipt. (Actually, it's a good idea to write your serial number down on your product's manual—and then keep that manual in a convenient place!)

➤ **Be polite!** I know you're frustrated and maybe a little bit angry, but put yourself in the position of the person on the other end of the line. That poor customer support person has to listen to angry, complaining customers for eight hours a day, every day. It's not that person's fault that your equipment isn't working—or that you had to listen to "The Girl from Impanema" for 10 minutes while you waited on hold. Be patient, be polite, and be nice—you'll get better service that way!

The Least You Need to Know

➤ Most problems with your home theater system are caused by bad or improper connections; always check the power cord and cable connections before you do anything else.

➤ It's important to track down where the problem really is; is it isolated to a particular component or speaker, or does it affect your entire system?

➤ If you can fix the problem yourself, call your dealer or installer, visit the manufacturer's Web site, or call the manufacturer's customer support line—just make sure you have your model number and serial number handy!

Chapter 24

Home Beautiful: Installing a Custom System

So far in this book we've talked a lot about hardware—projection TVs and a/v receivers and DVD players and the like. Equally important to the equipment you buy, however, is where you put that equipment. Should you buy a freestanding cabinet, or work with existing furniture, or go for a built-in installation—or do something else entirely? A home theater system does have to coexist with what's already in your home, after all.

In this chapter we'll look at some of the options you have when installing your home theater system—including the option of using a custom installer to do the work for you!

Flaunt It or Hide It: Where Do You Put Your Stuff?

Life was simpler before the home theater era, when all you had to worry about was which spot in your living room was the best place for your new console TV. (Typically, you put it right in front of where the cable connection came out of the wall.) Now you have to figure out where to put an entire stack of equipment—including a much-bigger video display—and how to position everything so that your favorite chair is in the proper listening position for full-blown surround sound. Not only is it a near-engineering challenge to position your TV and all those speakers, but you'll tax all your interior design skills trying to make all your audio/video components unobtrusively fit within your room's decor.

In terms of equipment storage, you have a number of options, from relatively cheap and easy to relatively expensive and involved. Which you choose depends as much on your design aesthetic as it does your pocketbook.

Input/Output

When selecting equipment storage, consider whether you want to show off your equipment or hide it from normal view. (Not to be sexist, but I have found this typically divides along gender lines.) If you like to show off your gear, you probably don't want an installation that hides your components behind wooden doors; if you don't want the equipment to dominate your living room, you probably don't want freestanding equipment racks.

In addition, you need to consider how often you'll be accessing your equipment. If you swap your components in and out frequently, a built-in installation can be a pain in the rear; if you're a "buy 'em and forget 'em" kind of person, a built-in installation may be preferable.

In any case, making your equipment fit with your decor is maybe the biggest challenge you'll face when building your home theater system. It's relatively easy to build a home theater that dominates a room; it's much harder to build a system that is both unobtrusive and delivers theater-quality picture and sound.

Obviously, using a custom installer and/or an interior designer can make this job a lot easier. You might also want to take a look at *Audio/Video Interiors* magazine for some decorating ideas; it's kind of the *Architectural Digest* for the home theater crowd.

Note that I haven't included furniture prices in the total costs of systems presented throughout this book, since you can truly spend as little or as much as you like on this essential part of your home theater system. At the low end, ready-to-assemble racks can cost as little as $100, while large all-wood audio/video cabinets can run upwards of $1,000 or more. For a truly custom installation, expect to spend at least a third of your total home theater budget—and a lot more if you want to build a dedicated home theater in your home!

What You Got Is Good Enough: Using Existing Shelves and Furniture

If you'll pardon my grammar, the least expensive option is to not buy any new equipment storage. Instead, look around your room and see if you have any handy bookshelves or existing furniture you can use to store your components.

Remember that your components (receiver, DVD player, VCR, and so on) don't have to be right next to your video display—even though running long cables between different parts of your system can be somewhat problematic. Still, if you have a nice cabinet or half-empty bookshelf on one wall and you want your new TV on another, it may be easier to run the cables than to buy or build a new cabinet to hold all your gear.

In addition, you shouldn't overlook the obvious equipment storage solution. If your system is small enough (and your TV large enough) you may be able to stack your components right on top of your TV cabinet!

Build It Yourself: Ready-to-Assemble Furniture

If you have to buy a new cabinet to hold your components, you don't have to spend a fortune if you don't want to. Many stores sell a wide selection of ready-to-assemble (RTA) furniture, some of which looks pretty good—especially for the price.

RTA furniture typically uses pressed wood components and a bunch of little screws and dowels to hold it all together. You'll probably spend a good evening assembling one of these pieces, find the instructions totally indecipherable, and end up with either too many or too few of the little connecting bits. You'll also find that none of the holes match up, which means you'll probably do some do-it-yourself drilling. Still, there's nothing more satisfying than building something with your own two hands (and a bunch of screwdrivers), and this type of storage won't put you in the poor house.

Overload!

Beware of running cables more than 6–12 feet between components. (It's okay to run speaker wire that long—and longer— assuming you're using a high-grade, well-insulated wire.) When you're sending low-voltage signals from an input device to an a/v receiver, those signals deteriorate quickly the longer the cable is run. For that reason, the closer you can put your other components to your receiver and video display, the better.

The downside to RTA furniture is that some of it looks pretty tacky, and you stand a good chance of having the whole thing dissemble itself over time. And particle board isn't a substitute for solid wood, of course. Still, when your budget's tight, RTA isn't a bad way to go.

You can typically find a selection of lower-priced RTA furniture at most consumer electronics stores and warehouse clubs. For higher-end RTA units—which can approach fine furniture quality and price—you should visit your local furniture store.

Power Up

Keep your screwdrivers and Allen wrenches handy—you should plan on periodically retightening all the screws and nuts in an RTA cabinet, as the various parts tend to work themselves loose with use.

Overload!

Don't forget to measure the *depth* of your TV and a/v components. There's nothing worse than buying an expensive new audio/video cabinet and finding out that you can't close the doors!

All Wood, All the Time: The Fine Furniture Option

When you want something of a little higher quality than RTA furniture—and you don't want to put it together yourself—it's time to take a trip to your local furniture store. Here you'll find all sorts of all-wood cabinets and armoires specifically designed to hold audio/video components.

This option is the way to go for a lot of consumers, and you'll typically find a large selection of units at most good-sized furniture retailers. Before you go shopping, however, grab your tape measure. You'll want to measure all your components—including your TV, if you're looking for an all-in-one unit—and make sure what you have will fit in what you buy.

As with all fine furniture, you'll find a wide range of both prices and quality. Some lower-end a/v furniture is actually made of pressed wood, just like most RTA products. As with all the furniture you buy, you should go with the sturdiest, highest-quality piece you can afford—you'll want it to last a long time!

When you're shopping for an a/v cabinet, take special note of how it manages your system's wiring. The better units have special channels or "pipes" to gather and route all your cabling and wiring; less-appropriate units force you to drill your own holes to run a cable from component A to component B. Look also for built-in cable connections, power outlets, and surge suppressors; these little extras can be worth their weight in gold!

Power Up

While closing a cabinet's doors to hide the ugly black panels and bright green lights of your components appeals to some, you'll find you'll need to keep the doors open to use and access your equipment—as well as to use your infrared remote control—which makes the doors somewhat superfluous. (Although, if your equipment is operated via RF remote—*not* infrared!—the RF signals can still reach the equipment even though your doors are closed.) Also question the pretty tinted glass doors found on some units—the glass is difficult to keep clean, and you'll still have to open the door every time you slap a new disc in your DVD player!

Spec It Yourself: Ordering Custom A/V Furniture

One problem with standard audio/video cabinets is that they're standard—and everybody's a/v system is different. Count yourself fortunate if you find a ready-made cabinet that perfectly fits your current equipment—and fear the day you add something *new* to your system!

Sometimes the only solution is to build a cabinet around your existing gear. Many high-end audio/video retailers and furniture stores offer custom-built cabinets for your audio/video equipment. You'll probably pay a little more for custom cabinets—or not, since some of this stuff is surprisingly affordable—but you'll get a storage solution that not only holds all your components, but also is a perfect fit for your living room's decor.

Interior Design Meets High Tech: Creating a Custom Installation

No matter what kind of cabinets and furniture you choose, many householders turn up their noses at how this type of home theater system intrudes into their living rooms. When you want your home theater to truly blend into your room, it's time to think about going with a built-in installation.

Power Up

An alternative to custom furniture is modular furniture. Several manufacturers offer combinations of different types of modules; just pick and choose from the various selections to create your own semi-custom cabinet or wall unit.

Built-in installations don't have to be overly involved. It's relatively easy to use wall-mounted or ceiling-mounted speakers to "hide" what are typically awkward surround-sound speakers; running speaker wire through a wall or basement serves to keep that ugly wire hidden, as well. In addition, many rear projection televisions come specially designed for flush-mount installation within a cabinet or fake wall.

Creating a built-in installation is as much of an interior-design challenge as it is a technology challenge. It's also a ton of work to retrofit an existing room for a built-in home theater system; for that reason, the majority of custom installations get green-lighted during new-housing construction. (It's a lot easier to run wire through unfinished walls than it is to snake the stuff behind the painted drywall.)

When you choose to design your own built-in installation, however, you have the ultimate in control over where things go, how they look, and how they work. Think the projection TV works best in that spot? Then that's where you build it in, no questions asked! Of course, this job isn't for the faint-hearted (or the aesthetically impaired); this is the perfect opportunity to bring in a custom installation specialist and an interior designer, and let them work their magic for you!

Power Up

Even if you can disguise your components, dealing with big brown speakers can be an additional challenge when building your system. I liked Shirley Jeane's solution, shown way back in Chapter 1, "It's More Than Just a Big TV: Home Theater Basics." She and her husband Harvey found (with no little difficulty) speakers with white cabinets (to fit with their room's color scheme), and then hung them from the ceiling!

Getting Fancy: More Sophisticated Installations

Once you're thinking about built-in installations, it's time to consider whether you want to stop with a "simple" single-room, single-purpose home theater setup—or go for something a bit more far-reaching.

Audio and Video Everywhere: Installing a Multiple-Room System

If your CD player sounds great in your living room, think how great it would sound out on your deck. And if you like watching satellite TV on your couch, contemplate how good that picture would look on the TV in your bedroom.

In other words, why limit your audio and video enjoyment to just one room of your house?

With a little bit of work—and the right custom installation firm—you can use your home theater's audio and video components to feed speakers and televisions all through your house. All it takes is some fancy switching devices, one of the whole-house remote control systems discussed back in Chapter 22, "Take Charge: Controlling

Your System," some video signal amplifiers, an extra audio amplifier or two, a fair amount of cabling, and the requisite satellite speakers and auxiliary TVs. Oh, and a little extra cash wouldn't hurt, either.

Input/Output

If all you want is to run audio or video to a second room—without wiring your whole house—there are some lower-cost options available to you.

For example, many receivers include both "A" and "B" speaker outputs; it's easy enough to use the "B" outputs to drive a second set of left and right (but *not* center!) speakers in another room. (Of course, this option forces you to listen to the same source material in both rooms—and you have to be sure to switch your receiver out of surround-sound and into two-channel stereo mode—but it's quick and easy!) You can also connect a spare set of audio output jacks from your receiver to a "slave" amplifier, and use that second amplifier to drive speakers in another location; this is how I power the speakers I have installed outside on my deck.

Some higher-end receivers feature multiroom/multisource outputs, which send line-level signals to an optional second amplifier. The benefit of this second output is that it can be switched to a different source than your receiver's main selection; push a button on your remote and send the sound from your CD player to a second room, while you watch cable TV in your main home theater room.

When you want to watch satellite TV in two different rooms, make sure you buy a system with dual LNBs. Each LNB can feed a separate satellite receiver; stick one receiver in your home theater room and another in your bedroom, and you can watch two different satellite channels at the same time. (You can also connect a multiplexer to a dual-LNB system and hook up any number of satellite receivers in multiple rooms.)

If you don't mind watching the same programming in your second room as you do in your main room, simply connect an extra video output from your a/v receiver (using either coax cable or composite video—whichever is free) to your second TV set in another room. As long as your a/v receiver is turned on, you'll be able to watch whatever source it's switched to. Of course, you might have a little trouble changing channels from the other room, but you can always buy an extra remote control and run an infrared blaster from your auxiliary room to your a/v receiver. (Or, if your equipment uses an RF remote, you can eliminate the infrared blaster—since RF signals can travel long distances and through walls.)

Wiring your entire house for audio and video is not a task I recommend for most consumers. It's complex and expensive and requires access to some sophisticated equipment (especially when it comes to controllers). This type of large-scale project is perfectly suited to a custom a/v installation firm, however; they do this sort of thing for a living.

When done right, however, it's a joy to behold. I've seen systems that use in-wall touchscreens to route the output of the CD player to one room and the signal from a digital broadcast satellite to another, all the while feeding a DVD or laserdisc to the projection TV in the main home theater room. You can't beat the convenience.

Of course, this sort of whole-house system doesn't come cheap—count on adding $10,000–$20,000 or more above the cost of the rest of your system. And it isn't easy to do, especially in existing homes; it's a lot easier to run the requisite cabling in a new house, before the walls get put up. Still, if you want the ultimate in whole-house audio/video convenience, check with your custom installer and see what's possible in your house.

Putting the "Home" in Home Theater: Integrating with Home Automation Systems

Running your audio/video system through your entire house is one thing, but connecting it to a system that controls other functions throughout your house is another. Home automation systems control not just your a/v system, but also your room lighting, home security, and much more—all from a central controller or set of controllers.

Home automation systems—such as the popular X-10 system—can be programmed to control virtually all electronic devices in your house. How would you like to push a single button and have your blinds close, your room lights dim, your projection TV fire up, and your DVD player start playing your favorite movie? Or how about, while you're watching that movie, pushing a button on your remote to put a picture-in-picture window on-screen to display the picture from a security camera mounted outside your front door? All this is possible with home automation systems; this technology essentially networks all your different devices.

Power Up

To learn more about home automation, check out the Home Toys Web site at www.hometoys.com.

As with whole-house a/v systems, home automation systems are probably best left to a custom installer. These systems aren't cheap, and they're not easy to install and program. But they are *really* neat—especially if you have a very large house, and the bucks that go with it!

When the Job's Just Too Big to Do Yourself: Thinking About Custom Installers

Most folks can set up an average home theater system all by themselves—all it takes is a bunch of cables, a free afternoon or two, and someone to tell you that you need to move that big cabinet another two inches to the left. When you get into sophisticated systems, however—such as multiple-room setups or systems with built-in speakers or displays—then it's time to consider calling in a pro to do the job for you.

Custom audio/video installation firms install home theater systems for a living. They know what equipment is best for specific types of rooms, they know where to find the best custom furniture for your system, and they're really good at running wires in places where you didn't think wires could be run. Beyond that, they know how to fully integrate all the components in your system, and give you total and user-friendly control over what you watch and listen to.

Of course, using a custom installer costs a little more than trying to do it yourself; you're paying for that expertise. Even though most custom installers will charge competitive prices for the equipment you purchase, expect to pay an extra 20 percent or so above the equipment price for the installation itself.

Why Use a Custom Installer?

If you have a large or complex system—or if you just don't want to fiddle with a messy installation—the extra price is worth it. Not only do custom installers help you install your system, they also help you build the right system for your needs, integrate the system into your room, provide expert setup for all the components in your system (including detailed convergence of your projection TV), show you how everything works, and take care of you after the sale—if and when something quits working, or you want to add something new to your system.

So, why should you use a custom installer for your home theater system instead of doing it yourself? Here are four good reasons:

➤ A custom installer deals with the cosmetic issues associated with home theater systems—how to make all those high-tech components fit in with the look and feel of your home.

➤ A custom installer helps to provide the best component matching for your system. Instead of just slapping together a lot of different equipment from different manufacturers, a good installer knows which components work best together—and which don't.

➤ A custom installer provides the control for your system—in the form of easy-to-use, preprogrammed remote control units that perform complex operations with a single touch.

➤ A custom installer provides support and service. When you have problems, these guys fix them!

229

I used a custom installer to design and install my home theater system when I built my house several years ago. They did a much better job than I could ever do in recommending the best equipment and coordinating the system's installation. They also spent a fair amount of time converging my new TV and calibrating my surround-sound system. To me, it was worth the money—and I'll use them again when I upgrade my system for HDTV.

Should You Use a Custom Installer?

When should you use a custom installer? While you can utilize the services of a custom installer for any size system, I'd definitely recommend custom installation in any of the following situations:

➤ You want one or more parts of your system (speakers, video display, etc.) to be built into a wall or ceiling

➤ You want your system to incorporate a front projection television

➤ You're spending more than $10,000 on your system

➤ You want to run audio or video into more than one room

➤ You want to integrate your home theater system with a home automation system

The best custom installers also work with interior designers and decorators to fully integrate your home theater into your home's decor. These experts can work together to effectively hide your system within a room—or turn a specific space into a dedicated home theater room. These services don't come cheap—but if you want the best results, you'll hire the best people to do the work.

Find a Firm: How to Choose a Custom Installer

Finding the right custom installation firm is a little more difficult than shopping for a new TV set. With a little digging, you're sure to find a wide variety of businesses doing some type of custom audio/video installation.

Some audio/video specialty stores do custom installation on the side—as do some general consumer electronics stores. You'll also find a number of firms that do nothing but custom installations; these businesses typically don't operate out of a storefront, and often specialize in higher-end installations.

How to Evaluate Different Firms

What should you look for in a custom installer? The most important factor to consider is experience. You want someone who's done this before, someone who isn't learning on the job, someone you can trust to see your project through from conception to completion. The experience factor holds true not only for the firm it-self, but also for the firm's employees; look for a crew who's been around for a while, and has installed a number of systems similar to the one you're contemplating.

You should also look for a firm that handles the brands of equipment you're inter-ested in, and one that is comfortable doing your type of installation. If you want a simple, more affordable system, you may want to skip the high-end specialists in your area; likewise, if you're installing a really sophisticated system, I wouldn't recommend the guy who delivers big-screens for that consumer electronics store in the strip mall.

When you're evaluating one or more custom installation firms, ask for references. Ask to see pictures of similar installations they've done; ask to talk to those customers, if possible. If you can talk to someone who's had a similar system installed by that firm, ask that person how he or she liked the firm's work, whether there were any prob-lems, whether the price came in as budgeted, how fast the work was completed, whether he or she is satisfied with the new system, and so on. There is no better way to find out about a firm's work than to ask its customers!

It also doesn't hurt to have a look around the firm's offices or showroom. Even if the firm doesn't have a storefront, it should still have some sort of showroom or demonstration center. What kind of equipment is installed in the showroom—and how is it installed? I'd have trouble trusting a custom installer that didn't do a good job on its own showroom!

Overload!

Beware of super-low bids. Any-thing that looks too good to be true probably is! Check the low bid to make sure it includes the specific equipment you want, and doesn't substitute an inferior model or brand. Also, make sure the bid includes *all* the installa-tion and labor—you don't want any surprises in the middle of the job!

Once you've narrowed your list down to a handful of firms, ask them each to prepare a bid for your work. Get this quote in writing, then compare the particulars between the firms. Since its unlikely that any two firms will bid the exact same equip-ment, this will be a little like comparing apples to Sherman tanks, but a close evaluation of the bids should help you decide who's giving you the most bang for the buck.

Where to Find a Custom Installer

Where do you find the perfect custom installer? Here are some tips:

➤ Ask friends who've had some custom installation work done; references are re-ally the best way to find a custom installer

➤ Look in the Yellow Pages or on the Internet

➤ Browse the dealer listings supplied by audio/video equipment manufacturers

➤ Use the CEDIA Finder Service at www.cedia.org

Input/Output

CEDIA is the Custom Electronic Design and Installation Association, an international trade association of companies specializing in planning and installing electronic systems for the home. CEDIA supports its member companies with courses and seminars on a wide variety of topics—from wiring and acoustics to home automation and future technologies. CEDIA also provides its members with other valuable resources, and honors the best firms and products with its yearly Industry Recognition awards.

Belonging to CEDIA is a good seal of approval for a custom installation firm. CEDIA companies subscribe to a strict code of professional conduct and ethics, and are typically among the best of the best in the consumer electronics industry. Using the CEDIA Finder Service to locate a CEDIA-member installer is a great place to start when you're looking for a custom installation firm.

Learn from a Pro: An Interview with an Award-Winning Custom Installer

One of CEDIA's top members is Tom Doherty, Inc. (TDI), of Indianapolis, Indiana. In fact, TDI was named CEDIA's Dealer of the Year for 1999—and also won a CEDIA award for Best Home Theater Electronic System Design over $150,000. (In addition, TDI's parent company, Escient, won the Best Video Product award for its PowerPlay system, discussed back in Chapter 10, "Digital Pictures on a Disc: DVD Players.")

TDI's award-winning installation was definitely on the high side of the home theater spectrum—the total cost ran close to $1 million! For that price, the owner got a theater-quality HDTV front projection system using a screen 16 feet wide by 9 feet tall. The speaker arrays are mounted behind the screen, which is acoustically transparent, and the viewers watch all the action from theater-style seating. It's a show-stopper system, melding the latest state-of-the-art technology with a striking design by Theo Kalomir-akis, one of the industry's premier designers.

(That million-dollar home theater is only *part* of this particular system, by the way; the complete installation features a whole-house system with audio and video—and corresponding touchscreen controllers—in practically every room!)

Tom Doherty's CEDIA award-winning installation—the screen is 16 × 9 feet!

(Courtesy of Tom Doherty, Inc.)

TDI is the firm I chose to install my home theater system, even though my system cost a mere fraction of the one that won CEDIA's top award. As I was preparing this book, I met with Jim Swearingen, TDI's sales manager and system designer, to ask him some questions about custom audio/video installations.

Michael Miller (MM): Jim, at what point should somebody consider going with a custom installer rather than doing it themselves?

Jim Swearingen (JS): We find that most of our clients come to us because they are much more interested in the end result than the parts, pieces, and processes used to create the theater system. So, my suggestion would be that if the process of education, component selection, room design, installation, and calibration become more than you are willing to risk to own a great home theater, it would be a great idea to talk to a custom installer.

Power Up

You can learn more about Tom Doherty, Inc. at their Web site, located at www.tdi-av.com. If you're in the Central Indiana area, give them a call at 317–848–7503 to discuss your home theater needs.

What a custom installer brings to the table is a knowledge of what components work well together, how to integrate components into a room, how to get the best performance possible from the combination of suggested components, how to make those components intuitively usable, and how to provide the support needed for our clients to understand and enjoy their systems.

Behind the scenes—just one of several banks of equipment that control the million-dollar home theater system.

(Courtesy of Tom Doherty, Inc.)

We bring the knowledge not only of individual component performance, but also of how combinations of components work together. We know what has worked well over time. We can help with cosmetic integration without affecting the performance of the system. We can take what would normally be a complicated system and make it easy for all family members to use. We provide coordination with other subcontractors, such as electricians, decorators, and cabinetmakers, to make sure that the end result is exactly as you hoped.

Televisions, surround processors, DVD Players, and control systems are becoming more and more sophisticated, which is both good and bad. It's good, because there is great flexibility and ability to match with other components and deliver great performance in a variety of environments. It's bad because there's an increased opportunity for components to *not* deliver the best possible performance. The performance you get by trial and error is nowhere near what could be experienced. We've done the trials, we can avoid the error.

MM: Take an identical system that a consumer might put together versus what a custom installer might put together. How much more will the customer pay for these services?

JS: For the components themselves, we all try to keep an eye on the advertised prices, so we're not charging more than a retailer for the same components. What you'll pay for from a custom installer is the labor to install components, the design of the system, the documentation of the installation, the interfacing with other subcontractors, and the programming and calibration of all components.

Typically, you'll be paying about twenty percent for labor, materials and engineering. What you'll get is a finished system that is programmed, calibrated, and fine-tuned, with no headaches.

MM: What's the main thing a custom installer brings to a home theater installation?

JS: There's a lot! Besides the obvious labor and design, though, I guess the issue I'd like to address is control. Control is ignored in the selection of the components, and too often what results is an otherwise great system that is incredibly difficult to use. Too often consumers are concentrating on the performance of each individual component, and paying no attention to how those components will work together. Even manufacturers who advertise that they've paid attention to control, in general, do a miserable job. What we can bring is the ability to easily and effortlessly control a collection of difficult, but high-performance components.

In a typical theater system, to watch a DVD one must turn on the television, select the proper input on the TV, turn on the surround receiver, select the proper input on the receiver, select the proper surround mode on the receiver, turn on the DVD player and then hit play. In more complex systems, add turning down the lights to the right level, lowering the screen for the projector, turning on the amplifier ... and turning everything off is just as complicated. Yes, you can consolidate your coffee table full of remotes into one remote, but you still have to press just as many buttons to make anything happen, and remember what those buttons do.

Control systems exist that allow one to press a single button to watch a DVD, cable, DSS, VCR, or any other source. These systems require the programming capabilities of a custom installer, as well as installation techniques to keep components in sync with each other.

Most custom installers are not just trying to sell you the largest stack of components, or the best or most expensive amplifier or projector. They truly concentrate on creating a high-quality system that is really usable, that can expand or change, and that stays working for a long time.

MM: What would be the minimum amount of money someone should spend to get a decent home theater system?

JS: I would define a really enjoyable, impactful home theater as one that delivers a semblance of what the film's producer intended. That's going to take at least four to five thousand dollars, and should include at least a 36-inch direct-view television. Speakers should be of high-enough quality that music could be enjoyed through them. There should be separate amplification with high-quality Dolby Digital surround processing for those speakers, rather than lower-end self-powered speakers. There should be a DVD player, and a subwoofer.

MM: If somebody has a little extra money to play with in their home theater budget, where should they put that money?

JS: There is no one place that I could suggest universally. You really have to examine the system to find out where the weak link is, and improve that weak link—and in every system that weak link's going to be different. It could be that you should move up a size in television, or a step up in quality of television. You may have a larger than normal room and need a larger subwoofer to fill it. It could be accessories you hadn't considered like cables or power conditioning. The key is to look at how the whole system operates together to improve the balance.

MM: Somebody doing this themselves, should they try to stay with a single manufacturer, or should they do a mix and match?

JS: There are pluses and minuses to both. Staying with a single manufacturer means that you have a better chance of things working together. But there is no one manufacturer that is great at everything ....

There are certain components where compatibility is not an issue. For example, using a Sony receiver with B&W speakers is not a problem. With other components, you run into more opportunities for trouble when mixing, especially when it comes to control. Many receivers' remotes, for example, will do an acceptable job of controlling their own brand of VCR, TV, or DVD player, but cause confusion and extra steps to control other brands. Performance is rarely the issue—usually control is the problem.

MM: How often should somebody look at his or her system and think about upgrading it, or reevaluating it?

JS: Just because something is newer and better than what you have doesn't mean that what you have isn't enjoyable any more. Take your laserdisc player, for instance. Just because few dealers still sell the players and you can't buy too many new discs anymore doesn't mean that it's not a viable piece of equipment for your home and that you won't continue to enjoy it.

There are so many implications in changing just one component in a large system that you want to be very careful about upgrades. Remember, if you have as many as a dozen components, changing one will affect the other eleven. The industry wants you to believe that there is something radically new every six months, but truly important improvements happen much more rarely.

My suggestion of when to upgrade is when a new format comes along. DVD, DSS, and high definition are all new formats that not only require one new component, but that also place new demands on other components in the system.

Let's use DVD as an example. Adding a DVD player is a great time to look at your surround processor. Does it have Dolby Digital decoding? Does it have the power and dynamics to handle a higher quality soundtrack? Dolby Digital decoding sends full-range audio to the rear channels—are your surround speakers up to the additional information? Can your television take advantage of a component video source? Will its weaknesses show with a higher-quality signal? These are the times to look at upgrades—not when a manufacturer changes from a black to a gold finish.

MM: It seems like one decision people have to make is between the best pure audio and the best video for home theater purposes. How do you deal with that?

JS: That's one that we struggle with a lot. The argument is that you cannot successfully address both—a speaker system that sounds great for audio will be compromised for use in a home theater, and vice versa. My view is that accuracy is the proper goal in either format—a speaker system should accurately reproduce what it is fed, without colorations to favor movies or music.

Unfortunately, it's not that simple—there are compromises that have to be made. No speaker does everything well, and trade-offs occur. Dynamics are important in a home theatre environment, more so than minor colorations in tonal accuracy. When listening to music, it is my feeling that tonal accuracy is more important than dynamics. Speakers for home theatre use should have a very focused dispersion, to pinpoint the location of sounds, especially in the front speakers. High-end audio speakers usually feature wide dispersion, to create the illusion of a three-dimensional sound stage with just two speakers.

While my choice for what to recommend for a client depends on his or her listening preferences, I usually err on the side of the high-end audio goals. I've found that high-end audio speakers also perform quite well with theatre sources, but that speakers colored purely for home theatre use sound lousy with a high-end audio source.

MM: Before we wrap up, is there anything else you'd like to talk about?

JS: My hope is that custom installers do not come off as elitist, like we're the only ones who know what's going on. What we do bring, however, is experience. Most custom installers tackle about a hundred projects a year. And even though each circumstance is different, we've learned what works and what doesn't. We know how well a component or a system will provide long-term pleasure—long past how cool it is when you first get it.

MM: Practice makes perfect?

JS: Right. And because a good custom installer lives and dies by his referrals, we'd better get it right.

The Least You Need to Know

➤ There are many ways to install your home theater components—from simple ready-to-assemble racks to custom furniture and built-in installations.

➤ More sophisticated—and more expensive—installations enable you to pipe audio and video throughout your entire house, and to control a variety of household functions.

➤ When your installation gets too complex to do it yourself, you should consider hiring a custom installation firm.

➤ Custom installers will cost you about 20 percent above the price of your equipment, but provide a high level of component selection, setup, and support.

Chapter 25

How Much Can You Afford: Putting Together the Perfect System for Your Budget

---

In This Chapter

➤ How much system can you buy for your particular budget?

➤ How much do you have to spend to get the kind of system you really want?

➤ Where to shop for the kind of system you can afford

If you've read this far, you're probably salivating as you contemplate finally building your dream home theater system. All that's left is to visit your audio/video dealer and write a check—or, if you're looking at a really high-end system, take out a sizeable loan!

The final question is: How big a check (or loan!) do you need? This last chapter pulls together everything you've learned so far and recommends some specific systems for your home theater budget.

Under $1,000: Home Theater on a Shoestring

Okay, let's be honest. You can't put together much of a home theater system for $1,000. Still, it *is* possible to build a minimal surround-sound system for about a grand, even if you won't get all the bells and whistles you see in the fancy audio/video magazines.

Here's what you can get for about $1,000 (provided you shop wisely):

➤ **27" direct view television.** You should be able to pick up a budget 27" set by any of the major consumer electronics manufacturers—Panasonic, RCA, Toshiba, and the like—for about $350. You can also find 27" sets for twice the price (and these sets will have better pictures and more features), but to keep your $1,000 budget, you'll have to shop for the lowest-price model you can afford.

Power Up

For simplicity's sake, I've priced all the systems in this chapter without cabinets, cables, and in-stallation. I typically budget an additional 20–30 percent to get everything plugged in and put away, so make sure you factor that into your calculations, as well.

➤ **VHS HiFi VCR.** VHS HiFi will deliver pretty good Dolby Pro Logic sound, and you can find a good selection of decks for around $150.

➤ **Home theater in a box.** As discussed back in Chapter 20, "Quick and Easy Systems: Home Theater in a Box," the lowest-priced way to get into home theater sound is with one of these all-in-one systems that package a bunch of speakers and a budget audio/video receiver. You won't get a lot of power or very big speakers, but you will be set with three front speakers (left, center, and right), two surrounds (left and right), and a small subwoofer. Look for budget boxes in the $500 range that include Dolby Digital surround sound.

The details of your under-$1,000 system are presented in the following table.

The Under-$1,000 Home Theater System

Component	Target Price	Suggested Manufacturers
27" direct view television	$350	Panasonic, RCA, Toshiba
VHS HiFi VCR	$150	Mitsubishi, Panasonic, RCA, Sony
Home theater in a box	$500	Aiwa, Kenwood, Pioneer, Sony

The best places to shop for your low-end system are mass merchants, consumer electronics stores, and warehouse clubs.

Under $2,500: The Budget System

Spend a little bit more money, and you start getting into "real" home theater systems, capable of playing high-quality DVDs with true 5.1 surround sound. Here's the sort of system you can expect to find for this price:

➤ **32" direct view television.** Look for budget models from the major manufacturers—or move down to a 27" set with high-end features, for the same price.

➤ **DVD player.** You can find pretty good DVD players for around $300 from Pioneer, Sony, Toshiba, and other manufacturers. As an added bonus, your DVD player can double as a CD player!

➤ **VHS HiFi VCR.** Even with a DVD player in your system, you probably still want a VHS HiFi VCR. There's no need to break the bank on this component, however, so keep the budget around $150.

Power Up

If you have a little extra money to spend, use it to choose a slightly better television. Stay in the 27" or 32" size, but upgrade to a set with a slightly better picture and a fancier remote.

➤ **Audio/video receiver.** When you go shopping for an a/v receiver, expect to spend around $350 for the lowest-priced Dolby Digital 5.1 models from Sony, Onkyo, Technics, and the like. Be careful when you're shopping, however, because you'll also find a lot of Dolby Pro Logic models for around the same price. (Given the choice, go with a lower-power Dolby Digital model over a higher-power Dolby Pro Logic—the Dolby Digital 5.1 is a noticeably superior surround-sound experience.)

➤ **Surround-sound speaker system.** For this budget, your best speaker bargains are likely to come from prepackaged systems. If you focus on the $1,000 price range, you can find fairly decent speaker packages from Bose, Infinity, Polk Audio, and others; look especially for systems that include all five speakers plus a subwoofer.

The details of your $2,500 system are presented in the following table.

The Under-$2,500 Home Theater System

Component	Target Price	Suggested Manufacturers
32" direct view television	$700	Panasonic, RCA, Sony, Toshiba
DVD player	$300	Pioneer, Sony, Toshiba
VHS HiFi VCR	$150	Mitsubishi, Panasonic, RCA, Sony
Audio/video receiver	$350	JVC, Kenwood, Onkyo, Sony, Technics, Yamaha
Surround-sound speaker system	$1,000	Bose, Definitive Technology, Infinity, KLH, Polk Audio

The best places to shop for your budget system are mass consumer electronics stores, audio/video specialists, and online/catalog retailers.

Under $5,000: Improving Performance

Most home theater experts agree that once you get into the $5,000 price range, you're getting a pretty good system. At this price level you can move up to a rear projection TV, add a digital satellite system, and pick a slightly more powerful receiver—as long as you choose a similar speaker system as you would for a $2,500 system.

Let's take a look at the components of a typical $5,000 system:

➤ **Rear projection television.** Moving to a bigger video display is the most significant improvement you can make in your system. If you target the $1,600 price range, you can find a good selection of 43–45" rear projection sets from Mitsubishi, RCA, and Sony. (At this price they won't be digital-ready, but what do you want—a free lunch?) Look for the set with the best picture and the highest-quality components, and you should be happy with your choice.

➤ **DVD changer.** Remember, your DVD player is doing double duty as a CD player, and it's awful nice to pop in five or six CDs for an evening's listening. You can budget around $600 and get a very good five-disc DVD/CD changer from Sony, Toshiba, and other manufacturers.

➤ **VHS HiFi VCR.** As long as you have a spare $150 in your budget, it's probably worth it to put a decent VHS HiFi VCR in your system. You'll find a wide variety of models to choose from at this price.

➤ **Digital satellite system.** With your new big-screen TV, the slight added investment in a satellite dish and receiver gives you a plethora of high-quality programming each month. Two bills will buy you a full system from RCA or Sony; just remember to budget another $40 or so a month for all that great programming!

➤ **Audio/video receiver.** In the $500 range, you get a good bang for your buck when it comes to a/v receivers. You should be in the 75–85 watt/channel range, with a lot of audio and video inputs, Dolby Digital 5.1 surround sound, and some sort of universal remote control. Look especially for digital inputs for your DVD changer and digital satellite dish.

➤ **Surround-sound speaker system.** A thousand dollars will buy you a pretty good prepackaged system from Bose, Polk, or other speaker manufacturers. For the best sound, look for a package that includes a powered subwoofer.

The details of your $5,000 system are presented in the following table.

The Under–$5,000 Home Theater System

Component	Target Price	Suggested Manufacturers
43–45" rear projection television	$1,600	Mitsubishi, RCA, Sony
DVD changer	$600	Panasonic, Onkyo, Sony, Toshiba
VHS HiFi VCR	$150	Mitsubishi, Panasonic, RCA, Sony
Digital satellite system	$200	RCA, Sony
Audio/video receiver	$500	JVC, Kenwood, Onkyo, Sony, Technics, Yamaha
Surround-sound speaker system	$1,000	Bose, Definitive Technology, Infinity, Polk Audio

The best places to shop for your improved-performance system are audio/video specialists, consumer electronics stores, and some custom installers.

Under $10,000: Bigger and Better

Ten grand will buy you one heck of a system today. (Much more than it bought me eight years ago!) For this price you can get a big digital-ready rear projection set, a reference-standard DVD player, a CD jukebox, and a really good-sounding speaker system.

Let's take a look at the individual components:

➤ **Digital-ready rear projection television.** Expect to write a check for about four grand—and in return, expect to get a digital-ready set that will display full HDTV broadcasts when you add an optional HDTV tuner. Look for a set with full 16:9 aspect ratio that can display full 1080i HDTV broadcasts without downconverting. This price range actually sees a lot of competition, so there should be a good number of sets to choose from by

Power Up

If you have some extra money to spend, use it to go with a better speaker system. In this price range, the speakers are probably the weakest link in your system, and a hundred or two extra can move you up to a better sounding set of speakers—or add a subwoofer to the mix.

just about every major manufacturer. (The one manufacturer missing from my list at this price range is Pioneer, whose digital-ready RPTV sets come in about 20 percent higher than competitors; their sets are pretty good, but I'm not sure they're really worth the added price.)

➤ **Reference-quality DVD player.** This is the one real extravagance in this system. Sure, you can go with the standard $300–$400 single-disc player (or the $600 carousel), but for a grand you get to play with the big boys. I particularly like Sony's high-end model (DVP-7700 as I write this, although the model number is likely to change with the new model year), which delivers superior picture quality and special effects in a sturdier package. Of course, you could save five hundred bucks by going with a normal model—but don't you deserve something special every now and then? (You might also want to examine the inputs on your rear projection TV; if you can hook up a progressive-scan DVD player, you might want to go that route to get rid of the scan lines in the picture.)

➤ **Digital satellite system.** The standard $200 DIRECTV satellite system from RCA or Sony should do just fine for this level system—although you might need to upgrade to the DIRECTV Plus system when you enable your system for full HDTV. (One slightly more expensive option is to upgrade to a satellite receiver with Dolby Digital 5.1 outputs, so you can receive the best surround sound off the dish.)

➤ **Audio/video receiver.** For $1,000, your a/v receiver can start to approach the performance level and feature set of separate components. You should be solidly in the 100 watt/channel range, with good clean sound, lots of inputs, both Dolby Digital and DTS decoding, on-screen displays, and some sort of universal or learning remote. Trust me—you'll really like the receivers in this price range!

➤ **CD jukebox.** Up till now our systems have relied on DVD players to do double-duty as CD players. Well, with this type of budget it's easy to divert $300 or so to a dedicated CD jukebox. There should be several models to choose from; go for a model that holds 200–400 discs.

➤ **Surround-sound speakers.** With a 10-grand system, you can spend $2,500 on speakers (with a little extra for a subwoofer, discussed next) and get really good sound. You're no longer limited to prepackaged sets (although you shouldn't rule them out—some high-end packages provide high-quality, perfectly matched sound), and now have a huge variety of options to choose from. In fact, the options are too numerous to mention here; you'll need to give all the $500 speakers in the store a good listening-to. (Remember, you need five speakers for a Dolby Digital 5.1 system—so that's $2,500 divided by five for a per-speaker budget of $500.)

➤ **Subwoofer.** At the lower price points, if you got a subwoofer it was part of a speaker package. Now that you've moved beyond prepackaged systems, you need to buy a subwoofer on its own. You don't have to stick to the same brand as your main speakers, although there's nothing wrong with that. Just set your budget ($300) and see what's available.

➤ **Programmable remote control.** When you spend this amount of money, you don't have to put up with the clutter of a half-dozen remote controls on your coffee table. Take $300 or so and buy a remote control that can be programmed to operate all your components; something like the Philips Pronto (discussed back in Chapter 22, "Take Charge: Controlling Your System") should do the job.

The details of a typical $10,000 system are presented in the following table.

The Under-$10,000 Home Theater System

Component	Target Price	Suggested Manufacturers
53–55" digital-ready rear projection TV	$4,000	Mitsubishi, Panasonic, RCA, Sony, Toshiba
DVD player	$1,000	Pioneer, Sony, Toshiba
VHS HiFi VCR	$200	Mitsubishi, RCA, Sony
Digital satellite system	$200	RCA, Sony
Audio/video receiver	$1,000	Onkyo, Pioneer, Sony, Yamaha
CD jukebox	$300	Pioneer, Sony, Yamaha
Surround-sound speakers	$2,500	Boston Acoustics, Definitive Technology, Infinity, Klipsch, Polk Audio
Subwoofer	$500	Definitive Technology, Infinity, Klipsch, Polk Audio, Velodyne
Programmable remote control	$300	Harmon/Kardon, Philips, Sony

The best places to shop for your bigger-and-better system are audio/video specialists and custom installation firms.

Under $25,000: High Definition

Now you're in the big leagues. Twenty-five grand buys you a full high-definition system, terrific sound, and just about any audio or video source you can think of. Here's what you should look for:

➤ **HDTV rear projection television.** Expect to spend around ten grand for a really big (65–70") rear projection set with built-in HDTV tuner. Look for a model that includes an IE1394 FireWire connection to receive digital signals from your cable company, as well as a built-in HDTV satellite receiver.

Power Up

If you have a spare $500 or so to spend, your best bet is to throw it in the speaker pile. You can either move up to $600 speakers, or split the difference and go for a really kickin' subwoofer—or with *two* subwoofers! Alternately, you can save the extra bucks until you're ready to buy an HDTV tuner for your big-screen TV.

➤ **DVHS video recorder.** Now that you have an HDTV TV, you want an HDTV VCR to record the new digital broadcasts. As I write this there aren't a lot of models out there (just one, as a matter of fact), but expect to see a wider choice over the coming months. As is, you'll spend in the $700 range for one of these new digital decks that record HDTV broadcasts—but you need one, don't you?

➤ **Reference-quality progressive-scan DVD player.** As in the $10,000 system, spending a thousand bucks for a DVD player is a bit of an extravagance, but the reference players at this price point are the cream of the crop, in terms of both performance and reliability. (And, if your projection television has the proper inputs, you can go with a progressive-scan DVD player, for even better picture quality.)

➤ **Digital satellite system.** Go with a high-end DIRECTV Plus satellite system from RCA or Sony that includes a built-in HDTV receiver and Dolby Digital 5.1 outputs.

➤ **Personal digital video recorder.** If you have an extra $700 or so to spend, drop it on one of these hard-disk recorders from TiVo and Philips. The convenience of rearranging and editing "live" broadcasts is something you'll wonder how you ever did without.

➤ **WebTV Plus.** Okay, this isn't a necessity, but for $200 bucks (plus about 25 bucks a month) you can check your e-mail and surf the Web without getting up from your easy chair!

➤ **CD jukebox.** For this level of system, you want to move up to the $700 models from Pioneer and Sony; you'll get 400-disc convenience, the best possible playback quality, good solid construction, and better control over what you want to listen to.

➤ **CD recorder.** When you want to make your own mix discs, you need a CD recorder. Philips and Pioneer will both get you going for around $600.

➤ **Audiocassette recorder.** Again, this isn't really a necessity, but it's nice to have a cassette recorder around just in case—and you'll only spend about $300 or so, for even the best decks.

➤ **Preamplifer.** Die-hard audiophiles will tell you that separate components sound better than integrated receivers. Well, in this price range, you can see (and hear) for yourself! Expect to spend around two grand for a full audio/video preamp that includes digital signal processing for all available types of surround sound.

➤ **Amplifier.** If you're going with separates, you need a separate power amplifier. For about $1,500 you can get a very clean 100 watts or more per channel—and one of the heaviest components in your new system!

➤ **Surround-sound speakers.** Now we're talking high end. Spend a grand a speaker (times five for Dolby Digital 5.1—that's a total of $5,000) and you'll get really clear sound that will please both movie buffs and audiophiles. The high-end speaker makers to look (and listen) for include Acoustic Research, Infinity, Klipsch, Paradigm, and many other respected names.

➤ **Subwoofer.** Spend somewhere between $500 and $800 and get a servo-controlled subwoofer that will disturb your neighbors—even if they live the next block over!

➤ **Remote control system.** Okay, here's the real cool part of buying a $25,000 system—you get your own custom remote control. Choose a system from Niles Audio or Lexicon, and your custom installer will program the remote control for your specific components—so you can perform most operations with a single touch!

Typical components for your $25,000 system are detailed in the following table.

The Under-$25,000 Home Theater System

Component	Target Price	Suggested Manufacturers
65–70" HDTV rear projection television	$10,000	Mitsubishi, Pioneer, Sony
DVD player	$1,000	Pioneer, Sony, Toshiba
DVHS VCR	$700	Panasonic
DIRECTV Plus digital satellite system	$400	RCA, Sony
Personal video recorder	$700	Philips
WebTV Plus	$200	Philips, Sony
CD jukebox	$700	Pioneer, Sony
CD recorder	$600	Philips, Pioneer
Audiocassette recorder	$300	JVC, Sony, Yamaha
Preamplifier	$2,000	B&K, Sony
Amplifier	$1,500	B&K, Sony
Surround-sound speakers	$5,000	Acoustic Research, Infinity, Klipsch, Paradigm, Polk Audio
Subwoofer	$750	Klipsch, Polk Audio
Remote control system	$1,500	Lexicon, Niles Audio

When you're purchasing a system in this price range, I recommend going straight to a custom installer—although some high-end audio/video specialists can also do a good job.

Unlimited Budget: Unlimited Performance

If money is no object, you can truly put together a dream system. (Of course, if money *really* is no object, what are you doing reading this cheap little book? Give me a call and I'll help you put together your system personally—for a hefty fee, of course!)

Just what will you find in a dream home theater system? Here's some of what you can expect:

➤ **HDTV front projection with line multiplier.** For the biggest picture possible, you'll need a high-end front projection system, from Runco or Sony or some other somewhat-exclusive manufacturer. Make sure you get high-quality construction (including 9" tubes if you go with a CRT model), and invest in a compatible line multiplier (Faroudja makes the best). The whole shebang, of course, should be hooked up to an HDTV tuner.

➤ **Multiple-jukebox DVD and CD controller.** Why settle with traditional DVD and CD jukeboxes? Link multiple jukeboxes together for high-volume storage, and manage the whole thing with the PowerPlay (for DVD) and TuneBase (for CD) products from Escient.

➤ **High-end audio/video separates.** Since you're in the nosebleed price range, spare no expense and go for the most expensive amplifiers, preamps, and digital signal processors money can buy, from manufacturers like Aragon, JBL, Krell, and Meridian. (Just make sure you don't hide them in a cabinet—especially if you want to impress your audiophile friends!)

➤ **Audiophile-quality speakers.** This is where you can really blow a load of dough. Start at ten grand minimum, and don't be surprised if you end up in the $40,000 range for some ultra-exotic speaker arrays from companies you've probably never heard of before. (But, boy, are these speakers cool-looking—and they sound great, too!)

➤ **Whole-house audio and video.** Naturally, you'll want to pipe audio and video throughout your entire house, so prepare to spend some extra bucks for additional video displays (including the obligatory plasma display) and speakers in however many rooms you want to wire. While you're wiring, make sure you include your AMX and Crestron whole-house control systems, complete with full-color touchpads in every room!

➤ **Integration with home automation system.** Finally, don't forget to link your a/v system with your home automation system—so you can use a single controller to raise your blinds, turn on the *Today* show, and start your coffeemaker!

The following table details just some of the potential components of an ultra high-end home theater system.

The Ultimate Home Theater System

Component	Target Price	Suggested Manufacturers
HDTV front projection television	$15,000+	Runco, Sony
DVHS VCR	$700+	Panasonic
Personal video recorder	$700+	Philips
WebTV Plus	$200+	Philips, Sony
Digital satellite system (bigger dish)	$400+	RCA, Sony
DVD jukebox and controller	$5,000+	Escient
CD jukebox and controller	$4,000+	Escient
CD recorder	$600+	Philips, Pioneer
Audiocassette recorder	$500+	JVC, Sony, Yamaha
Preamplifier	$2,500+	Aragon, JBL, Krell, Meridian
Amplifier	$2,000+	Aragon, Crown, JBL, Krell, Meridian
Surround-sound speakers and subwoofers	$10,000+	B&W, Cello, Cinepro, JBL, Legacy, M&K, Sonance, and others
Home automation and control system	$3,000+	AMX, Crestron

Where can you buy one of these dream systems? The *only* place to go is your CEDIA-certified home theater specialist—who can coordinate with your interior designer for your own truly custom installation!

The Least You Need to Know

➤ A thousand dollars will buy you a bare-bones system, consisting of a 27" TV, hi-fi VCR, and a "home theater in a box" speaker/receiver system.

➤ For $2,500 you get a slightly bigger direct view TV, DVD player, separate audio/video receiver, and surround-sound speaker package.

➤ With a $5,000 budget you can move up to a 45" rear projection TV and DVD changer, and add a digital satellite system to the mix.

➤ A $10,000 system lets you go digital-ready with a larger 16:9 rear projection set, better speakers, and a CD jukebox.

➤ If you can afford $25,000, you can go with a full HDTV system—including 65" rear projection TV, separate amp and preamp, and DVHS videocassette recorder.

➤ When money is no object, your system should include a really big front projection display (complete with HDTV tuner and line multiplier), DVD and CD jukebox control systems, whole-house audio and video, and integration with a home automation system.

Glossary

1.85:1   The most common wide-screen aspect ratio used in theatrical films.

1080i   One of the two main HDTV formats; transmits 1,080 lines of resolution with interlaced scanning.

16:9   The aspect ratio used in HDTV broadcasts; a 16:9 picture is 16 units wide by 9 units high. The 16:9 aspect ratio presents a wider image area than the traditional 4:3 ratio. Also measured as 1.78:1.

2.35:1   The widest possible aspect ratio used in theatrical films.

4:3   The NTSC standard aspect ratio for traditional TVs; a 4:3 picture is four units wide by three units high. Also measured as 1.33:1.

5.1   Dolby Digital produces five separate surround channels plus one subwoofer channel—thus, the "5.1" designation.

780p   One of the two main HDTV formats; transmits 780 lines of resolution with progressive scanning.

8mm   Recording format for camcorders that uses a videocassette with 8mm tape.

acoustic suspension   A type of speaker enclosure which uses a sealed box to provide accurate, tight bass response.

amplifier   A component that amplifies audio signals that are then output to one or more speakers.

analog   A means of transmitting or storing data using a continuously variable signal. Prone to signal degradation; does not always accurately reproduce the original.

anamorphic   A type of wide-screen display format available on selected DVD discs, which features increased resolution when played back on a 16:9 ratio TV.

aspect ratio   The ratio between the width and height of a video display. The NTSC television standard is 4:3, where HDTV uses a 16:9 ratio. Some wide-screen movies use an even wider ratio, either 1.85:1 or 2.35:1.

audio   Sound.

audio/video receiver   A combination of amplifier and preamplifier that controls both audio and video inputs and outputs. Most a/v receivers include some sort of surround-sound decoder, either Dolby Pro Logic or the newer (and slightly more expensive) Dolby Digital. Also called an *a/v receiver*.

bandwidth   Refers to the range of frequencies a component can reproduce, or the amount of information that can be carried by a circuit or signal. The larger the bandwidth, the better the sound or picture.

bass reflex   A type of speaker enclosure which includes a precisely designed or "tuned" opening in the enclosure. Typically louder—though less accurate—than acoustic suspension speakers.

bipole   A speaker design which generates equal amounts of in-phase sound both forward and backward. Typically used for rear-channel speakers in a surround-sound setup.

CD   Compact disc; a laser-based digital format for storing high-quality audio programming.

CD-R   CD-Recordable; compact discs that can be recorded (once) by home CD recorders.

CD-ROM   CDs specially formatted to store computer data.

CD-RW   CD-Rewritable; compact discs that can be recorded several times by computer-based CD recorders.

channel   One section of an audio track, usually carrying the sound for a single speaker.

chrominance   The color component of a video signal that includes information about the image's color (hue) and saturation.

comb filter   An electronic component in a television or other video display that removes residual chrominance (color) information from the luminance (brightness) signal, thus enhancing fine picture detail.

component video   A video signal which has been split into its component parts—red (Pr), green (Y), and blue (Pb). Component video connections—found on higher-end TVs and DVD players—reproduce the best possible picture quality, with improved color accuracy and reduced color bleeding.

composite video   A single video signal that contains both chrominance (color) and luminance (brightness) and information. Composite video is typically delivered through a single "video" RCA jack connection, and delivers a better-quality picture than an RF signal, but not as good as an S-Video signal.

CRT   Cathode ray tube, commonly called a picture tube. Used in all direct view, all rear projection, and some front projection televisions.

dB   Decibel, the standard unit of measure for expressing relative power differences—otherwise known as loudness. One dB is the smallest change in loudness most people can detect; a 10 dB difference produces twice the volume.

DBS   Digital broadcast satellite, or direct broadcast satellite; the satellite broadcasting system that uses a small 18" satellite dish to receive signals from a high-powered satellite in geosynchronous orbit.

digital   A means of transmitting or storing data using "on" and off" bits (expressed as "1" or "0"). Known for its highly accurate reproduction, with little or no degradation from the original.

Digital 8   Digital recording format for camcorders that utilizes standard 8mm or Hi8 cassettes.

digital compression   Any algorithm that reduces the storage space required to store or transmit information. MPEG2 is the most popular digital compression scheme today.

digital television   Television signals broadcast digitally; the U.S. TV standard that will become mandatory in 2006. DTV comes in several different formats, each with varying types of picture resolution and sound quality. The highest quality of these formats is called HDTV.

dipole   A speaker design that generates equal amounts of sound both forward and backward, with the two sounds being out of phase. Dipoles are often used as surround speakers.

DIRECTV   One of the two main providers of digital satellite programming.

DIVX   A type of DVD disc with regulated playback that is now obsolete.

DLP   Digital Light Processor, the technology that controls DMD front projection displays.

DMD   Digital Micromirror Device, a type of front projection video display that uses thousands of small mirrors, controlled by a DLP.

Dolby AC-3   The previous name for Dolby Digital.

Dolby Digital   Surround-sound format, sometimes referred to as 5.1. Incorporates six discrete digital audio channels: front left, front center, front right, surround left, surround right, and a "low frequency effects" channel for subwoofers.

Dolby Digital EX   Extended version of the Dolby Digital surround-sound format, with 6.1 channels. The extra channel is a matrixed rear surround channel positioned at the rear of the room, behind and between the left and right surrounds.

Dolby HX Pro   This circuit adjusts cassette tape bias during recording to extend dynamic headroom (the difference between the loudest and the softest audible signals) and improve the tape deck's ability to record high frequencies without distortion. Dolby HX Pro requires no decoding.

253

Dolby noise reduction   Noise reduction systems used on audiocassette decks. There are several different types of Dolby noise reduction, including Dolby B, Dolby C, Dolby S, and Dolby HX Pro.

Dolby Pro Logic   The predecessor to Dolby Digital, with only four channels: front left, front center, front right, and a single "surround" channel. The single surround channel is typically sent to two or more rear speakers. Dolby Pro Logic channels are matrixed into a left and right output, where Dolby Digital uses six discrete outputs.

DSP   Digital Signal Processing, computer-based circuitry used in some surround-sound receivers that creates different simulated sound fields.

DSS   Digital satellite system; see *DBS*.

DTS   Digital Theater Systems, a 5.1 surround-sound format that competes (some-what unsuccessfully) with Dolby Digital.

DTS ES   A 6.1 version of DTS surround sound; the extra channel is a matrixed rear surround positioned behind and between the left and rear surrounds.

DTV   See *digital television.*

DVD   An audio/video laser-based disc format with storage capacities ranging from 4.7 gigabytes to 17 gigabytes. (The initials DVD, which initially stood for digital video disc—and then digital versatile disc—currently don't stand for anything.)

DVD-Audio   New audio-only DVD format that delivers better-than-CD quality sound; competes with SA-CD.

DVD-ROM   DVD discs specially formatted to store computer data.

DVHS   New videocassette format that can record and play back 16:9 HDTV pro-gramming.

DVR   Digital video recorder, a device that records programming digitally on a large hard disk. Also known as personal video recorder (PVR) or personal television receiver (PTR).

dynamic range   The difference between loud and soft sounds.

EchoStar   Through the DISH Network, one of the two main providers of digital satellite programming.

field   When using interlaced scanning, half of a *frame* of picture information.

FPTV   Front projection television, a video display device that projects a picture onto the front of a separate screen.

frame   One single still image, that when played in rapid succession with other frames, creates a moving picture.

frequency response   The range of frequencies accurately reproduced by a particular component; the wider the range, the better.

HDTV   High-definition television, a subset of the new digital TV standard that reproduces pictures in either 780p or 1080i resolution, with a 16:9 aspect ratio and Dolby Digital 5.1 surround sound.

Hi8   High-resolution version of the 8mm camcorder format.

home theater   The attempt to reproduce, as accurately as possible, the experience of watching a film in a movie theater. Typically involves a high-quality video source (such as DVD), audio/video receiver, surround-sound speakers, and a large video display device.

horizontal resolution   The sharpness of a video display, measured in terms of horizontal lines that can be resolved from one side of the screen to the other. Broadcast television has a horizontal resolution of 330 lines; DVDs deliver 500 lines; and HDTV can deliver up to 1,080 lines of horizontal resolution.

Hz   Hertz, a unit of measurement for the frequency of sounds. One Hz is equal to one cycle per second, and the range of human hearing is typically 20–20,000 Hz.

interlaced scanning   A method of displaying television pictures where the picture is displayed in two halves (one of odd-numbered lines, one of even-numbered lines) that are interlaced together to create the full picture.

laserdisc   An older laser-based format for delivering audio/video programming on 12" discs. Laserdiscs deliver 425 lines of nondigital horizontal resolution, where DVDs deliver 500 lines, digitally.

LCD projector   A type of front projector that generates a picture using a liquid crystal display, which is then projected through a magnifying lens.

LD   See *laserdisc*.

letterbox   A method of displaying an entire wide-screen image on a narrower screen, using black bars above and below the picture.

light-valve projector   A type of front projector that combines LCD and CRT projection technology.

line doubler   See *line multiplier*.

line multiplier   A circuit that doubles, triples, or quadruples the number of lines that make up a picture, perceptively increasing picture detail while decreasing the incidence of flicker and visible scan lines.

LNB   Low Noise Blocker, a small amplifier located on the arm of a satellite dish that receives digital satellite transmissions.

luminance   The brightness or black-and-white component of a color video signal; determines the level of picture detail.

Mini DV   Digital video recording format for camcorders that uses an ultra-small cassette.

monopole The most common type of speaker that fires in only one direction (forward); compare with *bipole* and *dipole* speakers that fire in two opposing directions.

MPEG2 The method of compressing digital video signals used by DVDs, digital broadcast satellites, and digital and high-definition television.

NTSC National Television System Committee, the industry group that established the current North American analog broadcast TV standard. Sometimes refers to the standard itself.

PAL The European broadcast standard.

pan-and-scan A technique used to display the most important parts of a widescreen image on a narrower 4:3 ratio screen. The name comes from the panning and scanning necessary to keep the focus on the most important part of the scene, which is not always in the direct center of the picture.

PIP Picture-in-picture, the display of a second picture in a small window within a larger picture.

pixel The individual picture elements that make up a video image.

plasma display A flat-panel video display that uses plasma gas to "light up" individual pixels in a picture.

preamplifier A component that controls or switches the various inputs from audio and video sources.

progressive scanning A method of displaying television pictures where the picture is displayed in a single pass, instead of the two fields used with *interlaced scanning*. A progressively scanned picture more accurately reproduces fast action, and minimizes the visibility of flicker and scan lines.

PTR Personal television receiver. See *DVR*.

PVR Personal video recorder. See *DVR*.

receiver A component that combines a preamplifier, amplifier, and radio in a single chassis. Receivers that include inputs and outputs for video sources and display are called *audio/video receivers*.

region codes The codes embedded in DVD discs that define what global regions in which the disc can be played.

ReplayTV One of the two systems using a hard disk drive to record television programming digitally. These units are alternately referred to as digital video recorders (DVRs) or personal video recorders (PVRs).

resolution The measurement of picture detail, typically measured in terms of horizontal lines that can be seen or resolved on a display. See *horizontal resolution*.

RPTV Rear projection television, a video display device that uses three CRTs to project a picture backwards within a cabinet onto a mirror, which then reflects the picture onto the back of a translucent screen.

SA-CD   Super-audio CD; a new CD-based format that delivers better-than-CD quality sound. Competes with *DVD-Audio.*

scan lines   The horizontal lines, scanned one after another, that comprise the picture on a video display. (Don't confuse with *horizontal resolution,* which measures the visible number of lines in a display.)

signal-to-noise ratio   A measure of the content portion of an audio or video signal in relation to the noise contained in the signal, expressed in decibels (dB). A higher S/N ratio indicates a quieter or less noisy signal. As an example, VHS VCRs have S/N ratios in the 40 dB range, where DVDs have S/N ratios approaching 65 dB.

subwoofer   A speaker specially designed to reproduce a range of very low frequencies— typically 20–200 Hz. Subwoofers are common in home theater systems, to enhance the reproduction of low bass in movie soundtracks.

surround sound   The experience of being surrounded by sound from a video or audio source. Typically achieved with a surround-sound decoder (either Dolby Digital or Dolby Pro Logic) and multiple speakers.

S-VHS   Super VHS, a variation on the standard VHS format that delivers sharper pictures (400 lines of resolution vs. 240 lines for standard VHS).

S-Video   A four-pin connection that transmits the chrominance (color) and luminance (brightness) portions of a video signal separately, for improved color accuracy and reduced distortion.

THD   Total harmonic distortion, a measurement of the noise generated by an amplifier or receiver. The lower the number, the better.

THX   A set of high-fidelity standards, above and beyond the Dolby Digital standard, for both home theater equipment and prerecorded programming.

TiVo   One of the two systems using a hard disk drive to record television programming digitally. These units are alternately referred to as digital video recorders (DVRs) or personal television receivers (PTRs).

tweeter   A small, lightweight driver within a speaker enclosure that reproduces the highest musical frequencies.

V-Chip   Government-mandated chip included in newer television sets that can block the display of inappropriate programming.

VCR Plus+   VCR technology that uses preassigned codes to record specific programs.

VHS   Today's standard videocassette format.

VHS-C   A recording format for camcorders that uses standard VHS-format tape in a smaller-shelled cassette.

VHS HiFi   A variation on the standard VHS format that includes high-fidelity stereo sound. VHS HiFi VCRs can also play back tapes encoded with Dolby Pro Logic surround sound—although they can't reproduce Dolby Digital soundtracks.

video   Picture.

WebTV   Devices that access the Internet using a television set as the main display.

wide-screen   A picture with an aspect ratio wider than 4:3 or 1.33:1.

woofer   A driver within a speaker enclosure that uses a large cone to reproduce bass frequencies.

wow and flutter   Measures the accuracy of a cassette deck's playback speed; the lower, the better.

Home Theater Resources

If you want more information about home theater systems, you've come to the right place! This appendix lists the best audio/video magazines, Web sites, manufacturers, and online retailers.

Magazines

The following are some of the leading audio/video magazines, along with their related Web sites:

➤ *Audio Video Interiors* (www.audiovideointeriors.com)

➤ *Home Cinema Choice* (www.homecinemachoice.com)

➤ *Home Theater* (www.hometheatermag.com)

➤ *Sound & Vision* (www.soundandvisionmag.com)

➤ *The Perfect Vision* (www.theperfectvision.com)

➤ *Widescreen Review* (www.widescreenreview.com)

General Web Sites

The following Web sites are good general sources of information about home theaters and audio/video systems:

➤ About.com Home Electronics
   (homeelectronic.about.com/hobbies/homeelectronic/mbody.htm)

➤ Active Buyer's Guide: Home Theater Systems
   (www.hometheatersystems.activebuyersguide.com)

➤ AmateurHomeTheater.com (www.amateurhometheater.com)

➤ AudioREVIEW (www.audioreview.com)

➤ CEDIA Home Theater Automation (www.cedia.org)

➤ DBSDish.com (www.dbsdish.com)

➤ Digital Theater (www.digitaltheater.com)

➤ eTown (www.e-town.com)

➤ Remote Central (www.remotecentral.com)

➤ Sam's Digital Television Report (www.teleport.com/~samc/hdtv/index.html)

➤ Stereophile Guide to Home Theater (www.guidetohometheater.com)

Manufacturers' Web Sites

The following are Web sites for selected manufacturers of audio and video equipment:

➤ Bose (www.bose.com)

➤ DIRECTV (www.directv.com)

➤ EchoStar/DISH Network (www.dishnetwork.com)

➤ Escient (www.escient.com)

➤ JVC (www.jvc-america.com)

➤ Loewe (www.loewetv.com)

➤ Mitsubishi (www.mitsubishi-tv.com)

➤ Onkyo (www.onkyousa.com)

➤ Panasonic (www.panasonic.com/host/consumer.html)

➤ Philips (www.philipsusa.philips.com)

➤ Pioneer (www.pioneerelectronics.com)

➤ RCA (www.rca.com)

➤ ReplayTV (www.replaytv.com)

➤ Runco (www.runco.com)

➤ Sony (www.sel.sony.com/SEL/consumer/)

➤ Technics (www.panasonic.com/consumer_electronics/technics_audio/index.htm)

➤ TiVo (www.tivo.com)

➤ Toshiba (www.toshiba.com/tacp/)

➤ Yamaha (www.yamaha.com)

Retailers' Web Sites

The following are Web sites for selected online retailers of audio and video equipment and software:

- ➤ Amazon.com (www.amazon.com)
- ➤ AVIA Home Theater Search Engine (www.avia.org)
- ➤ Best Buy (www.bestbuy.com)
- ➤ CDNow (www.cdnow.com)
- ➤ Circuit City (www.circuitcity.com)
- ➤ Crutchfield (www.crutchfield.com)
- ➤ DishDirect (www.dishonline.com)
- ➤ DVD City (www.dvdcity.com)
- ➤ DVD Express (www.dvd.com)
- ➤ GetPlugged.com (www.getplugged.com)
- ➤ hifi.com (www.hifi.com)
- ➤ J&R Music World (www.jandr.com)
- ➤ ROXY.com (www.roxy.com))

Index

Symbols

1080i, 48-49
  formats, 68
  HDTVs, 48-49
27" televisions, costs, 240
2look4, Web site, 168
32" televisions, costs, 241
5.1 audio
  connections, RCA jacks, 187-188
  DVDs, 98-99
8mm, 106
  batteries, 106
  camcorders, 106
  Hi8, 106
  qualities, 106
  recording times, 106
  sound systems, 81-82, 106
  video resolutions, 81-82
  video sources, 81-82

A

A connections, speakers, 155
ABC, 65
About.com Home Electronics, Web site, 259
accurate reproductions, digital videos, 74-75
acoustic-suspension speaker design, 150
Acoustics Research, speakers, 247
Active Buyer's Guide: Home Theater Systems, Web site, 259
adapters, VHS-C, 105-106
advantages
  broadcast televisions, 76
  cable televisions, 76
  DBS, 77
  DVD, 77-78
  DVR, 79-80
  VCR, 78-79
advertisements, research, 19-21
Aiwa, HTIB, 180, 240
Allen wrenches, RTA furniture, 224
AM/FM tuners, 6-7
Amateur Home Theaters, Web site, 259
Amazon, Web site, 100, 110, 261
amplifiers, 13-14, 138-139
  costs, 247-248
  integrated, 140
  speakers, 138-139
subwoofers, 155-156
THD, 141
THX, 134
AMX
  custom remote controls, 206
  home automation systems, 249
analog
  broadcasts, 60-61
  line audio connections, 187
  video sources, 74-75
anamorphic discs and modes, DVDs, 90-91
antennae, 118-119, 143
  connections, 192-193
  televisions, 15
anti-copy circuit, DVDs, 96-97
Aragon, amplifiers, 248-249
askMP3, Web site, 168
assembling the connections, 177-178
audio, 126. *See also* audio/video; sound systems; surround-sound systems; video
  5.1 connections, 187-188
  channels
    Dolby Digital, 127-130

Dolby Digital EX, 129-130
Dolby Pro Logic, 131-132
DTS systems, 132-133
CD
    changers, 160-161
    players, 6-7, 14-15, 159
    recorders, 161, 167
digital connections, 188-189
equipment, Web sites, 260-261
formats, DVDs, 91-92
home automation systems, 228
line connections, 187
multiple-room installations, 226-228
sources, 4-5
    AM/FM tuners, 6-7
    amplifiers, 13-14
    audiocassette decks, 5-7, 15-17, 165-166
    costs, 5-7
    DVD players, 14-15, 91-92, 162
    DVD-A players, 163-164
    MiniDisc recorders, 167
    MP3 recorders, 167-169
    receivers, 6-7, 13-14
    SACD players, 162-164

satellite receivers, 115-117
shopping lists, 16-17
speakers, 6-7, 14, 126, 156-157
    connections, 189-190
    surround-sound systems, 8
troubleshooting, 212-213
    audiocasettes, 215
    bad sound, 214
    buzzing, 213-214
    CDs, 214-215
    rear speakers, 215-216
    speaker hookups, 212
Audio Video Interiors, magazine and Web site, 222, 259
audio/video. *See also* audio; sound systems; surround-sound systems; video
    equipment, 22
    furniture, 225
    receivers, 6-7, 13-16, 120, 135, 138-139
        amplifiers, 138-139
        bandwidth, 140
        buying, 23
        connections, 142-145, 191-192, 196
        costs, 140-145, 241-244

DTS circuitry, 132-133
    HTIB systems, 180
    inputs, 142-145
    output power, 140
    outputs, 142-145
    performance specifications, 140-141
    power, 145
    preamplifiers, 138
    remote controls, 144-145
    setup, 191-192, 196
    shopping, 145-146
    sound, 146
    surround-sound systems, 8, 141-145
    weight, 141
shopping, equipment, 22
specialists, retailers, 21
audiocassette players, 165-166
    costs, 5-7, 246
    frequencies, 165-166
    troubleshooting, 215
Audiofind, Web site, 168
AudioREVIEW, Web site, 20, 259
automatic clock sets, 107-108
auxiliary satellites, 119
available sources (video), 82-83
AVIA Home Theater Search Engine, Web site, 261
awards, CEDIA, 232-238

B

B connections, speakers, 155

B&K
   amplifiers, 247
   preamplifiers, 247

B&W, speakers, 249

backward-compatible DVDs, 93-94

balance (tonal), speakers, 156

bandwidth
   audio/video receivers, 140
   digital broadcasts, 60-61
   Dolby Digital, 127-130

bass
   reflex speaker design, 150
   subwoofer selecting, 155-156

batteries
   8mm, 106
   remote controls, 211
   VHS-C, 106

Best Buy, 20-22, 261

Best Home Theater Electronic System Design, TDI, 232-238

Best Video Product, Escient, 232-238

bipole speaker designs, 148-151, 155

bits, information, 74-75

black bars, DVDs, 90-91

bookshelf speakers, 150

Bose Corporation, 150-153
   speakers, 182, 241-243
   Web site, 260

Boston Acoustics, speakers, 245

boxes, cable, 118-119

brand names, televisions, 42-43

broadcast
   analog, 60
   digital, 60
   HDTVs, 65-66
   recording, DVRs, 111-113
   television, 86-87
      advantages, 76
      disadvantages, 76
      sound systems, 81-82
      video resolutions, 81-82
      video sources, 74-76, 81-82

budgets, 23, 239-249

buying 23, 145. *See also* shopping
   FPTV, 52
   HDTV, 66-68
   receivers, 23
   RPTV, 49
   speakers, 23
   televisions, 23
   video sources, 82-83

buzzing, troubleshooting, 213-214

C

cable
   boxes, 118-119, 143, 194, 223
   coaxial, 115-117, 119, 184-189
   connections, 192-193
   digital, 74-75
   fiber-optic, 188-189

cable televisions, 15, 86-87
   advantages/disadvantages, 76
   sound systems, 81-82
   VHSs, 104
   video resolutions, 81-82
   video sources, 74-76, 81-82

camcorders, 144
   8mm, 106
   cameras, 105
   connections, 106-107
   Digital 8, 106-107
   Hi8, 106
   input/output, 80-81
   Mini DVs, 107
   VCR, 78-79
   VHS-C, 105-106
   video recorders, 105
   video sources, 80-81

cameras, camcorders, 105

carousels, DVDs, 95-96

cassette decks, 165-166

catalog merchants, 21

cathode ray tube. *See* CRT, 35

CBS, 62-65

CD Now, Web site, 100, 261

CD-R discs (CD-recordable discs), 93-94, 161, 167

CD-Recordable discs. *See* CD-R discs

CD-Rewritable discs. *See* CD-RW discs

CD-ROM drives, computers, 97

CD-RW discs (CD-Rewritable discs), 161, 167

CDs (compact discs), 161-162
  changers, 160-161
  costs
    CD players, 5-7, 159
    CD recorders, 161, 167, 246
    jukeboxes, 160-161, 244-246
  DVD changers/players, 93-96, 162
  DVD-A, 163
  jukeboxes, 160-161, 244-246
  players, 6-7, 14-17, 142
    connections, 192
    costs, 5-7, 159
  recorders, 143, 161, 167, 246
  skipping, 215
  Super Audio, 162
  troubleshooting, 214-215

CEDIA (Custom Electronic Design and Installation Association), 22, 232

awards, 232-233, 235-238
  Home Theater Automation, Web site, 259
  Web site, 22, 231, 259

Cello, speakers, 249

changers
  CD, 160-161
  DVDs, 94

ChannelMaster, 121

channels
  audio
    Dolby Digital, 127-130
    Dolby Digital EX, 129-130
    Dolby Pro Logic, 131-132
    DTS systems, 132-133
    low-frequency effects, 129
    matrixing, 126
    Dolby Digital, 127-130
    Dolby Digital EX, 129-130
    Dolby Pro Logic, 131-132

chips, surround-sound decoders, 141-142

choosing
  custom installers, 230
  video sources, 82-83

chrominance
  component video, 185-186
  composite video connections, 184-185
  RGB video, 187
  S-Video, 185

cinemascope, wide-screen formats, 30, 32

Cinepro, speakers, 249

circuit breakers, troubleshooting, 210-211

Circuit City, 20-22, 87-89, 261

coaxial cable, 115-119, 185-186
  digital audio connections, 188-189
  RF connections, 184

comb filters
  FPTVs, 53-54
  RPTVs, 53-54
  televisions, 43-45

compact discs. *See* CDs

compact VHS. *See* VHS-C

compatibilities, video sources, 82-83

Complete Idiot's Guide to Surfing the Internet with WebTV, The, book, 80

component videos
  connections, 185-186
    chrominance, 185-186
    luminance, 185-186
    RCA jacks, 185-186
  DVDs, 98-99

composite videos
  connections, 184-185
    chrominance, 184-185
    luminance, 184-185
    RCA jacks and plugs, 184-185
  DVDs, 98-99

computers
  CD-ROM drives, 97
  DVD drives, 97
  DVD-ROMs, 93-94
  flat-screen plasma displays, 58
connections, 184. *See also* inputs/outputs; outputs
  5.1 audio, 187-188
  A, speakers, 155
  antennae, 192-193
  assembling, 177-178
  audio/video receivers, 142-145, 191-192, 196
  B, speakers, 155
  cables, 192-193
  camcorders, 106-107
  CD players, 192
  component videos, 185-186
  composite videos, 184-185
  diagrams, 190-194
    audio/video receivers, 191-192, 196
    televisions, 192-193
  digital audio, 188-189
    coaxial cable, 188-189
    fiber-optic cable, 188-189
  digital satellite receivers, 192-193
  DVD players, 98-100, 192-193
  FireWires, 66-68, 245
  line audio, 187

Mini DVs, 107
RF, 184
RGB video, 187
S-Video, 185
speakers, 189-190
  A connections, 155
  B connections, 155
  negative leads, 189-190
  positive leads, 189-190
  subwoofers, 190
televisions, 192-193
VCR players, 192-193
contents, flat-screen plasma displays, 55-56
control processors, custom remote controls, 204-207
converges, CRTs, 50-52
converters, digital formats, 62-64
costs
  amplifiers, 247-248
  audio/video receivers, 140-145, 241-245
  audiocassette recorders, 246
  CD jukeboxes, 160-161, 244, 246
  CD players, 159
  CD recorders, 161, 167, 246
  custom installers, 235
  Digital 8, 106-107
  DIRECTV, 117-119, 244
  Dolby Digital, 135
  DSS, 242-246
  DVD changers, 242-243

DVD players, 77-78, 94-95, 241, 244-247
DVD-A, 163
DVHS video receivers, 246
DVRs, 79-80, 110-112
EchoStar, 117-119
flat-screen plasma displays, 57
  televisons, 36-37
FPTVs, 36-37, 52-54, 248
furniture, home theater system storage, 221-223
HDTVs, 31-32, 66-68, 245-248
home automation systems, 249
HTIB systems, 180, 240
IntelliControl (Niles Audio), custom remote controls, 205
MiniDisc recorders, 167
multiple jukeboxes, 248
personal digital video recorders, 246
preamplifiers, 246-248
programmable remote controls, 245
projectors, 50-52
remote controls, 197-199, 205, 245-247
RPTVs, 36-37, 47, 52-54, 242-245
SACD players, 162
speakers, 182, 241-249
subwoofers, 244-247

surround-sound speaker systems, 241-247
televisions, 38-39, 42, 240-241
27", 240
32", 241
VCRs, 78-79, 240-245
VHS HiFi VCRs, 240-242
video sources, 75-76, 82-83
WebTV Plus, 246
whole-house audio and video installations, 226-228
countries, DVDs, 92-93
creating a home theater room, 174-175
Creston
custom remote controls, 206
home automation systems, 249
Crown, amplifiers, 249
CRT (cathode ray tube), 35, 42, 48-50
converges, 50-52
FPTVs, 36, 49-50
LCDs, 36
projectors, 50-52
RPTVs, 48-49
televisions, 35-36
Crutchfield, Web site, 261
custom a/v furniture, 225
Custom Electronic Design and Installation Association. *See* CEDIA
custom installations, 226

equipment storage, 225-226
home automation systems, 228
home theater systems, 229-236
choosing, 230
costs, 235
evaluating, 230-231
finding, 231
retailers, 21
TDI, interviews, 232-238
multiple-room systems, 226-228
custom remote controls, 199, 204-207
AMX, 206
control processors, 204-207
Creston, 206
IntelliControl, 205
system controllers, 204-207

D

DAILYMP3, Web site, 168
dark tubes, televisions, 43-45
DBS Dish, Web site, 260
DBS (digital broadcast satellite) systems, 17, 62-68, 74-75, 115-117. *See also* DSS; satellite systems
advantages, 77
DIRECTV, 77, 117-119
disadvantages, 77

DISH Network (from EchoStar), 117-119
dishes, 15
Dolby Digital format, 77
EchoStar, 77, 117-119
pay-per-view-movies, 77
receivers
Dolby Digital 5.1, 115-117
Dolby Pro Logic, 115-117
sound systems, 77, 81-82
video resolutions, 81-82
video sources, 74-77, 81-82
deals, 24
decoders
digital formats, 62-64
Dolby Digital, 5.1 audio connections, 187-188
Dolby Digital EX, 152
Dolby Pro Logic, 131-132
DTS, 132-133
DVD players, 99-100
receivers, 130
surround-sound audio/video receivers, 141-142
preamplifiers, 138
Definitive Technology speakers, 182, 241-245
subwoofers, 245
demonstration materials, 23

designs (speakers),
150-151
  acoustic-suspension,
  150
  bass reflex, 150
  bipole, 148, 151, 155
  dipole, 151, 155
  monopole, 148
development, DVDs,
87-89
diagrams, connections,
190-191, 194
  audio/video receivers,
  191-192, 196
  televisions, 192-193
diaphragms, speakers,
148
digital
8
  camcorders,
  106-107
  costs, 106-107
  qualities, 106-107
  sound systems,
  81-82, 106-107
  video resolutions,
  81-82
  video sources, 81-82
  audio connections,
  188-189
  coaxial cable,
  188-189
  fiber-optic cable,
  188-189
  RCA jacks, 188-189
  audios, DVDs, 98-99
  broadcasts, 60-64
  bandwidth, 60-61
  compressions,
  60-61

HDTVs, 74-75
inputs/outputs,
60-61
timetables, 65-66
cable, 74-75
formats
  converters, 62-64
  decoders, 62-64
  inputs/outputs,
  62-64
recording, DVDs,
96-97
televisions, 31-33,
43-45, 62-68
videos, 74-75
digital broadcast satellite
systems. *See* DBS systems
digital light processing.
See DLP
digital micromirror
device. *See* DMD
digital-ready
televisions, 31-32
digital satellite systems.
See DSS
digital signal processing
chips. *See* DSP chips
digital sound processing
modes. See DSP modes
Digital Theater, Web
site, 5, 260
digital theater sound
systems. *See* DTS systems
digital versatile discs. *See*
DVDs
digital VHS. *See* DVHS
digital video recorders.
See DVRs
Dimension Music, Web
site, 168

dipole speaker designs,
151, 155
direct view televisions,
35-36, 42
DIRECTPC systems, 119
DIRECTV, 60-61,
117-122
  bandwidth, 118
  costs, 117-119, 244
  DBS, 77
  HDTV programming,
  121
  local network stations,
  118-119
  receivers, 117-119
  satellite systems,
  32-33, 62-65
  services, 118
  shopping, 121-122
  tuners, 117-119
  Web site, 119, 260
DIRECTV Plus, 119-122
disadvantages
  broadcast televisions,
  76
  cable televisions, 76
  DBS, 77
  DVD, 77-78
  DVR, 79-80
  VCR, 78-79
discs
  CD-R, 161, 167
  CD-RW, 161, 167
  DVD, 87-89
DISH 500, 121-122
Dish Direct, Web site,
261
DISH Network services
(from EchoStar),
117-121
  bandwidth, 118

costs, 117-119
HDTV programming, 121
local network stations, 118-119
receivers, 112, 117-119
Web site, 119
dishes
DBS, 15
DIRECTPC, 119
multiple-LNB, 121
satellites, 115-117
installation, 119-120
mounting, 119
distorted television pictures, troubleshooting, 219
DIVXs, 87-89
DLP (digital light processing), 50-52
DMD (digital micromirror device), 50-52
Dolby B, noise reduction, 166, 215
Dolby C, noise reduction, 166, 215
Dolby Digital sound, 4, 117, 122, 126-129, 133, 141-142
5.1 audio connections, 187-188
audio channels, 127-130
bandwidth, 127-130
costs, 135
decoders, 86-87, 130

DVDs, decoders, 86-87
formats
DBS, 77
DVD, 77-78, 86-87
HDTV programming, 121
HTIB systems, 181
installation, 127-130
matrixing channels, 127-130
preamplifiers, 138
receivers, 115-117, 130
satellite receivers, 115-117
speakers, 128, 154-155
subwoofers, 155-156
surround-sound systems, 12-14, 86-87
Dolby Digital 5.1. *See* Dolby Digital sound
Dolby Digital 6.1. *See* Dolby Digital EX
Dolby Digital EX, 126-129, 133-135, 141, 152
audio channels, 129-130
installation, 129-130
matrixing channels, 129-130
speakers, 129-130
Dolby noise reduction, audiocassettes, 165-166
Dolby Pro Logic, 4, 117, 126-134, 141-145
audio channels, 131-132
decoders, 131-132

DVD formats, 86-87
HDTV programming, 121
HTIB systems, 181
installation, 131-132
matrixing channels, 131-132
preamplifiers, 138
satellite receivers, 115-117
speakers, 128, 131-132, 154-155
surround-sound systems, 12-14
Dolby S, noise reduction, 166
drivers, 148
midrange, 148
speakers
in phase, 149
out of phase, 149
tweeters, 148
woofers, 148
DSP (digital signal processing) chips, 126
DSP (digital sound processing) modes, 181
DSS (digital satellite systems), 6-11, 38-39, 42-45, 115-117. *See also* DBS systems; satellite systems
costs, 5-7, 242-246
DIRECTV, 117-119
DISH Network (from EchoStar), 117-119
EchoStar, 60-61
installation, 121

MPEG-2 digital compressions, 60-61
receivers
    Dolby Digital 5.1, 115-117
    Dolby Pro Logic, 115-117
DTS (Digital Theater Sound) systems, 4, 132-133, 142
    audio channels, 132-133
    audio/video receivers, 132-133
    decoders, 132-133
    movie theaters, 132-133
    preamplifiers, 138
    speakers, 132-133
dual LNB, 120-121
dual-side DVDs, 87-91
DVD City, Web sites, 261
DVD Express, Web site, 100, 261
DVD-A (DVD-Audio), 163
    costs, 163
    formats, 97-98
    shopping, 164
    technologies, 97-98
DVD-Audio. *See* DVD-A
DVD-ROMs, 93-97
DVDs (digital versatile discs), 32-33, 38-39, 43-45, 60-61, 66-68, 74-75, 78-80, 86-89
    5.1 audio, 98-99
    advantages, 77-78
    anamorphic discs and modes, 90-91

anti-copy circuits, 96-97
audio formats, 91-92
backward-compatible, 93-94
black bars, 90-91
carousels, 95-96
CD-Rs, 93-94
CDs, 93-94
changers, 94-96, 242
component videos, 98-99
composite videos, 98-99
computers, drives, 97
connections, 98-99
    component videos, 98-99
    composite videos, 98-99
    RF (coax), 98-99
    S-Videos, 98-99
costs, 5-7, 77-78, 94-95, 241-246
countries, 92-93
development, 87-89
digital audios, 98-99
digital recording, 96-97
disadvantages, 77-78
discs, 87-89
    dual-side, 87-91
    movie ratings, 93
    personal identification numbers, 93
    ratings, 93
DIVXs, 87-89
Dolby Digital
    decoders, 86-87
    format, 77-78
    sound, 86-87

Dolby Pro Logic format, 86-87
drives, computers, 97
dual-side, 87-91
DVD-ROMs, 94
Escient's PowerPlay, 95-96
formats, 86-87, 92-93
home theater systems, 86-87
information, dual-side, 87-91
inputs/outputs, 86-87, 90, 94-95, 98-99
instructions, 93-94
jukebox-type, 95-96
laserdiscs, 80-81, 87-89
letterboxed, 87-91
MP3 discs, 93-94
MPEG-2 digital compressions, 60-61
multiple camera angles, 90
multiple languages, audio formats, 92
NTSC, 77-78, 86-87
options, 90
picture qualities, 86-87, 94-95
pits, 87-89
pixels, 90-91
players, 6-9, 12-17, 94, 142
    CDs, 161-162
    connections, 99-100, 192-193
    costs, 5-7, 94-95, 241-246
    decoders, 99-100

DVD players,
letterboxing, 30, 32
DVD-ROMs, 97
easy operations,
99-100
features, 94-95
interlaced scanning,
94-95
performances,
94-95
playing CDs, trou-
bleshooting,
214-215
progressive-
scanning, 94-95
single-play or
changer, 99-100
THX, 134
troubleshooting,
214-218
videophiles, 99-100
video sources, 30,
32
programming, 90
quality pictures, 87-89
recorders, 94-97
resolutions, 86-87,
96-97
region codes, 92-93
resolutions, 86-87,
96-97
RF (coax), 98-99
S-Video, 98-99
side/layer combina-
tions, 87-89
sound systems, 77-78,
81-82, 86-89
special effects, 87-89
special features, 90
storage capacity, 90
subtitle tracks, 92
technologies, 74-75,
87-89

traditional audios,
98-99
TuneBase, 95-96
two in one, 93-94
VHSs, 104
video resolutions,
81-82
video sources, 74-82
wide-screen formats,
90-91
DVHS (digital VHS),
78-79, 105
HDTVs, 105
sound systems, 81-82
video recorders,
66-68, 246
video resolutions,
81-82
video sources, 81-82
digital video recorders.
See DVRs
DVRs (digital video
recorders), 78-79,
109-113
advantages, 79-80
costs, 5-7, 79-80, 110,
112, 246
disadvantages, 79-80
hard disks, 113
installing, 112-113
Philips, 110
ReplayTV, 109-112
shopping, 113
sound systems, 79-80
TiVo, 109-112
video sources, 79-80

E

E! Online, Web site, 111
easy operations, DVD
players, 99-100

echoes, 174-175
EchoStar
bandwidth, 118
costs, 117-119
DBS, 77
DISH Network (from
EchoStar), 117-119
DISHplayer satellite
receivers, 112
DSS, 60-61
local network stations,
118-119
receivers, 117-119
shopping, 121-122
WebTV, 112
EchoStar/DISH Network,
Web site, 260
editing features, Mini
DVs, 107-108
efficiency, speakers, 157
eight-track players, 16
enclosures, 149-150
bookshelf speakers,
150
floor-standing
speakers, 149
in-wall speakers, 150
satellite speakers with
subwoofers, 150
equalizers, 134, 145
equipment
audio/video, 22
buying tips, 22-25
storage, 221-223
a/v furniture, 225
custom installation,
225-226
fine furniture,
224-225
RTA furniture,
223-224

Escient, 160
  Best Video Product, 232-238
  CD jukebox and controllers, 249
  DVD jukebox and controllers, 249
  PowerPlay, DVDs, 95-96
  Web site, 161, 260
eTown, Web site, 20, 260
evaluating custom installers, 230-231
extra features, DVDs, 86-87
extraneous noises, 174

F

fading satellite picture, troubleshooting, 217-218
features
  automatic clock sets, 107-108
  DVD players, 94-95
  four heads, 107-108
  HDTVs, 68
  Mini DVs, 107
  projectors, 50-52
  super VHS, 107-108
  VCR plus, 107-108
  VHS HiFi, 107-108
fiber-optic cable, digital audio connections, 188-189
fine furniture, 224-225
FireWires
  connections, 66-68, 245

digital cable, 74-75
IE1394, 66-68
firms, custom installers
  choosing, 230
  evaluating, 230-231
  finding, 231
  TDI, 232-238
five-disc carousels, CD changers, 160-161
flat sound speakers, 157
flat tubes, televisions, 43-45
flat-screen plasma televisions, 8, 12, 16, 36-37, 55-57
  computer compatibilities, 58
  contents, 55-56
  costs, 5-7, 36-37, 57
  HDTV compatibilities, 58
  inputs/outputs, 55-56
  measurements, 36-37
  picture qualities, 57-58
  prices, 57
  sizes, 36-37
  weight, 55-56
flicker, HDTVs, 64
floor-standing speakers, 149
FM sensitivity, 141
formats
  1080i, 68
  digital broadcasts, 62-64
  DVD, 86-87
  HDTV, 68
  Hi8, 106
  Mini DV, 107
  VHS, 104
four heads, features, 107-108

FOX, 62-65
FPTV (front projection television), 8, 12, 16, 36-37, 49-52
  buying advantages/disadvantages, 52
  comb filters, 53-54
  considerations, 37
  costs, 5-7, 36-37, 52-54, 248
  CRTs, 49-50
  HDTV capabilities, 53-54, 248
  inputs/outputs, 49-50, 53-54
  LCDs, 36
  line doublers, 53-54
  line multiplying, 49-50
  measurements, 37
  physical sizes, 53-54
  picture qualities, 53-54
  picture-in-picture, 53-54
  remote controls, 53-54
  screen sizes, 53-54
  sizes, 37, 49-52
  sound systems, 53-54
  V-Chip parental controls, 53-54
  viewing angles, 53-54
  viewing distances, 53-54
Frasier, television show, 112
frequencies
  audiocassette recorders, 165-166
  Dolby Digital ranges, 127-130

HTIB systems, 181
ranges, Dolby Digital, 127-130
speakers, 157
subwoofers, 155-156
tweeters, 148
woofers, 148
front left speakers, layout, 151-153
front projection televisions. *See* FPTVs
front right speakers, layout, 151, 153
furniture, equipment storage, 221-223
a/v, 225
fine, 224-225
RTA, 223-224
fuses, troubleshooting, 210-211
fuzzy television picture, troubleshooting, 217

G

GE, 32-33, 42-43
geosynchronous satellites, 115-117
Get Plugged, Web site, 261
gigabytes, information, 87-89
government-mandated HDTVs, 65-66
grainy television picture, troubleshooting, 217
gray market goods, 24

guides
on-screen, 117
programs, satellite receivers, 121

H

hard disks, DVRs, 113, 117
hard surfaces, home theater systems, 174
Harman/Kardon, remote controls, 203, 245
HBO, 66, 86
HDTVs (high-definition televisions), 9-12, 15-16, 31-32, 34-37, 48-49, 52, 55-57, 60-68, 78-79, 86-87
1080i, 48-49
antennas, 15
broadcasts, 65-66, 74-77
sound systems, 81-82
video resolutions, 81-82
video sources, 74-75, 81-82
buying, 66-68
costs, 31-32, 66-68, 243, 248
digital broadcasts, 74-75
DVHSs, 105
expectations, 64
features, 68
FireWires, connections, 68
flat-screen plasma displays, 58
flicker, 64

formats, 68
FPTVs, 53-54, 248
government-mandated, 65-66
high resolution, 31-32
inputs/outputs, 30, 32, 64-65, 68
manufacturers, 68
MPEG-2 digital compressions, 60-61
NTSC signals, 68
picture, 64
pixel resolutions, 68
programming, 121-122
Dolby Digital, 121
Dolby Pro Logic, 121
ratios, 30, 32
recommendations, 66-68
recorders, 66-68
RPTVs, 53-54, 243-245
sound, 64
technologies, 74-75
transmissions, 66-68
tuners, 31-32, 64-68
wide-screen productions, 64
height, video displays, 176
Hi8
8mm, 106
camcorders, 106
formats, 106
qualities, 106
sound systems, 81-82
SVHS, 106
video resolutions, 81-82
video sources, 81-82

HiFi
  VCR players, 5-9, 12-13, 16
  VHSs, 104
  Web site, 261
high-definition televisions. *See* HDTVs
high resolution HDTV, 31-32
hissing, audiocassette recorders, 165-166
home automation systems
  costs, 249
  installations, 228
  X-10 systems, 228
Home Cinema Choice, magazine and Web site, 259
Home Theater, magazine and Web site, 259
home theater in a box systems. *See* HTIB systems
home theater systems, 4-7, 15-16, 75-76
  audio sources
    amplifiers, 13-14
    audio/video receivers, 13-14
    audiocassette decks, 165-166
    CD players, 14-15
    CD recorders, 167
    DVD players, 14-15
    MiniDisc recorders, 167
    MP3 recorders, 167-169
    speakers, 14
  audio/video receivers, 139

amplifiers, 138-139
connections, 142-145
costs, 140-145
performance specifications, 140-141
preamplifiers, 138
remote controls, 144
shopping, 145-146
surround-sound, 141-142
buying equipment, tips, 23-25
connections, 184
  5.1 audio, 187-188
  assembling, 177-178
  component video, 185-186
  composite video, 184-185
  diagrams, 190-194, 196
  digital audio, 188-189
  line audio, 187
  RF, 184
  RGB video, 187
  S-Video, 185
  speakers, 189-190
costs, 5-7, 239-249
creating a home theater room, 174-175
DVDs, 86-87
DVRs, 109-113
  installing, 112-113
  shopping, 113
equipment storage, 221-223
  a/v furniture, 225
  custom installation, 225-226

fine furniture, 224-225
RTA furniture, 223-224
hard surfaces, 174
HTIB, 179
  costs, 180
  shopping, 181-182
installations, 226
  custom installers, 229-231
  home automation systems, 228
  multiple-room systems, 226-228
layouts, 176
light, 174
positioning your system, 176
remote controls, 197-199
  custom remotes, 204-207
  learning remotes, 201
  multiple-component remotes, 200
  programmable remotes, 202-203
  shopping, 207
  single-brand remotes, 200
  standard remotes, 200
  universal remotes, 200-201
research, 19-21
resources
  magazines, 259
  Web sites, 259-261

retailers, 21-22
satellites, connecting multiple receviers, 120-121
shopping lists, 17
speakers, 147, 156
 costs, 182
 designs, 150-151
 drivers, 148
 enclosures, 149-150
 layout, 151, 153
 selecting front speakers, 153-154
 selecting rear speakers, 154-155
 selecting subwoofer speakers, 155-156
 shopping, 157
stores, 21-22
surround-sound systems, 8, 134-135
televisions, 8, 11-12, 29-30, 32
troubleshooting, 210
 professional help, 219-220
 remote controls, 211
 sound, 212-216
 specific components, 211
 video, 216-219
video displays, 8, 11-12
video sources, 9
 DVD players, 12-13
 hi-fi VCR players, 12-13
Home Toys, Web site, 228

horizontal resolutions, 104
HTIB (home theater in a box) systems, 179
 costs, 180, 240
 Dolby Digital, 181
 Dolby Pro Logic, 181
 frequencies, 181
 shopping, 181-182
 speakers, 180
 subwoofers, 180-181
Hughes, 117

I

IE1394, FireWires, 66-68
in-wall speakers, 150
Infinity
 speakers, 241-247
 subwoofers, 245
information
 bits, 74-75
 DVDs, pits, 87-89
 gigabytes, 87-89
 microscopic pits, 87-89
 pits, 87-89
infrared remote controls, 198, 205, 211
inputs/outputs, 30, 32, 66-68. *See also* connections; outputs
 analog broadcasts, 60-61
 audio/video receivers, 142-145
 camcorders, 80-81

composite videos, 184-185
digital broadcasts, 60-61
digital cable, 74-75
digital formats, 62-64
DVDs, 86-87, 98-99
flat-screen plasma displays, 55-56
FPTVs, 49-50, 53-54
HDTVs, 64-65
HDTV tuners, 68
line multiplying, 49-50
preamplifiers, 138
RBGs, 64-65
RPTVs, 53-54
S-Video, 11-12, 16, 120, 181
televisions, 30, 32, 35-36, 43-45
VHS-Cs, 105-106
videogame systems, 81
installations, 226
 custom, 229-236
 choosing, 230
 costs, 235
 evaluating, 230-231
 finding, 231
 Dolby Digital, 127-130
 Dolby Digital EX, 129-130
 Dolby Pro Logic, 131-132
 DSS, 121
 dishes, 119-120
 receivers, 119-121
 DVRs, 112-113
 Escient, 232-238

home automation
systems, 228
multiple-room sys-
tems, 226-228
TDI, 232-238
whole-house systems,
226-228
instructions, DVDs,
93-94
integrated amplifiers,
140
IntelliControl, custom
remote controls, 205
interactivity, televisions,
32-33
interlaced scanning,
DVD players, 94-95
Internet
merchants, 21
MP3 recorders,
167-169
research, home the-
ater systems, 19-21
WebTV, 80-81, 117
interview with Jim
Swearingen, 232-238

J

J&R Music World, Web
site, 261
jacks
RCA
5.1 audio, 187-188
component video,
185-186
composite video,
184-185
digital audio,
188-189
line audio, 187
speakers, 189-190

JBL, speakers, 248-249
jukeboxes
CDs, 160-161
costs, 160-161, 248
DVDs, 95-96
multiple, 248
JVC, 20
a/v receivers, 241-243
Web site, 260

K

Kenwood
a/v receivers, 243
HTIB, 180, 240
KLH, speakers, 241
Klipsch speakers,
245-247
Krell amplifiers,
248-249

L

laserdisc players, 15-16,
86-87
DVDs, 80-81, 87-89
sound systems, 81-82
THX, 134
troubleshooting, 218
video resolutions,
81-82
video sources, 74-75,
80-82
laws, Satellite Home
Viewer Improvement
Act of 1999, 118-119
layouts
home theater systems,
176
speakers, 151-153

LCD
CRT, 36
FPTV, 36
screens, 55-56, 144
pixellation, 50-52
projectors, 50-52
learning remote con-
trols, 198, 201
LED, 120
left front speakers,
selecting, 153-154
left surround speakers
layout, 151-153
selecting, 154-155
Legacy, speakers, 249
letterbox
DVDs, 30, 32, 87-91
movies, 8
televisions, 30, 32
Lexicon, remote con-
trols, 247
light, home theater sys-
tems, 174
light valves, projectors,
50-52
line audio connections,
187
line doublers
FPTVs, 53-54
RPTVs, 53-54
line multiplying
FPTVs, 49-50
inputs/outputs, 49-50
technology, 34-35
LNB (Low Noise
Blocker), 115-122
local network stations,
118-119
Loewe, 42-43, 260
low-frequency effects,
127-129. *See also* sub-
woofers

Low Noise Blocker. *See* LNB

Lucasfilm, THX, 133-134

luminance
component video connections, 185-186
composite video connections, 184-185
RGB video connections, 187
S-Video connections, 185

Lycos Music MP3 Search, Web site, 168

M

M7K, speakers, 249

macros, remote controls, 199

magazines, 259
Audio Video Interiors, 222, 259
Home Cinema Choice, 259
Home Theater, 259
Perfect Vision, The, 259
research, home theater systems, 19-21
Sound & Vision, 259
Widescreen Review, 259

main satellites, 119

makes and models, 38-39, 43-45

manufacturers'
advertisments, 19-21
brand names, 42-43
HDTVs, 68
remote controls, 144, 200

televisions, 42-43
Web sites, 260

mass merchants, 21

matrixing channels, 126
Dolby Digital, 127-130
Dolby Digital EX, 129-130
Dolby Pro Logic, 131-132

measurements
flat-screen plasma televisions, 36-37
FPTVs, 37
RPTVs, 37
televisions, 30, 32, 35-36

menus, satellite receivers, 121

merchants
catalog, 21
home theater systems, 21-22
Internet, 21
mass, 21

Meridian, amplifiers, 248-249

microscopic pits, information, 87-89

midrange drivers, 148

Mini DVs, 107

MiniDisc players, 143

MiniDisc recorders, 5-7, 167

Mitsubishi, 35-36, 49
HDTVs, 247
RPTVs, 242-247
VCRs, 240-241, 243
Web site, 260

models (speakers), front speakers, 153-154

modes (DSP), stimulated surround, 181

monopole speaker designs, 148

Monty Python's Life of Brian, movie, 92

mounting satellite dishes, 119

movies, 9
DTS systems, 132-133
DVDs, 93
letterbox, 8
pay-per-view, 115-117
ratings, 93
THX, 133-134

MP3, Web site, 168

MP3 discs, DVDs, 93-94

MP3 Place, Web site, 168

MP3 recorders and Web sites, 167-169

MP3now, Web site, 168

MPEG-2
digital compressions, 60-61
video compressions, 87-89

MultiAudio, Web site, 168

multibrand remotes, 144

multiple camera angles, DVDs, 90

multiple languages, audio formats (DVDs), 92

multiple LNB, dishes, 121

multiple-component remote controls, 200

multiple jukeboxes, costs, 248

multiple-room audio and video installations, 226-228

multiplexers, 120-121

Musicseek, Web site, 168

N

Napster, Web site, 168

National Television Standards Committee. *See* NTSC

NBC, 62-65

negative leads, speakers, 149, 189-190

NetFlix, Web site, 100

networks (local), satellites, 118-119

new technologies, DVD-Audio, 97-98

newspapers (research), home theater systems, 19-21

Niles Audio, remote controls, 205, 247

noise reduction, audio-cassettes, 165-166
Dolby B, 166
Dolby C, 166
Dolby S, 166

noises, extraneous, 174

NTSC (National Television Standarts Committee), 61
DVDs, 77-78, 86-87
pictures, 60-61
signals, HDTVs, 68
tuners, 64-65

O

Onkyo
DVD changers, 243
receivers, 241-245
Web site, 260

on-screen guides, 117

options, DVDs, 90

outlets, 177-178

outputs. *See also* connections; inputs/outputs
amplifiers, 138-139
audio/video receivers, 140-145
S-Video, 181
subwoofers, 144, 190

P

Palavista Digital Music Metacrawler, Web site, 168

Panasonic
DVD changers, 243
DVHS VCRs, 247-249
RPTVs, 245
televisions, 240-241
VCRs, 240-243
Web site, 260

panavision, wide-screen formats, 30, 32

Paradigm, speakers, 247

parental controls, V-Chips, 11-12

pay-per-view movies, 77, 115-117

Perfect Vision, The, magazine and Web site, 259

performances
audio/video receivers, 140-141

DVD players, 94-95
RPTVs, 47

personal DVRs, costs, 246

personal identification numbers, DVD discs, 93

personal television receivers. *See* PTRs

personal video recorders. *See* PVRs

Philips, 78, 162
CD recorders, 247-249
DVRs, 110
personal video recorders, 247-249
programmable remote controls, 245
Pronto remote controls, 202
Web site, 260
WebTV, 112
WebTV Plus, 247-249

phone lines, satellites, 115-117

physical sizes
FPTVs, 53-54
RPTVs, 53-54
televisions, 43-45

picture qualities
DVDs, 86-87, 94-95
flat-screen plasma displays, 57-58
FPTVs, 53-54
RPTVs, 53-54
televisions, 43-45

picture-in-picture. *See* PIP

picture (television), troubleshooting, 216-217

Pioneer, 49
  a/v receivers, 245
  CD jukeboxes, 245-247
  CD recorders, 247-249
  DVD players, 241, 245-247
  HDTV RPTVs, 247
  HTIB, 180, 240
  Web site, 260
PIP (picture-in-picture), 11-12, 43-45, 53-54
pits, 87-89
pixel resolutions, 60-64
  DVDs, 90-91
  HDTVs, 68
  LCDs, 50-52
plasma flat-screen televisions. *See* flat-screen plasma televisions
plugs
  RCA, composite video, 184-185
  speakers, 189-190
Polk Audio, 153
  speakers, 182, 241-247
  subwoofers, 245-247
positioning your system, 176
positive leads, speakers, 149, 189-190
power
  audio/video receivers, 140, 145
  speakers, 151
  strips, 177-178, 210
powered towers, 149
PowerPlay systems, 232-238

preamplifiers, 138
  costs, 246-248
  surround-sound decoders, 138
  THX, 134
prepackaged speaker systems, 182
prices. *See* costs
professional help, repairing equipment, 219-220
program guides, 11-12, 32-33, 43-45
programmable remote controls, 144, 198-203, 245
programming
  DVDs, 90
  VCRs, 104
  VHSs, 104
programs
  guides, satellite receivers, 121
  HDTV, 121
  pay-per-view, 115-117
  television, DVRs, 111-113
progressive-scanning, DVD players, 94-95
projectors, 50-52
Pronto (Philips), remote controls, 202
ProntoEdit software, 202
Proscan, 32-33, 42-43
PTRs (personal television receivers), 110
PVRs (personal video recorders), 110

Q

qualities
  8mm, 106
  Digital 8, 106-107
  Hi8, 106
  Mini DVs, 107
  pictures, DVDs, 87-89
  VHS-Cs, 105-106
  video sources, 82-83

R

R/L audio connections, 120
radio frequency. *See* RF
ratings, speaker power, 151
ratios, HDTV, 30, 32
RBGs, inputs/outputs, 64-65
RCA, 20, 32-33, 42-43, 49, 60-61, 64-68, 117, 121
  DIRECTV Plus DSS, 247
  DSS, 242-249
  HDTV DIRECTV tuners, 122
  jacks
    5.1 audio, 187-188
    component video, 185-186
    composite video, 184-185
    digital audio, 188-189
    line audio, 187
  plugs, composite video, 184-185

RPTVs, 242-245
televisions, 240-241
VCRs, 240-245
Web site, 260
ready-to-assemble furniture. *See* RTA furniture
rear projection television. *See* RPTV
rear speakers
surround-sound, selecting, 154-155
troubleshooting, 215-216
receivers, 6-7
audio/video, 6-7, 16, 120, 135, 138-139
amplifiers, 138-139
bandwidth, 140
connections, 142-145, 191-192, 196
costs, 140-145, 241-244
DTS circuitry, 132-133
HTIB systems, 180
inputs, 142-145
outputs, 140-145
performance specifications, 140-141
power, 145
preamplifiers, 138
remote controls, 144-145
shopping, 145-146
surround-sound systems, 141-146
weight, 141
buying, 23
decoders, Dolby Digital, 130

digital satellites, connections, 192-193
DIRECTV, 117-119
DISH Network (from EchoStar), 117-119
DVHS video, costs, 246
EchoStar, 117-119
satellites, 115-117, 120-122
DISHplayer, 112
Dolby Digital 5.1, 115-117
Dolby Pro Logic, 115-117
installations, 119
menus, 121
program guides, 121
THX, 134
recommended screen sizes, televisions, 34-35
recorders
audiocassette, 15-17
frequencies, 165-166
costs, 246
CD, 161, 167, 246
DVDs, 94-97
hard disk drives, TiVo, 117
HDTVs, 66-68
MiniDisc, 167
MP3, 167-169
video, digital, 246
videocassettes, 66-68
recording
8mm, 106
DVR, 111-113
VHS-C, 105-106

reflections, sound, 174-175
region codes, DVDs, 92-93
Remote Central, Web site, 203, 260
remote controls, 6-7, 117, 197-199
audio/video receivers, 144-145
CD players, 160-161
costs, 197-199, 245-247
custom, 199, 204-207
AMX, 206
control processors, 204-207
Crestron, 206
IntelliControl, 205
system controllers, 204-207
FPTVs, 53-54
Harman/Kardon Take Control, 203
infrared, 198, 205
learning, 198-201
macros, 199
manufacturers, 200
multiple-component, 200
Philips Pronto, 202
programmable, 198, 202-203, 245
RPTVs, 53-54
shopping, 207
single-brand, 198-200
standard, 198, 200
Take Control software, 203
televisions, 43-45
troubleshooting, 211

281

two-way operations, 202

universal, 198, 200-201

whole-house installation systems, 226-228

repairing equipment, tips, 219-220

ReplayTV, 113
  DVRs, 109-112
  PVRs, 110
  Web site, 111, 260

research, home theater systems, 19-21

resolutions, DVDs, 86-87, 96-97

retailers
  advertisments, 19-21
  audio/video specialists, 21
  catalog merchants, 21
  custom installers, 21
  home theater systems, 21-22
  Internet merchants, 21
  mass merchants, 21
  Web sites, 261

return policies, 24

RF (radio frequency), 184
  coaxial connections, 98-99, 120-121
  DVDs, 98-99
  remotes, 205

RGB video connections, 187

right front speakers, selecting, 153-154

right surround speakers
  layout, 151-153
  selecting, 154-155

rooms
  creating a home theater room, 174-175
  size, 175

ROXY, Web site, 110, 261

RPTVs (rear projection televisions), 4-8, 12, 16, 36-37, 42, 48-52, 57, 60-61
  buying advantages/disadvantages, 49
  comb filters, 53-54
  considerations, 37
  costs, 5-7, 36-37, 47, 52-54, 242-243
  CRTs, 36, 48-49
  HDTV capabilities, 53-54
  inputs/outputs, 53-54
  line doublers, 53-54
  measurements, 37
  performances, 47
  physical sizes, 53-54
  picture quailities, 53-54
  PIPs, 53-54
  remote controls, 53-54
  screen sizes, 52-54
  sizes, 37, 52
  sound systems, 53-54
  V-Chip parental controls, 53-54
  viewing angles, 53-54
  viewing distances, 53-54

RTA (ready-to-assemble) furniture, 223-224

Runco
  HDTV FPTVs, 248-249
  Web site, 260

S

SA-CDs (Super Audio CDs), 97-98, 162-164

salespersons, 23

Sam's Digital Television Report, Web site, 260

Satellite Home Viewer Improvement Act of 1999, 118-119

satellite systems, 15. *See also* DBS systems; DSS
  auxiliary, 119
  DBS systems, 115-117
  digital receivers, connections, 192-193
  DIRECTV, 32-33, 62-65
  dishes, 115-117
    installation, 119-120
    mounting, 119
  DISHplayer receivers, 112
  DSS, 115-117
  geosynchronous, 115-117
  installation, 119-121
  LNB, 115-117
  local network stations, 118-119
  main, 119
  mounting, 119
  phone lines, 115-117
  pictures, troubleshooting, 217-218

receivers, 115-117, 122
    connecting multiple receviers, 120-121
    Dolby Digital 5.1, 115-117
    Dolby Pro Logic, 115-117
    installation, 119-120
    shopping, 121-122
    speakers, 150
    technologies, 74-75
screen sizes
    FPTVs, 53-54
    RPTVs, 53-54
    televisions, 34-35, 43-45
        width ratios, 30, 32
screwdrivers, RTA furniture, 224
SDTV (standard-definition television), 62-64
sharper pictures, HDTVs, 64
shopping, 17, 23, 145. *See also* buying
    audio/video equipment, 22
    audio/video receivers, 145-146
    DIRECTV, 121-122
    DVD-A, 164
    DVRs, 113
    EchoStar, 121-122
    home theater system equipment, 23-25
    HTIB systems, 181-182

remote controls, 207
SACD, 164
satellite systems, 121-122
speakers, 157
Showtime, 86
side/layer combinations, DVDs, 87-89
signal-to-noise ratios. *See* S/N ratios
single center-channel speakers
    layout, 151-153
    selecting, 153-154
single-brand remote controls, 198-200
single-play DVD players, 99-100
sizes
    flat-screen plasma televisions, 36-37
    FPTVs, 37, 49, 52
    rooms, 175
    RPTVs, 37, 52
skipping CDs, troubleshooting, 215
S/N (signal-to-noise) ratios, 181
sockets (wall), troubleshooting, 210
software
    ProntoEdit, 202
    Take Control, 203
Sonance, speakers, 249
Sony, 20, 42-43, 49, 97-98, 117, 162
    a/v receivers, 241-245
    amplifiers, 247
    audiocassette recorders, 247-249
    CD jukeboxes, 245-247

DIRECTV Plus, 247
DSS, 242-249
DVD changers, 242-243
DVD players, 241-247
HDTV DIRECTV tuners, 122
HDTV FPTVs, 248-249
HDTV RPTVs, 247
HTIB, 180, 240
MiniDisc recorders, 167
preamplifiers, 247
programmable remote controls, 245
RPTVs, 242-245
speakers, 182
televisions, 241
VCRs, 240-245
Web site, 260
WebTV Plus, 247-249
Sound & Vision, magazine and Web site, 259
sound systems. *See also* audio; audio/video; surround-sound systems; video
    8mm, 81-82, 106
    audio/video receivers, 146
    broadcast television, 81-82
    cable television, 81-82
    Digital 8, 81-82, 106-107
    digital broadcast satellites, 81-82
    Dolby Digital, 126
    Dolby Digital DTS ES, 126

Dolby Digital EX, 126
Dolby Pro Logic, 126
DVDs, 81-82, 86-89
DVHSs, 81-82
DVRs, 79-80
flat speakers, 157
FPTVs, 53-54
HDTVs, 64, 81-82
Hi8, 81-82
laserdiscs, 81-82
reflections, 174-175
RPTVs, 53-54
SVHSs, 81-82
televisions, 43-45
troubleshooting,
212-213
    audiocasettes, 215
    bad sound, 214
    buzzing, 213-214
    CDs, 214-215
    rear speakers,
    215-216
    speaker hookups,
    212
VCRs, 78-79, 104
VHSs, 81-82, 104
sources
audio, 17
    audiocassette decks,
    165-166
    CD changers,
    160-161
    CD players, 14-15,
    159
    CD recorders, 161,
    167
    Dolby Digital,
    115-117
    Dolby Pro Logic,
    115-117

DVD players, 14-15,
    162
    DVD-A, 163-164
    MiniDisc recorders,
    167
    MP3 recorders,
    167-169
    SACD, 162-164
video
    DVD players, 12-13
    hi-fi VCR players,
    12-13
    shopping lists, 17
space (rooms), creating a
home theater room,
174-175
speakers, 6-8, 14-16,
143, 147, 156
    amplifiers, 138-139
    audio channels,
    127-130
    bookshelf, 150
    buying, 23
    connections, 189-190
    A, 155
    B, 155
    costs, 248
    designs, 150-151
        acoustic-
        suspension, 150
        bass reflex, 150
        bipole, 148-151,
        155
        dipole, 151, 155
        monopole, 148
    diaphragms, 148
    Dolby Digital,
    127-130, 154-155
    Dolby Digital EX,
    129-130

Dolby Pro Logic,
    128-132, 154-155
    drivers, 148
        tweeters, 148
        woofers, 148
    DTS systems, 132-133
    efficiency, 157
    enclosures, 149-150
        bookshelf, 150
        floor-standing, 149
        in-wall, 150
        powered towers,
        149
        satellite speakers
        with subwoofers,
        150
    flat sound, 157
    floor-standing, 149
    frequencies, 157
    front, 151-154
    home theater systems,
    costs, 182
    HTIB systems, 180
    in phase, 149
    in-wall, 150
    jacks, 189-190
    layout, 151, 153
    out of phase, 149
    plugs, 189-190
    power ratings, 151
    powered towers, 149
    rear, troubleshooting,
    215-216
    satellite with sub-
    woofers, 150
    shopping, 157
    single center-channel
    speakers, 151-154
    subwoofers, 151-153
        connections, 190
        selecting, 155-156

surround-sound, 4-7, 126, 151-153
  costs, 5-7, 241-247
  selecting, 154-155
  THX, 134
  tonal balance, 156
  troubleshooting, 212
  video shielding, 157
  voice coils, 148
  wires, 189-190, 194
special effects/features, DVDs, 87-90
specialists (audio/video), retailers, 21
specifications (performance), audio/video receivers, 140-141
standard remote controls, 198-200
standard-definition television. *See* SDTV
stations (local networks), satellite, 118-119
Stereophile Guide to Home Theater, Web site, 260
storage
  DVDs, capacity, 90
  equipment, 221-223
    a/v furniture, 225
    custom installation, 225-226
    fine furniture, 224-225
    RTA furniture, 223-224
  MPEG2 video compressions, 87-89

stores, home theater systems, 21-22
sub-pixels, 55-56
subtitle tracks, DVDs, 92
subwoofers, 14, 126-130, 143. *See also* low-frequency effects
  amplifiers, 155-156
  costs, 5-7, 244-247
  Dolby Digital, 155-156
  Dolby Pro Logic, 131-132
  DTS systems, 132-133
  floor-standing speakers, powered towers, 149
  frequencies, 155-156
  HTIB speakers, 180-181
  layouts, 151-153
  outputs, 144, 190
  satellite speakers, 150
  selecting, 155-156
  speaker connections, 190
Super Audio CDs. *See* SA-CDs
Super VHS. *See* SVHS
surge suppressors, 177-178, 210
surround-sound systems, 4-8, 126-127. *See also* audio; audio/video; sound systems; video
  amplifiers, 13-14
  audio/video receivers, 8, 13-14, 141-145

CD players, 14-15
costs, 5-7, 241-247
decoders, 138
Dolby Digital, 12-14, 115-117, 127-130, 138, 181
Dolby Digital EX, 129-130
Dolby Pro Logic, 12-14, 115-117, 131-132, 138, 181
DSP modes, 181
DTS systems, 132-133
DVD players, 14-15
  features, 86-87
  preamplifiers, 138
  speakers, 8, 14, 241-247
  THX, 133-134
  tips, 134-135
SVHS (Super VHS), 105-108
  costs, 105
  Hi8, 106
  sound systems, 81-82
  VCRs, 105
  video resolutions, 81-82
  video sources, 81-82
S-Video connections, 143, 181, 185
  chrominance, 185
  DVDs, 98-99
  inputs, 11-12, 16, 120, 181
  luminance, 185
  outputs, 181
Swearingen, Jim, interview with, 232-238

switches (wall), troubleshooting, 210
systems
audio, 4-5
AM/FM tuners, 6-7
amplifiers, 13-14
audiocassette recorders, 6-7
CD players, 6-7
costs, 5-7
receivers, 6-7, 13-14
shopping lists, 16-17
speakers, 6-7, 14, 156-157
surround-sound, 8
controllers, 204-207
home automation, 249
home theater, 4-7, 15-16
assembling the connections, 177-178
audio sources, 14-15, 165-169
audio systems, 13-14
audio/video receivers, 138-146
buying equipment, 23-25
connections, 184-196
costs, 5-7
creating a home theater room, 174-175
hard surfaces, 174
layout, 176
light, 174
merchants, 21-22
positioning your system, 176
reasearch, 19-21
remote controls, 197-207
resources, 259-261
retailers, 21-22
shopping lists, 17
speakers, 147-157
surround-sound systems, 8
video displays, 8, 11-12, 29-30, 32
video sources, 9, 12-13
home theaters
costs, 239-249
DVRs, 109-113
equipment storage, 221-226
installation, 226-231
satellites, 120-121
stores, 21-22
surround-sound, 134-135
troubleshooting, 210-220
HTIB, 179
audio/video receivers, 180
costs, 180
frequencies, 181
shopping, 181-182
speakers, 180
subwoofers, 180-181
remote controls, 204-206
speakers, 180-182
surround-sound, 4-5
amplifiers, 13-14
audio/video
receivers, 8, 13-14, 145
CD players, 14-15
costs, 5-7, 241, 243-244, 247
Dolby Digital, 12-14, 115-117, 127-130, 138, 181
Dolby Digital EX, 129-130
Dolby Pro Logic, 12-14, 115-117, 131-132, 138, 181
DTS systems, 132-133, 138
DVD players, 14-15
speakers, 8, 14
THX, 133-134
tips, 134-135

T

Take Control, remote controls and software, 203
TDI (Tom Doherty, Inc.), 232-238
Best Home Theater Electronic System Design, 232-238
Web site, 233
Technics
receivers, 241-243
Web site, 260
technologies
CD players, 159
digital videos, 74-75
DVDs, 74-75, 87-89
HDTVs, 74-75
infrared, 205
satellites, 74-75

surround-sound, 127
Dolby Digital, 127-130
Dolby Digital EX, 129-130
Dolby Pro Logic, 131-132
DTS systems, 132-133
THX, 133-134
televisions, 4-12, 16, 29-30, 32, 143-144
27", costs, 240
32", costs, 241
antennas, 15
brand names, 42-43
buying, 23
cable, 15
comb filters, 43-45
connections, 192-193
costs, 5-7, 38-39, 42
CRT, 35-36
dark tubes, 43-45
diagonal measurements, 30-32
digital, 31-33, 43-45, 62-68
digital-ready, 31-32
direct view, 35, 42
DIRECTV tuners, 117-119
display technologies, 35
direct view, 35-36
flat-screen plasma, 35-37
FPTVs, 36
front projections, 35
rear projection, 35-36
RPTVs, 36
e-mail, WebTV, 32-33

flat tubes, 43-45
FPTVs, front projection, 5-8, 12, 16
height, 176
high-definition, 30, 32
HDTV, 30, 32
inputs/outputs, 30, 32, 35-36, 43-45
cost, 38-39
manufacturers, 42-43
measurements, 30, 32, 34-35
screens, 34-35
width, 30, 32
physical sizes, 43-45
screens, 34-35
widths, 30-32
picture
quality, 43-45
troubleshooting, 216-217, 219
PIPs, 43-45
plasma, flat-screen, 5-8, 12, 16
prices, 42
program guides, 32-33, 43-45
rear projection, 36
recommended screen sizes, 34-35
RPTVs, 4-8, 12, 16, 242
remote controls, 43-45
satellites, 15, 120-121
screens
cost, 38-39
measurements, 30, 32, 34-35
sizes, 43-45
width ratios, 30, 32

sound systems, 43-45
costs, 38-39
types, 35
direct view, 35-36
flat-screen plasma, 35-37
FPTVs, 36
front projection, 35
rear projection, 35-36
RPTVs, 36
V-Chip parental controls, 43-45
WebTV, 32-33
e-mail, 32-33
width, measurements, 30, 32
THD (total harmonic distortion), 141, 181
There's Something About Mary, movie, 31
THX, 133-135
tips. *See also* troubleshooting
buying equipment, 23-25
DVD-A shopping, 164
installation
satellite dishes, 119-120
satellite receviers, 120-121
remote control shopping, 207
repairing equipment, 219-220
SACD shopping, 164
speaker shopping, 157
surround-sound systems, 134-135
troubleshooting
sound, 212-216
video, 216-219

287

TiVo, 113
  DVRs, 109-112
  hard disk drive
    recording, 117
  PTRs, 110
  Web site, 111, 260
Tom Doherty, Inc. *See*
  TDI
tonal balance, speakers,
  156
Toshiba
  DVD changers,
    242-243
  DVD players, 241-247
  RPTVs, 245
  televisions, 240-241
  Web site, 260
total harmonic distor-
  tion. *See* THD
touchscreen custom
  remote controls,
  204-207
transmissions, HDTVs,
  66-68
troubleshooting, home
  theater systems, 210.
  See also tips
  professional help,
    219-220
  remote controls, 211
  sound, 212-216
  specific components,
    211
  video, 216-219
TuneBase, 95-96, 160
tuners
  DIRECTV, 117-119
  HDTVs, 31-32, 64-68
  NTSCs, 64-65
turntables, 16, 143, 214
TV show, *Frasier*, 112

tweeters, 148
two in one, DVDs, 93-94
two-way operations,
  remote controls, 202
types of televisions, 35

U

universal remote con-
  trols, 198-201
upgrading
  VHSs, 104
  video sources, 82-83
Usenet newsgroups, Web
  site, 168
USSB, 118

V

V-Chip parental con-
  trols, 11-12
  FPTVs, 53-54
  RPTVs, 53-54
  televisions, 43-45
VCRs (videocassette
  recorders), 6-9, 16,
  66-68, 78-80, 86-87,
  96-97, 142
  advantages/
    disadvantages, 78-79
  camcorders, 78-79
  connections, 192-193
  costs, 5-7, 78-79, 105,
    240-242
  hi-fi, 12-13
  horizontal resolutions,
    104
  programming, 104
  sound systems, 78-79,
    104

SVHSs, 105
troubleshooting,
  218-219
VCR plus, features,
  107-108
VHSs, 66-68, 78-79,
  104
video sources, 78-79
Velodyne, subwoofers,
  245
VHS-C (compact VHS),
  105-106
  adapters, 105-106
  batteries, 106
  camcorders, 105-106
  inputs/outputs,
    105-106
  qualities, 105-106
  recording times,
    105-106
VHSs, 66-68, 86-87,
  96-97, 104-106
  cable television, 104
  DVDs, 104
  DVHSs, 105
  formats, 104
  HiFi, 12-13, 104
    costs, 104, 240-242
    features, 107-108
    sound systems, 104
  horizontal resolutions,
    104
  programming, 104
  sound systems, 81-82,
    104
  upgrades, 104
  VCRs, 78-79, 104
  video resolutions,
    81-82
  video sources, 74-75,
    81-82

video. *See also* audio; audio/video; sound systems; surround-sound systems
  component connections, 185-186
  composite connections, 184-185
  compressions, MPEG2, 87-89
  digital recorders, costs, 105, 246
  displays, 4-7
    costs, 5-7
    height, 176
    shopping lists, 17
    televisions, 8, 11-12 29-30, 32
  DVHS recorders, costs, 66-68, 246
  equipment sources (Web sites), 260-261
  home automation systems, 228
  manufacturers' Web sites, 260
  multiple-room installations, 226-228
  recorders
    camcorders, 105
    digital, 105, 246
    DVHS, 66-68
  resolutions, 81-82
  retailers, Web sites, 261
  RGB connections, 187
  shielding, speakers, 157
  sources,
    8mm, 81-82
    available sources, 82-83

    broadcast television, 74-75, 81-82
    buying, 82-83
    cable television, 74-75, 81-82
    camcorders, 80-81
    choosing, 82-83
    compatibilities, 82-83
    costs, 75-76, 82-83
    Digital 8, 81-82
    digital broadcast satellites, 74-75, 81-82
    DSS, 6-9
    DVD players, 6-9, 12-13, 74-75, 81-82
    DVHS, 81-82
    HDTV broadcasts, 74-75, 81-82
    Hi-Fi VCR players, 6-9, 12-13
    Hi8, 81-82
    laserdiscs, 74-75, 80-82
    qualities, 82-83
    shopping lists, 17
    SVHS, 81-82
    upgrading, 82-83
    VHS, 74-75, 81-82
  video game systems, 81
  WebTV, 80-81
  troubleshooting, 216
    DVDs, 218
    laserdiscs, 218
    picture, 216-217
    satellites, 217-218
    sound, 212
    televisions, 216-217, 219

    VCR players, 218-219
    Web sites, 260-261
videocassette recorders. *See* VCRs
videocasettes, troubleshooting, 218-219
video game, systems, 81, 144
videophiles, DVD players, 34-35, 99-100
viewing angles
  FPTVs, 53-54
  RPTVs, 53-54
viewing distances
  FPTVs, 53-54
  RPTVs, 53-54
voice coils, speakers, 148

W

wall sockets, troubleshooting, 210
wall switches, troubleshooting, 210
Web sites, 259-261
  2look4, 168
  About.com Home Electronics, 259
  Active Buyer's Guide: Home Theater Systems, 259
  Amateur Home Theater, 259
  Amazon, 100, 110, 261
  askMP3, 168
  Audio Video Interiors, 259
  Audiofind, 168

AudioREVIEW, 20, 259

AVIA Home Theater Search Engine, 261

Best Buy, 261

Bose, 260

CD Now, 100, 261

CEDIA, 22, 231

CEDIA Home Theater Automation, 259

Circuit City, 261

Crutchfield, 261

DAILYMP3, 168

DBS Dish, 260

Digital Theater, 5, 260

Dimension Music, 168

DIRECTV, 119, 260

Dish Direct, 261

DISH Network, 119

DVD City, 261

DVD Express, 100, 261

E! Online, 111

EchoStar/DISH Network, 260

Escient, 161, 260

eTown, 20, 260

Get Plugged, 261

HiFi, 261

Home Cinema Choice, 259

Home Theater, 259

Home Toys, 228

J&R Music World, 261

JVC, 260

Loewe, 260

Lycos Music MP3 Search, 168

Mitsubishi, 260

MP3, 168

MP3 Place, 168

MP3 recorders, 167-169

MP3now, 168

MultiAudio, 168

Musicseek, 168

Napster, 168

NetFlix, 100

Onkyl, 260

Palavista Digital Music Metacrawler, 168

Panasonic, 260

Perfect Vision, The, 259

Philips, 260

televisions, 32-33

Pioneer, 260

RCA, 260

Remote Central, 203, 260

ReplayTV, 111, 260

ROXY, 110, 261

Runco, 260

Sam's Digital Television Report, 260

Sony, 260

Sound & Vision, 259

Stereophile Guide to Home Theater, 260

TDI, 233

Technics, 260

TiVo, 111, 260

Toshiba, 260

Usenet newsgroups, 168

Widescreen Review, 259

Yamaha, 260

WebTV

e-mail, 80-81

EchoStar, 112

Internet, 80-81

Internet terminals, 117

Philips, 112

video sources, 80-81

WebTV Plus, costs, 246

weight

audio/video receivers, 141

flat-screen plasma displays, 55-56

whole-house audio and video installations, 226-228

wide-screen

formats

cinemascope, 30, 32

DVDs, 30, 32

movies, 30, 32

panavision, 30, 32

production, HDTVs, 64

Widescreen Review, magazine and Web site, 259

wires, speakers, 189-194

wood (fine furniture), equipment storage, 224-225

woofers, 148

wrenches (Allen), RTA furniture, 224

X-Z

X-10 systems, home automation systems, 228

Yamaha

a/v receivers, 241, 243, 245

audiocassette recordes, 247, 249

jukeboxes, 245

Web site, 260